Gayatri Spivak

Gayatri Spivak

Deconstruction and the Ethics of Postcolonial Literary Interpretation

By

Ola Abdalkafor

**Cambridge
Scholars**
Publishing

Gayatri Spivak:
Deconstruction and the Ethics of Postcolonial Literary Interpretation

By Ola Abdalkafor

This book first published 2015

Cambridge Scholars Publishing

Lady Stephenson Library, Newcastle upon Tyne, NE6 2PA, UK

British Library Cataloguing in Publication Data
A catalogue record for this book is available from the British Library

ISBN (10): 1-4438-7467-1
ISBN (13): 978-1-4438-7467-0

TABLE OF CONTENTS

ACKNOWLEDGEMENTS

My biggest thanks and gratitude should go to Professor Peter Hulme, Professor Sanja Bahun, the Department of Literature, Film and Theatre Studies at the University of Essex and The Albert Sloman Library. As for my parents, there are no words that really express how grateful I am to them. They did everything possible to keep me going on with determination. I also thank my dear husband Abdulrahman Razouk, my sister Reem and two brothers Alaa Aldeen and Mohammad for their tender feelings; they always cheered me up and encouraged me. Finally, although they cannot read and understand what I am writing now, I thank my precious children, Talal and Mariam, because their smiles always gave me the strength and determination to go on. I want them to know that I love them and will stand by them as long as I live.

INTRODUCTION

The post-colonial critic and theorist, Gayatri Chakravorty Spivak, is a well-known scholar in diverse fields of academic research. She was born in 1942 in Calcutta, India. Her education started at a missionary school that was not an upper-class one. Before leaving for Cornell, the United States, she continued her education and got her B.A. at Presidency College which according to her was left-influenced and politically active.[1] In 1961, she went to the United States at a time when there "was nothing – no multiculturalism, no academic feminism."[2] Yet, she admits that she was fortunate enough to be taken seriously, especially by the literary critic Paul De Man (1919-1983), who was her PhD supervisor. After obtaining her PhD at Cornell in 1967, Spivak joined the department of Comparative Literature at the University of Iowa as an Assistant Professor, beginning an intellectual career which has already lasted more than four decades.

Mark Sanders, author of one of the four book-length studies of Spivak, notes that: "[b]y the late 1980s Spivak had become not only an academic 'star' in the United States, garnering a series of prestigious university appointments, but also a major international intellectual, highly sought after as a speaker at conferences and other gatherings in culture and the arts all over the world."[3] Spivak's work is rich in topics that can be the focus of many books. It has covered historiography, literature, cultural politics, and translation. She is renowned for her engagement with post-structuralism, deconstruction, feminism, Marxism, psychoanalysis and subaltern studies. Moreover, much of what is now known as postcolonial literary criticism is indebted to her analysis of both western and non-western literary texts. Although reading and interpreting literary texts has been one of Spivak's central and significant contributions to postcolonial theory, there has as yet been no concerted effort to understand how she

---

[1] Gayatri Chakravorty Spivak, *The Spivak Reader: Selected Works of Gayatri Chakravorty Spivak*, ed. Donna Landry and Gerald Maclean (London: Routledge, 1996), 16-17.

[2] Swapan Chakravorty et al, *Conversations with Spivak* (London: Seagull, 2006), 13.

[3] Mark Sanders, *Gayatri Chakravorty Spivak: Live Theory* (London: Continuum International Publishing Group, 2006), 6.

approaches the task of literary criticism and how that approach has developed over the course of her career.

This book, *Gayatri Spivak: Deconstruction and the Ethics of Postcolonial Literary Interpretation,* is concerned with Spivak's approach to literary analysis illustrated in her readings of: Charlotte Brontë's *Jane Eyre* (1847), Jean Rhys's *Wide Sargasso Sea* (1966), Mary Shelley's *Frankenstein* (1818), J. M. Coetzee's *Foe* (1986) and Mahasweta Devi's "Pirtha, Puran Sahay and Pterodactyl" (translated by Spivak in 1993). These readings were compiled in the chapter entitled: "Literature" which appears in Spivak's book: *A Critique of Postcolonial Reason: Towards a History of the Vanishing Present* (1999). Although Spivak has written about many literary texts, these five texts are particularly important because the essays discussing them are reproduced in the major work, *A Critique of Postcolonial Reason,* where Spivak strives to offer her critique of postcolonial reason after more than three decades as a teacher of literature and as a critic. Spivak wrote this book with the aim of providing postcolonial readers with an approach to the reading of great western texts. When Spivak reproduced her analyses of these five texts in "Literature," many changes occurred in the reproduction at different levels. However, for the purposes of this book, the focus will be on two major and significant changes. First, when Spivak compiled all these studies together, she juxtaposed western texts with non-western ones for the aim of contrasting them rather than discussing each group of texts separately. In this manner, she paved the way for detecting possible connections or disconnections between the two sides. Second, she places these readings in the second chapter of her book, immediately after the chapter "Philosophy" where she reads the philosophy of Immanuel Kant, Karl Marx and Friedrich Hegel. Ordering "Philosophy" and "Literature" in this way may allow readers to establish connections between western philosophy and Spivak's literary analysis. In other words, the way Spivak orders the two chapters sheds new light on what Spivak does when she analyses a literary text. This book will focus both on "Literature" as a whole and on the separate articles combined in it.

Most of the previous brief studies of and commentaries on Spivak's chapter "Literature" or the articles it includes agree that deconstruction is a constant reference point for Spivak. Stephen Morton, for instance, argues that "Spivak's ongoing engagement with deconstruction has not only enabled her to produce a theoretical vocabulary with which to criticize the cultural, political and economic legacy of colonialism, but it has also allowed her to develop an ethic that is sensitive to the singular position of the subaltern."[4] Indeed, deconstruction has influenced Spivak's writings since her translation of Derrida's *de la grammatologie – Of Grammatology* – in 1976. Spivak herself admits her being indebted to deconstruction on many occasions. For example, in 1988, Spivak says: "[t]here would have been no 'other worlds for me' if something now called deconstruction had not come to disrupt the diasporic space of a postcolonial academic."[5] The existing studies that discuss deconstruction in Spivak's thought deal with deconstruction as a general approach that is clear in Spivak's writing in the various disciplines she has been involved in. However, there is no study that tries to show how exactly Spivak uses deconstruction in approaching "Literature." Again, most of these studies do not explore whether Spivak has used deconstruction consistently and whether it has referred to the same thing in all the times it is deployed in Spivak's criticism. Therefore, focusing on "Literature" which contains Spivak's articles starting from 1985 to 1999, the questions that this book aims to address are: How did Spivak as a literary critic approach literature? Is deconstruction the main approach she used during that period? Does 'deconstruction' always mean the same thing, or are different forms of deconstruction prominent at different stages of her career? What theory of literary interpretation can be adduced from this set of readings?

To address these questions, this book will dedicate one chapter to each of the five texts which Spivak discusses, attempting in each case to understand how she uses deconstruction. The aim is to disentangle the knots within Spivak's literary analysis, showing the tools and concepts she finds useful for each move she makes. The book is divided into eight chapters. Chapter One provides the relevant background, first by examining Spivak's deconstruction of Kant's *Critique of Judgment*, an exercise which provides the essential terms and techniques which Spivak uses in analysing *Jane Eyre, Wide Sargasso Sea* and *Frankenstein*; and second by examining the feminist debates to which Spivak contributed before writing about the those three literary texts. Chapters Two, Three, and Four explain Spivak's deconstruction of the three texts in light of the background provided in the first chapter. Chapter Five provides the theoretical background explaining how Derrida's deconstruction contributes to understanding Spivak's readings of *Foe* and "Pterodactyl." The chapter will attempt at revealing the connections between Derrida's deconstruction and Spivak's discussion of the two final texts. Chapters Six

---

[4] Stephen Morton, *Gayatri Spivak: Ethics, Subalternity and the Critique of Postcolonial Reason* (Cambridge: Polity Press, 2007), 69.
[5] Gayatri Chakravorty Spivak, *In Other Worlds: Essays in Cultural Politics* (London: Routledge, 1988), xxi.

and Seven examine her analyses of *Foe* and "Pterodactyl" respectively, investigating whether Spivak's approach to these two texts is the same one she used in reading the first three texts. Chapter 8 concludes the book by clarifying whether an approach can be extracted from the scrupulous analysis of how Spivak approaches the literary texts included in "Literature." This chapter will also refer to Spivak's *An Aesthetic Education in the Era of Globalisation* (2012) to find out whether or not Spivak has changed her approach.

Apart from chapters Two and Five which provide the theoretical backgrounds of Spivak's criticism of the texts under discussion, this book will present the discussion of Spivak's readings of the literary texts according to the dates of their publication. The order of the chapters is also thematic: the first three texts are western ones through which Spivak critiques the marginalisation of the 'native subaltern female.' What is different in her analysis of *Foe* is that the text was written by a South African writer where Spivak detects a perspective of subaltern representation that differs from the one demonstrated in the first three. *Foe* was written as a rewriting of Daniel Defoe's *Robinson Crusoe,* a canonical English text which is often read as containing colonial themes. Therefore, *Foe,* in a way, is still connected to the western canon. However, Spivak's analysis of "Pterodactyl" seems to be the radical shift in her literary criticism because the novella was written by Devi who, both as a writer and activist, has been deeply involved in issues related to the poorest people in India. Through analysing Devi's "Pterodactyl," Spivak demonstrates the literary representation of the subaltern which is in contrast with the eighteenth-century and nineteenth-century western texts which depended on the exclusion of the Other.`

Previous book-length studies of Spivak's thought have examined her literary criticism only as one aspect of her work. So, for example, in his book: *Gayatri Spivak: Ethics, Subalternity and the Critique of Postcolonial Reason* (2007), Morton discusses in a very important chapter of twenty-six pages Spivak's reading of some literary texts showing the importance of Spivak's approach in terms of pedagogy. Again in twenty-seven pages, Mark Sanders' *Gayatri Chakravorty Spivak: Live Theory* (2006) attempts to examine whether Spivak's approach to reading literature can lead to a responsible global literacy. Sangeeta Ray, for her part, presents a chapter in her book, *Gayatri Chakravorty Spivak: In Other Words* (2009), where she concentrates on the pedagogical significance of "Three Women's Texts" if read alongside Spivak's well-known essay, "Can the Subaltern Speak? Speculations on Widow Sacrifice." As these and other critics agree, Spivak's literary theory has implications for pedagogy, which she herself goes on to draw out in her book *An Aesthetic Education in the Era of Globalization* (2012). However, the value of Spivak's literary criticism cannot be fully appreciated and apprehended only by predicting its consequences and prospects. There is no work or study that presents an in-depth analysis of the steps which Spivak follows when analysing these texts, an analysis that is necessary for figuring out whether there was a consistent theoretical practice which underlay Spivak's literary criticism during that period (1985-1999) and to identify the terms and characteristics of such a practice.

The background of "Literature" (1999)

"Literature" is the second chapter of *A Critique of Postcolonial Reason,* and it is a combination of Spivak's "Three Women's Texts and a Critique of Imperialism" (1985) and "Theory in the Margin: Coetzee's *Foe* Reading Defoe's Crusoe/ Roxana" (1988) in addition to her analysis of "Pterodactyl" (1999). Spivak's declared aim when she first wrote "Three Women's Texts and a Critique of Imperialism" was to offer a critique of the influence of imperialism on the representation of the 'native subaltern female' as an object of knowledge in eighteenth- and nineteenth-century British fiction, as well as, in twentieth-century feminist criticism. Critique here is used according to Spivak's definition of it as "a careful description of the structures that produce an object of knowledge."[6] With this aim, Spivak discusses *Jane Eyre, Wide Sargasso Sea,* and *Frankenstein.* "Three Women's Texts" was written at a time when a new wave of feminism started to appear and was called third-wave feminism. Whereas first-wave feminism was seen as essentialising the woman to fight for political rights such as suffrage, and second-wave feminism as giving the woman an essence depending on the social construction of the woman, third-wave feminism rebuffed essentialism and underscored the heterogeneity of women's experiences.

The second article included in "Literature" is "Theory in the Margin: Coetzee's *Foe* Reading Defoe's Crusoe/Roxana" where Spivak examines *Foe* (1986) by the South African novelist J. M. Coetzee. This article was written in 1988 as a paper for the English Institute 1987-1988, and was published in *Consequences of Theory* in 1991. The title of the book was derived from "Some Consequences of Theory," the title of the first English Institute panel designed by Jonathan Arac. Arac suggested that "since theory has taught us the groundlessness of truth, what we must have

---

[6] Spivak, *Conversations,* 60.

instead are consequences."[7] In other words, theorists have lost the fixed ground that they can start from since their intellectual effort is always guarded by the margins as Spivak herself wanted to prove in her study of *Foe*. Barbara Johnson, one of the book's editors, comments on Spivak's study of *Foe* saying: "Spivak notes the current centrality of philosophical and political margins in literary theory and criticism."[8] Therefore, one can argue that Spivak reads Coetzee's text as an example of the shift from the centre to the margins of literary theory. Spivak also added her 1999 reading of Devi's "Pterodactyl" to "Literature." She had expressed some of her ideas about "Pterodactyl" in the preface and appendix of her 1993 translation of *Imaginary Maps,* a collection of three stories by Devi. However, in 1999, she elaborates on the novella and contrasts it with the texts studied in "Three Women's Texts." On the one hand, *Foe,* as Spivak's reading shows, presents a different way of representing the subaltern through its insistence on the un-representability of the subaltern's story. Spivak's translation of and commentary on Devi's "Pterodactyl," on the other hand, is the shift to reading a text written by "the descendent of the colonial female subject that history did in fact produce."[9]

To clarify the significance of Spivak's chapter "Literature" and to justify selecting it as the focus of this book, it must be located within the wider trajectory of Spivak's literary criticism. The significance of "Literature" lies in the importance of the period ranging from 1985 to 1999 during which Spivak's criticism changed its focus from colonial to postcolonial texts. A quick skim of the texts studied by Spivak before this period helps us realise how "Literature" can be distinguished from what preceded it. Starting from 1967, Spivak's PhD thesis tackled the Irish poet W. B. Yeats. Her writings were mainly concerned with Yeats until 1975, and a year later Spivak's translation of *de la grammatologie* was published. After this year, deconstruction started to show its influence on Spivak's literary analysis. Between 1977 and 1980, Spivak concentrated on analysing romantic English poets like Samuel Coleridge and William Wordsworth. Apart from Spivak's translation of Devi's story "Draupadi," which was published in 1981, Spivak's writing between 1981 and 1985

---

[7] Barbara Johnson, "Introduction: Truth or Consequences" in *Consequences of Theory,* edited by Jonathan Arac and Barbara Johnson (London: The John Hopkins University Press, 1991), viii.

[8] Johnson, "Introduction," xii.

[9] Gayatri Chakravorty Spivak, *A Critique of Postcolonial Reason: Towards a History of the Vanishing Present* (Cambridge: Harvard University Press, 1999), 140.

focused on theoretical topics such as 'the subaltern' and 'representation', resorting to the work of philosophers like Michel Foucault, Karl Marx and Jacques Derrida. Another important theoretical field that Spivak approached during the period between 1981 and 1985 was French feminism. In 1981, Spivak wrote "French Feminism in an International Frame" where she criticises high French feminism for excluding what at that time was known as the 'Third-World woman.'

In 1983, Spivak presented "Can the Subaltern Speak? Speculations on Widow Sacrifice," a paper which marked the shift of Spivak's attention to issues of subaltern women, the disenfranchised women who cannot speak for themselves. During that time, Spivak was involved in the work of the Subaltern Studies Group, a group of South Asian scholars interested in reviving the voice of the subaltern from official records documenting insurgency during the British rule of India. This group was founded by Ranajit Guha, the Indian historian who migrated to the UK in the 1960s. They have published many volumes on subaltern issues since 1983. Spivak herself co-edited the fourth volume and had an introductory chapter in it in 1985: "Subaltern Studies: Deconstructing Historiography." The year 1985 witnessed the publication of "Three Women's Texts and a Critique of Imperialism" in which Spivak's attention was directed to nineteenth- and twentieth-century English fiction. Since that year, Spivak started analysing texts coming from other parts of the world, juxtaposing them to canonical English texts as was the case in her reading of *Foe* in "Theory in the Margin." Meanwhile, Spivak continued her translation of and commentary on Devi's works like "Stanadayini," "Douloti the Bountiful" and "The Hunt." Her translation efforts culminated in *Imaginary Maps* (1993).

While Spivak's analyses of other literary texts are rarely evoked or discussed by critics, "Literature" remains the chapter to which most references to Spivak are made. "Three Women's Texts" and "Theory in the Margin" have often been reprinted. The texts that these two articles tackle open the way for a critique of imperialism since they contain slippages which evoke, for a critic like Spivak, colonial spaces like the Caribbean and India. In addition these texts contain figures of Otherness: Bertha in *Jane Eyre*, Christophine in *Wide Sargasso Sea*, the monster in *Frankenstein*, Friday in *Foe* and Bikhia and the pterodactyl in "Pterodactyl". In brief, "Literature" is significant because, as Spivak herself says in the preface of *A Critique of Postcolonial Reason*, it is a chapter which "reads a cluster of literary texts to show how colonialism and postcoloniality are figured."[10]

---

[10] Spivak, *Critique*, x.

As Morton argues, Spivak has "made an important contribution to the development of a critical vocabulary and theoretical framework through which to read postcolonial texts."[11] Whereas most of the Spivakian vocabulary will be explained in detail in the coming chapters, it is essential here to introduce 'the native subaltern female,' the key concept which Spivak introduced to the field of postcolonial criticism and which will be recurrently used in this book. Introducing this concept and explaining some of its particularities may answer the question of why Spivak uses 'the native subaltern female' to the exclusion of 'the Third-World woman.' Spivak declares that her literary analysis in "Literature" is concerned with the 'native subaltern female.' She used 'the Third-World woman' until the year 1981 and, in 1985 she used the 'native female' without 'subaltern.' It is in *A Critique of Postcolonial Reason* where she used both the 'native subaltern female' and "the-native-informant-as-woman-of-the-South."[12] The following paragraphs will start by giving an example of the female about whom Spivak writes. Then the theoretical nuances of this example will be explained.

The example is taken from Spivak's participation in the International Conference on Population and Development (ICPD) in Cairo, 1994. In the paper which Spivak presented in this conference, the 'native subaltern female' is the poorest woman of the South. Spivak criticises the issue of reducing reproductive rights to abortion which was under discussion in this conference. She argues that abortion is immaterial in the South where poor women consider children a source of social security. She accuses the proponents of reducing the reproductive rights to abortion of not taking into account the heterogeneity of poor women in the South. The proponents of such a solution view the poor woman of the South as a copy of themselves: "[f]ocusing reproductive rights so intensely on abortion assumes that the able woman of the North is a person endowed with subjectivity and that the poor woman of the South should of course want what she herself wants."[13] The female about whom Spivak was speaking is a good example of the 'native subaltern female' because she cannot represent herself in such international conferences. The poorest women of the South do not have access to the dominant discourses of the globalising system. Many world organisations and local non-govermental organisations speak in these women's names. Organisations suggest solutions for what

---

[11] Morton, *Gayatri Spivak,* 15.

[12] Spivak, *Critique,* 13, n. 20. I will use the 'native subaltern female' throughout the book because this is the term Spivak uses in the text of the book.

[13] Gayatri Chakravorty Spivak, "Public Hearing on Crimes Against Women," *WAF* 7 (1995): 3-4.

they evaluate as these poor women's problems without listening to them. In brief, the voice of the poorest women of the South is lost and this loss is filled by western women and organisations. Of course, the poorest woman of the South is only one example of the 'native subaltern female' and it cannot be generalised as the norm. Now that the example has been presented, an explanation of why Spivak uses 'the native subaltern female' instead of 'the Third-World woman' will be offered by clarifying how she uses the terms 'native informant,' 'subaltern,' and 'South.'

Spivak borrows the term 'native informant' from ethnography. Morton contends that "the label 'native informant' is conventionally used in ethnography to describe indigenous people who provide information about non-western societies to western ethnographers."[14] In Spivak's opinion, ethnography takes the 'native informant' seriously, considering that the latter has a cultural identity, an identity that can be inscribed only by the West. However, she thinks that in other disciplines – philosophy for instance – the 'native informant' was exploited merely to consolidate western theories and then s/he was excluded from the species of mankind. Hence, when Spivak wrote "Three Women's Texts," she used the 'native female' implying the female whose voice cannot be retrieved since this voice was manipulated by western imperialism. Later, in *A Critique of Postcolonial Reason*, specifically in her chapter on literature, Spivak describes the woman she wants to track in her study as the 'native subaltern female.' Sanders argues that adding the term 'subaltern' is significant here because Spivak seems to have become aware that not all native women are unrepresentable due to class and caste distinctions.[15]

'Subaltern' refers to social groups like peasants, workers and tribals who are subject to the power of the ruling classes.[16] It is the term which was associated with the prominent Marxist thinker, Antonio Gramsci (1891-1937). Gramsci was one of the leaders of the Communist Party of Italy and was imprisoned by Mussolini's fascist regime. Gramsci developed the concept of cultural hegemony which is a means used by capitalist systems to present bourgeois values as common sense in society. By this, the capitalist system achieves the coercion of the subaltern classes. Gramsci describes the subaltern classes saying: "[t]he subaltern classes, by definition, are not unified and cannot unite until they are able to become a 'State': their history, therefore, is intertwined with that of

---

[14] Morton, *Gayatri Spivak*, 142.
[15] Sanders, *Gayatri Chakravorty Spivak*, 84.
[16] The following three paragraphs draw on my MA dissertation, "Representing the Subaltern: Spivak's Reading of Foucault and Marx in "Can the Subaltern Speak?" (University of Essex, 2008).

civil society, and thereby with the history of States and groups of States."[17] Gramsci's analysis of the subaltern makes them appear only as allies to be won by other social groups striving for domination. Spivak used this term after her involvement with the Subaltern Studies Group whose effort since the 1980s has been directed to the retrieval of the voices of the subaltern in India during the British rule in India. Spivak's contribution to the work of this group is her endeavour to avoid the essentialism of defining the subaltern merely by its difference from the élite. To her, the subaltern is a heterogeneous term which may include women, tribals, and the unemployed who, she concludes, cannot represent themselves. She maintains that there is always a group in formation at the margin contending that: "the name subaltern for everything that is different from organised resistance is a warning that tells us that as we organize, as we *must* organize, there is something beyond the margin of organizability that begins to construct itself."[18]

Moreover, the 'native subaltern female' cannot be referred to as 'the Third-World woman' because Spivak replaces 'the Third World' by 'the South.' Spivak's reservation concerning the term 'Third World' is associated with her ideas about imperialism which, she claims, inscribed the earth dividing it into three worlds. Postcolonial critics offer different definitions and perspectives of imperialism. However, the common point is that the hegemony that imperialism imposed on the so-called 'Third World' was not confined to economics, but its effects can be detected in other cultural fields, including literature. They claim that imperialism was motivated by "the desire for, and belief in, European cultural dominance – a belief in a superior right to exploit the world's resources."[19] The imperial discourse, they think, was powerful and could monopolise the means of representation.[20] Spivak, as argued by Laura Chrisman, discusses imperialism as "a territorial and subject-constituting project."[21] Spivak does not spend much ink defining imperialism, preferring instead to work out the effects

---

[17] Antonio Gramsci, *Selections from the Prison Notebooks*, edited and translated Quintin Hoare and Geoffrey Nowell Smith (London: Lawrence and Wishart, 1971), 52.

[18] Gayatri Chakravorty Spivak, "Gayatri Spivak on the Politics of the Subaltern," edited by Howard Winant, *Socialist Review* 20:3 (1990): 90.

[19] Bill Ashcroft et al, *Key Concepts in Post-Colonial Studies* (London: Routledge, 1998), 126.

[20] Ashcroft et al, *Key Concepts*, 126.

[21] Laura Chrisman, *Postcolonial Contraventions Cultural Readings of Race, Imperialism and Transnationalism* (Manchester: Manchester University Press, 2003), 52.

of imperialism as they appear in different cultural fields. In literature, for instance, she illustrates how imperialism influences fictional structures like moving a white female character from the margin to the centre at the expense of another racially marginalised character.

Spivak perceives the 'Third World' which we speak of, or may imagine that we know, as only fiction, something which is constructed and which does not copy any real essence since imperialism monopolised both philosophical and political representation of the so-called 'Third World.'[22] Two concepts that belong to Spivak's critique of imperialism are 'worlding' and 'epistemic violence.' She believes that it is European imperialism that produced the division of worlds which were not present before colonisation. This worlding was followed by epistemic violence which can be defined as "an interested construction, rather than 'the disinterested production of facts.'"[23] In other words, the West started to create and sustain certain images of the colonised peoples. These images gave European societies the stereotypes of the uncivilised Other and led them to justify and support the civilising mission which was the pretext of colonisation. Epistemic violence was enabled by the subject/object binary in which one side is collapsed into the other, leading imperialism to apply the same technique to the binary opposition self/Other. In claiming that the Other can be collapsed into the self, imperialism was underlain by a claim of knowing Europe's Others and a right to represent them, since it is a technique of power to "know and represent the Other."[24] By this process, imperialism domesticated the Other; hence Spivak's perseverance that this Other cannot be retrieved in its pure identity or consciousness:

> No perspective *critical* of imperialism can turn the Other into a self, because the project of imperialism has always already historically refracted what might have been the absolutely Other into a domesticated Other that consolidates the imperialist self. [25]

In her literary readings, Spivak repeatedly evokes the idea of domesticating the Other to argue against the possibility of making the Other as a copy of

---

[22] Gayatri Chakravorty Spivak, "Can the Subaltern Speak? Speculations on Widow Sacrifice" in *Marxism and the Interpretation of Culture*, edited by Cary Nelson and Lawrence Crossberg (London: Macmillan Education Ltd., 1988), 271-313.

[23] Peter Childs and Patrick R.J. Williams, *An Introduction to Post-colonial Theory* (Essex: Pearson Education Limited, 1997), 165.

[24] Chrisman, *Postcolonial Contraventions*, 57.

[25] Gayatri Chakravorty Spivak, "Three Women's Texts and a Critique of Imperialism," *Critical Inquiry* 12 (1985): 253.

the self and she calls this 'selfing the Other.'[26] For her, it is only possible
to turn the Other into a domesticated version of the western self. Spivak
refuses the label 'Third World' – and consequently avoids 'Third-World
woman' – as a fictional construction, occasionally replacing it with 'the
South', a term resulting from the new economic division of the world into
the North and the South.[27] Thus, Spivak tries to avoid the theory of the
'three worlds' in dealing with the 'native-informant-as-woman-of the-
South' keeping, with vigilance, the South:

> It is beyond the scope of this book [*A Critique of Postcolonial Reason*] to
> demonstrate how the new North-South divide in the post-Soviet world
> imposes new limitations, although my argument will constantly seek to
> escape that caution. We may, however, suggest that our grasp on that
> process is made more secure if we in the humanities [...] see the "third
> world" as a displacement of the old colonies as colonialism proper
> displaces itself into neocolonialism.[28]

Hence, there are three reasons for Spivak's exclusion of the term 'Third-
World woman.' First, the 'Third World' is an imperialist construction.
Second, the modern economic division of the world leaves us with only
the North and the South. Third, not all 'Third-World women' are subaltern
figures and not all of them are unrepresentable. Spivak jettisons this kind
of homogeneity.

Spivak uses a variety of terms when to refer to the Other. These terms
will be used throughout this book and therefore there is a need to briefly
clarify the differences among them before moving to the main argument.
First, 'the native informant' is the Other when s/he is viewed and tackled
as a source of information. Spivak uses this term when she deals with a
text that marginalises the Other and renders her/him as a passive object of
knowledge. Second, the Other is divided into two types in Spivak's
thought: the Other who can be domesticated and made a copy of the self
and the 'wholly,' 'absolutely' or 'quite' Other who cannot be domesticated.
Spivak stresses that "[b]y definition, we cannot – no self can – reach the
quite-other."[29] The subaltern and the 'native subaltern female' belong to

---

[26] Spivak also uses the word 'self' as a verb in expressions like 'to self the Other'
to indicate that someone is trying to make the Other as a copy of the self.
[27] Gayatri Chakravorty Spivak, "Appendix" in Mahasweta Devi, *Imaginary Maps*,
translated by Gayatri Chakravorty Spivak (Calcutta: Thema, 2001), 200.
[28] Spivak, *Critique*, 3.
[29] Gayatri Chakravorty Spivak, "A Moral Dilemma" in *What Happens to History:
The Renewal of Ethics in Contemporary Thought*, edited by Howard Marchitello
(London: Routledge, 2001), 215.

this 'wholly' Other. The last three terms are used interchangeably in this book due to the fact that Spivak uses all of them to refer to characters that cannot be represented or contained by the literary text since their consciousness or voice cannot be revived.

Aware of these ideas about the terms used by Spivak and about the 'native subaltern female' who was at the forefront of Spivak's mind while she was approaching the five literary texts and even when she was compiling the essays into "Literature," we can move to Chapter One: "Spivak's Engagement with Kant's *Critique of Judgment* and Western Feminist Discourses." The discussion of how Spivak approached the literary texts in the period between 1985 and 1999 can be better understood by highlighting the relationships which Spivak establishes between the philosophy of Enlightenment and literature and by applying de Man's version of deconstruction both to philosophy and canonical literary texts. This can be discussed through Spivak's reading of some of Kant's ideas since she repeatedly evokes Kant in her analysis of the texts under discussion. Furthermore, Spivak's attention to the exclusion of the 'native subaltern female' was triggered during her involvement in western feminism. This makes it also essential to understand how the feminist background during that time influenced Spivak's literary criticism, Chapter One will also attempt to provide this feminist background with special attention to the period between 1981 and 1985 when Spivak realised that western feminism excluded the female who was known at that time as the 'Third-World woman' from feminist freedom.

CHAPTER ONE

SPIVAK'S ENGAGEMENT WITH KANT'S *CRITIQUE OF JUDGMENT* AND WESTERN FEMINIST DISCOURSES

Spivak's understanding of the foreclosure of the 'native informant' in Kant's *Critique of Judgment* greatly influences her criticism of the representation of the 'native subaltern female' in eighteenth- and nineteenth-century British literature and twentieth-century western feminist criticism. This chapter first explains Spivak's deconstruction of Kant's *Critique of Judgment*. It is important to explain this deconstruction because Spivak makes several references to Kant's critique in "Three Women's Texts" and this draws our attention to the fact that there must be thematic and methodological connections between Spivak's reading of Kant and her criticism of the literary texts. Then, the chapter will demonstrate that what Spivak does to Kant's text is de Man's tropological deconstruction. This point is also important because though in the 1985 version of "Three Women's Texts" Spivak does not mention Paul de Man's tropological deconstruction, a careful reading of the article illustrates her resort to tropological deconstruction in approaching the three texts. In *A Critique of Postcolonial Reason,* Spivak mentions tropological deconstruction in her reading of Kant which comes first in the book and then in the chapter on literature. Spivak also makes connections between Kant's critique and twentieth-century Anglo-American feminism in which she herself was involved. Therefore, another aim of this chapter is establishing the relationship between Spivak's reading of Kant's text and the way in which she changed her position within the feminist discourses up to the moment of writing "Three Women's Texts." By establishing these connections, this chapter will provide a comprehensive background that will pave the way for a better understanding of Spivak's argument in "Three Women's Texts."

Spivak's engagement with Kant's *Critique of Judgment*

Spivak repeatedly evokes Kant in her readings of *Jane Eyre* and *Frankenstein*. Her reading of some ideas of Kant's philosophy is essential to understand her literary interpretation since she assumes that the imperialist project of soul-making, the civilising mission, started in the eighteenth century and the source is the construction of the Other as savage by the philosophy of Enlightenment. When Spivak speaks about the imperialist project of soul-making, she means that imperialism constituted the European subject as civilised and free at the expense of the 'native informant' who was constituted as uncivilised and bound. This project supported the imperialist civilising mission which was the pretext for colonial expansion. The first time Spivak evoked Kant in her reading of literature associating him with imperialism was in 1985 in her discussion of *Jane Eyre*. However, Spivak's most detailed explanation of what she sees as Kant's foreclosure of the 'native informant' comes in her chapter on philosophy in *A Critique of Postcolonial Reason*. This book was written fourteen years after "Three Women's Texts." Nonetheless, it provides a background that clarifies the relationship between Spivak's understanding of Kant and what she wrote on *Jane Eyre*, especially that she includes "Three Women's Texts" in a later chapter of the same book.

The key text for Spivak's literary analysis is Kant's *Critique of Judgment* (1790), which is the third of his critiques, following *Critique of Pure Reason* (1781) and *Critique of Practical Reason* (1788). In Spivak's opinion, the three critiques form a cultural self-representation of western man's capacity for aesthetic judgment. However, it is in the third critique that she detects the slippage which demonstrates Kant's need for the foreclosure of the 'native informant' in the interest of consolidating this western self. Spivak describes this slippage as "an unacknowledgeable moment that [she] will call 'the native informant' [which] is crucially needed by the great texts; and it is foreclosed."[1] To better understand this last statement, one needs to know how Spivak uses the term 'foreclosed.' She borrows the term 'foreclosure' from psychoanalysis, namely in the Lacanian sense as explained in *The Language of Psycho-Analysis* (1974). Lacan introduced this term, *forclusion* in French, as an equivalent to Freud's *verwerfung* or repudiation, which refers to a psychic defence, meaning that the ego rejects an idea with its affect and pretends that the idea never occurred to it. It is a two-step process which includes the idea's introduction to and then its expulsion from the subject. Lacan, for his part,

---

[1] Spivak, *Critique*, 4.

defines foreclosure as the rejection of a fundamental signifier resulting in the expulsion of this signifier from the subject's symbolic order. However, this foreclosed signifier remains in the real.[2] The real is an important term in relation to Spivak's approach to the 'native subaltern female' because according to Lacan, the real is "that which resists symbolization absolutely."[3] Because the world of words is what creates things, the real remains outside language. The real cannot be considered a meaning and this means that it cannot be subject to representation or symbolisation. The real belongs to the impossible. Accordingly, the 'native informant' and consequently the 'native subaltern female' are foreclosed symbolically from the Name of Man by a philosopher, like Kant. However, the native figure returns in the real, haunting the philosopher's text without surrendering to any kind of representation. Therefore, the 'native informant' belongs to the impossible in as much as s/he cannot be represented any more.[4]

To prove that Kant forecloses the 'native informant,' Spivak follows two steps. First, she chooses two instances from his *Critique of Judgment* and deliberately wrenches them out of their philosophical context. The first instance is the appearance of "*der rohe Mensch,*" which she translates as "man in the raw," in the "Analytic of the Sublime."[5] The second is naming 'man in the raw' as the New Hollander, the Australian aboriginal, and the Fuegian, the indigenous inhabitant of Tierra de Fuego in South America, in the "Analytic of Teleological Judgment." She takes 'man in the raw,' the New Hollander and the Fuegian as variables for the 'native informant.' Second, Spivak introduces the discourse of anthropology to conclude that these two instances demonstrate the foreclosure of the 'native informant.' In the following paragraphs, the philosophical context of each of the two examples chosen by Spivak will be briefly explained according to Kant's text, and then Spivak's intervention will be discussed.

The sublime and 'man in the raw' in Kant's text

'Man in the raw' is presented in Kant's explanation of the sublime, which hinges on the relationship between two faculties of the mind: imagination

---

[2] Jean Laplanche and J. B. Pontalis, *The Language of Psycho-Analysis* translated by Donald Nickleson Smith (New York: Norton, 1974), 166-169.
[3] Jacques Lacan, *The Seminar of Jacques Lacan, Book II: The Ego in Freud's Theory and in the Technique of Psychoanalysis 1954-1955,* edited by Jacques-Alain Miller, trans. Sylvana. Tomaselli (New York: W.W. Norton), 66.
[4] Lacan, *The Seminar of Jacques Lacan, Book II.*
[5] Spivak, *Critique,* 13.

and reason. The explanation is divided into the mathematically sublime and the dynamically sublime. In the mathematically sublime, Kant defines the sublime as the absolutely large or the magnitude that is beyond all comparison and "equal only to itself. It follows that the sublime must not be sought outside itself."[6] Thinking of the sublime cannot be achieved by imagination, which depends on appearances. Therefore, Kant insists that the sublime is to be sought in crude nature not in works of art because in art both the form and magnitude are determined by human purposes. For example, thinking of the infinite, which is absolutely large, needs the human mind to be super-sensible; that is, it has to surpass all sensibility on which imagination depends. Because the sublime is large beyond any standard of sense, and because imagination fails to judge it, what we judge as sublime is not the object but "the mental attunement in which we find ourselves when we estimate the object."[7] The natural object is only what prompts this attunement of the mind and it is only reason that can receive the idea of the sublime as in the case of the infinite. That is why the respect for the object is replaced with the respect for the human mind. Thus, judging the sublime results in displeasure because of the inadequacy of imagination but it also gives pleasure because it elevates reason as Kant explains: "[w]hat makes this possible is that the subject's own inability uncovers in him the consciousness of an unlimited ability which is also his, and that the mind can judge this ability aesthetically only by that inability."[8]

In the part dealing with the dynamically sublime, Kant contests that nature can be considered dynamically sublime because it can be seen as an object of fear threatening our life and health and calling forth our strength to resist it. However, this fear caused by nature's might does not dominate the human mind; we feel superior to nature by thinking we are able to overcome the natural obstacles and this is the basis for self-preservation. The ability to feel superior to nature is part of human nature but it must be developed. Therefore, Kant proposes: "the predisposition to this ability [to feel the sublime] is part of our nature, whereas it remains up to us, as our obligation, to develop and exercise this ability."[9] It is man's capacity for overcoming the fear of the abyss of nature and for judging the sublime that leads to man's freedom. Kant adds that in order to be attuned to feel the sublime, the mind must be receptive to ideas and this requires culture:

---

[6] Immanuel Kant, *Critique of Judgement,* translated by Werner S. Pluhar (Cambridge: Hackett Publishing Company, 1987), 105.
[7] Kant, *Critique of Judgement,* 112.
[8] Kant, *Critique of Judgement,* 116.
[9] Kant, *Critique of Judgement,* 121.

It is a fact that what is called sublime by us, having been prepared through culture, comes across as merely repellent to a person who is uncultured and lacking in the development of moral ideas [...] But the fact that a judgment about the sublime in nature requires culture [...] still in no way implies that it was initially produced by culture and then introduced to society by way of (say) mere convention. Rather, it has its foundation in human nature: in something that, along with common sense, we may require and demand of everyone, namely, the predisposition to the feeling for (practical) ideas, i.e. to moral feeling.[10]

What is translated as 'the uncultured' in the above quotation appears in Kant's text as '*der rohe Mensch.*' Spivak insists that this term – "generally translated 'uneducated,'" – should be translated as "man in the raw," a term which, in her opinion, includes the savage or the primitive.[11] Building on her translation of *der rohe Mensch* and maintaining that it includes the 'native informant,' Spivak further argues that the 'native informant' is excluded from this 'programmed' passage to freedom since Kant claims that a person who is not prepared through culture will view the sublime as repellent. Because Spivak is convinced that culture in Kant's text refers only to western culture excluding other cultures, she concludes: "[i]t is not possible to *become* cultured in this culture [which, for Spivak, refers to western culture], if you are *naturally* alien to it."[12]

However, Kant's example of the uncultured man or *der rohe Mensch* is the Savoyard peasant from a part of France located in the western Alps. Kant had read about the Savoyard peasant in *Voyages dans les Alpes* by the Swiss geologist Horace Bénédict de Saussure. Since he is not prepared by culture to judge the sublime, this peasant describes any person enjoying the view of the snowy mountains as a fool.[13] Apart from Spivak's translation, this peasant would be described as 'uneducated' rather than 'not prepared by culture' in the meaning Spivak intends, western culture. In fact, Spivak does not offer any kind of evidence about what Kant refers to by his use of the term 'culture.' Besides, her conclusion is based on the assumption that man in the raw "can, in its signifying reach, accommodate the savage and the primitive."[14] Kant's text does not discuss cultural difference overtly and Spivak admits this, stressing that there is an implicit rather than explicit presupposition of cultural difference. She says: "Kant's philosophical project, whether sublime or bourgeois, operates in terms of

---

[10] Kant, *Critique of Judgement,* 124-5.

[11] Spivak, *Critique,* 13.

[12] Spivak, *Critique,* 12.

[13] Kant, *Critique of Judgement,* 124.

[14] Spivak, *Critique,* 13.

an implicit cultural difference."[15] Actually, what she presents is not
evidence but an assumption which she justifies by explaining that she sees
an implicit racial difference underlying the manner in which manhood is
defined in the third critique. Spivak imagines the 'native informant,' the
retrieval of whose voice is impossible, arguing that Kant's text "uses a
peculiar thinking of what man is to put him [the 'native informant'] out of
it."[16] Spivak imagines the 'native informant' emphasising that Kant's text
defines the introduction into humanity as the passage from fearing the
abyss of nature to appreciating the sublime followed by realising the
presence of God. This is a passage from savagery to Christian faith, a
passage enabled by western culture. Thus, Spivak imposes the figure of
the 'native informant' on Kant's text despite him not mentioning such a
figure at all. In this way, Spivak gives a geo-political dimension to Kant's
philosophical text.

She also argues that Kant's text deconstructs itself by showing that
freedom happens through obligation. Spivak tries to prove this by making
some modifications to the usual translation of Kant's terms. For example,
she states that a programme or blueprint is implied in the word *anlage* in
Kant's text. Whereas *anlage* is usually translated as 'tendency' or
'predisposition' in a clause like "the predisposition to feel the sublime,"
Spivak finds in it an indication of obligation in the following manner:
when encountering a natural sublime, a lack in imagination is revealed due
to imagination's failure to feel the sublime. Reason is compelled, rather
than inclined, to supplement this lack. Then, the respect for the object of
nature is replaced with a respect for the human mind for its ability to
supplement this lack. This in Kant's opinion happens by a certain
subreption which Spivak defines, depending on the *Oxford English
Dictionary*, as the suppression of truth. Thus, since the whole process of
judging the sublime, in Spivak's estimation, is based on the suppression of
truth, and since it excludes the primitive informant who is not prepared by
western culture, this means that the freedom offered by Kant's text is
merely a truth-claim. Spivak defines the truth-claim as "a trope that passes
itself off as truth."[17] She thinks that supplementing the gap in this manner
is what philosophy is based on. Further, in *An Aesthetic Education in the
Era of Globalization* (2012), Spivak argues that this way in which reason
supplements the gaps is the kind of an intended 'mistake' on which the
philosopher depends for his theories to be consolidated. She quotes Kant's

---

[15] Spivak, *Critique*, 32.

[16] Spivak, *Critique*, 26.

[17] Spivak, *Critique*, 147.

definition of the word 'maxim' – which is a truth-claim – in the following manner:

> I call all subjective grounding propositions [*Grundsätze*] that are found [*hergenommen*] not from the nature [*Beschaffenheitt*] of the object [Latin spelling] but from the interest of reason in regard to a specific [*gewiss*] possible perfection of the cognition of the object [Latin spelling], maxims of reason. Thus there are maxims of speculative reason's speculative reason, which rest unsupported [*lediglicl*] on reason's speculative interest, even though it may seem as if they were objective principles [*Principien*].[18]

Of course, Spivak here concentrates on the fact that most English translations of this passage hide the strong wording of Kant because, unlike *Principien* which are objective principles, *Grundsätze* refers to subjective principles. The fact that, according to Spivak's translation of *Grundsätze,* maxims are subjective principles which are used by the philosopher as if they were objective leads Spivak to conclude that a "'maxim' is something that the philosopher devises in order to come to terms with the transcendental gap at the origin of philosophy."[19] Then, she argues that "Kant's own text can also be described as an intended mistake."[20]

The philosopher is aware of the maxim, or the mistake, used by him to supplement the gap in his theory but the danger lies in such maxims being exploited by politicians because politicians are not aware of why such maxims are existent.[21] For example, in her reading of the third critique, Spivak explains that since freedom is achieved through man's ability to judge the sublime without fearing it and since this happens via culture, Kant's text provides an alibi for correcting the mistake of 'man in the raw' who views the sublime as fearful, in order to civilise and enable him to pass to freedom. In other words, the relationship between the western subject and the 'native informant,' "the not-yet-subject," is established on the former's conviction that the latter's mistake must be corrected by culture through the civilising mission.[22] Spivak contends:

---

[18] Immanuel Kant, "Toward a Perpetual Peace," in *Political Writings,* translated by H. B. Nisbet (Cambridge: Cambridge University Press, 1991), 130, quoted in Spivak, *An Aesthetic Education in the Era of Globalization* (London: Harvard University Press, 2012), 14.

[19] Spivak, *An Aesthetic Education,* 16.

[20] Spivak, *An Aesthetic Education,* 20.

[21] Spivak, *An Aesthetic Education,* 16.

[22] Spivak, *Critique,* 14.

[T]he mistake made by the *raw* man, for whom the abyss of the infinite is fearful rather than sublime, must be corrected through culture itself, although on the threshold of such a project [the project of correcting the mistake committed by the 'native informant'] stands the peculiar relationship between productive and natural culture cited earlier. (One of the ideological consequences of this relationship might be the conviction that the cultural mission of imperialism can never really succeed, but it must nonetheless be undertaken.[23]

Therefore, Spivak believes that the seeds for the civilising mission were sown by the philosophy of Enlightenment and she traces the influence of this idea on the literary texts discussed in her chapter on literature.

The New Hollander and the Fuegian

Spivak draws her second example of Kant's foreclosure of the 'native informant' from "Analytic of Teleological Judgment," the part in which Kant proposes that we must assume an intelligent Being who is the author of the world, and who is beyond the sensible. Kant reaches this conclusion through viewing nature as governed by a final intentional end. He argues that although we can discover the mechanical laws which control the material objects of nature, we cannot depend on such laws for all objects to explain organisms. For example, we can know by mechanical laws that a tree sheds its leaves to store water, but these laws cannot be used to understand how the tree has been organised in a way that makes this process possible. Therefore, Kant resorts to the theory of purposes which govern nature, suggesting that an object is a natural purpose if it produces and is produced by itself. The tree, for example, produces another tree and can grow by its ability to separate and recombine the materials it takes from nature. The tree then is an organised and self-organising being in which every part is there for the sake of other parts and for the sake of the whole. Knowing this internal purposiveness of the tree is called by Kant the intrinsic purposiveness and if it is present, the object is called a natural purpose. A natural purpose is different from an object or being that is a purpose of nature. A purpose of nature can be judged according to extrinsic purposiveness which refers to the external purposive relations between things. In order to be able to describe an object or a being as a purpose of nature, we need to know the final purpose of nature itself. But

---

[23] Spivak, *Critique*, 14.

this final purpose can be sought only super-sensibly beyond nature since we do not know why nature itself should exist.

Kant supposes that nature is designed in accordance with the human mind and its pleasure, so man is the purpose of nature. However, Kant admits that the theory of purposes is complicated by the presence of the New Hollanders and the Fuegians as he explains:

> The internal form of a mere blade of grass suffices to prove to our human judging ability that the blade can have originated only under the rule of purposes. But we arrive at no categorical [but only a hypothetical] purpose if we disregard the internal form and organization, and consider instead extrinsic purposive relations as to what use other natural beings make of the grass: how cattle need grass, and how people need cattle as a means for their existence. We cannot arrive at a categorical purpose in this way because, after all, we cannot see why people should have to exist (a question it might not be so easy to answer if we have in mind, say, the New Hollanders or the Fuegians).[24]

In his review of Spivak's *A Critique of Postcolonial Reason,* Vijay Mishra contends:

> We know from other sources (for example, Rousseau) that the inhabitants of these newly discovered lands were considered to be particularly savage and we also know that the New Hollander is the Australian aborigine. Although the passage quoted [Kant's passage on the New Hollander] is given in parenthesis and is a minor aside (for philosophers), it has considerable anthropological significance because these examples of absolute rawness, the irredeemable native Others, are presented as figures who cannot be the subject of speech or judgment in the *Critique* [*Critique of Judgment*].[25]

Kant chooses the New Hollanders and the Fuegians, rather than man in general or western man, to show his confusion about the final purpose of nature. If man is the purpose of nature but still it is not clear why the New Hollander should exist, Spivak comments, it means that Kant does not consider the New Hollander to be a human being. It is this selection of examples that troubles Spivak, who objects to considering them as merely casual rhetorical examples. She asserts that Kant in this passage expels the aboriginal from the species of the rational human in order to prove the universality of the rational man who is capable of judgment. In other

---

[24] Kant, *Critique of Judgement,* 258.
[25] Vijay Mishra, "Review of Gayatri Chakraborty Spivak, *A Critique of Postcolonial Reason,*" *Textual Practice* 14:2 (2000): 416.

words, she means that Kant needed the exclusion of the 'native informant' in order to consolidate western man as a moral rational self. So, immediately after introducing the 'native informant,' Kant excludes him/her from the Name of Man and this is what foreclosure means. Nonetheless, since for Lacan foreclosure happens only symbolically, the 'native informant' is also excluded only from the symbolic order. As the foreclosed idea in Lacan's theory appears in the real as the impossible that cannot be represented, the 'native informant' in the real appears but s/he becomes the subaltern whose consciousness cannot be retrieved and represented. We can conclude that the foreclosure of the 'native informant' makes the rational being in Kant's theory a false universal.

Spivak's anthropological intervention

As explained above, Spivak takes the moment of the emergence of the 'native informant' in Kant's text not as a casual example, but as an anthropological moment underlain by racial difference. Thus, the second step, following the selection of her examples, is Spivak's anthropological intervention. The clearest influence on Spivak's anthropological intervention while reading Kant is the anthropologist Johannes Fabian to whom Spivak refers twice in *A Critique of Postcolonial Reason*. Fabian blames the philosophy of Enlightenment for absenting the 'native informant' as he makes clear in his book: *Time and the Other: How Anthropology Makes its Subject* (1983). In his opinion, Enlightenment philosophy's source of the representation of the Other was anthropology in which the Other was empirically present as a 'native informant' giving information. Then, this philosophy exploited the 'native informant's' empirical presence and theorised him/her. This, Fabian stresses, caused a contradiction in anthropological principles because the philosophy of Enlightenment changed the presence of the 'native informant' in anthropological studies into a theoretical absence in philosophy. Fabian contends:

> On the one hand we dogmatically insist that anthropology rests on ethnographic research involving personal, prolonged interaction with the Other. But then we pronounce upon the knowledge gained from such research a discourse which construes the Other in terms of distance, spatial and temporal. The Other's empirical presence turns into his theoretical absence [...][26]

---

[26] Johannes Fabian, *Time and the Other: how Anthropology Makes its Object* (New York: Colombia University Press, 1983), xi.

Spivak's anthropological intervention is inspired by Fabian's take on the philosophy of Enlightenment because turning the 'native informant' into an absence is exactly what Spivak criticises in her reading of Kant's third critique. Introducing anthropology, using the term 'native informant' and referring to Fabian denote that Spivak thinks that Kant constructed the 'native informant' from the anthropological studies of his time and then changed this figure into a theoretical absence. In this respect, Simon Swift lists many studies that were published in the twentieth century explaining relations between Kant's philosophy and anthropology. Swift argues that these relations "have been significantly qualified through closer attention to Kant's involvement in debates about the growth of philosophical anthropology in the German academy from the 1760s onwards, and in particular during the composition of the *Critique of Judgment* after 1785."[27] For Spivak, Kant absents the 'native informant' theoretically when he finds that the existence of the 'native informant' is inexplicable, thereby dismissing the 'native informant' not only from the text but also from the human species. Therefore, Spivak wants to situate the moment when this dismissal happens in Kant's text, opposing thereby the recommendations of the literary critic and theorist Paul de Man who insists that Kant's text must be read as purely dealing with epistemological concepts.

Paul de Man: tropological deconstruction and misreading

Bart Moore-Gilbert argues that "following the lead of her teacher Paul de Man in *Allegories of Reading* (1979), Spivak is equally interested in the ways that the rhetoric or style of texts [...] interrupt and contradict their logical or thematic propositions."[28] Moore-Gilbert's statement is plausible since de Man was Spivak's supervisor during her PhD and this is how she defines her relation with him: "I am not a scholar of de Man. I am his student, perhaps his first PhD."[29] In addition, the fact that de Man is one of the two people to whom she dedicates *A Critique of Postcolonial Reason* requires attention to the contribution of his work to Spivak's own critical practice mainly concerning the dichotomy literature/philosophy, and to her reading of Kant, which enriched her reading of three of the five texts tackled in this book. In an article discussing contours of learning in

---

[27] Simon Swift, "Kant, Herder, and the Question of Philosophical Anthropology," *Textual Practice* 19:2 (2005): 219.

[28] Bart Moore-Gilbert, *Postcolonial Theory: Contexts, Practices, Politics* (London: Verso, 1997), 84.

[29] Spivak, "Learning from de Man: Looking Back," *Boundary 2* 32:3 (2005): 27.

Spivak's works, Simon Swift says that Spivak for a long time seemed to be wavering between esteeming and renouncing de Man.[30] Actually, Swift's conclusion is not far from true because, as will be explained in the following paragraphs, Spivak applies de Man's two-step deconstruction although she renounces his insistence on philosophical correctness and his warning against introducing empirical discourses into philosophy.

In reading Kant, Spivak's effort is associated with de Man's criticism in a way that she makes use of his theories to disobey his instructions to readers of philosophy and literature. First, Spivak benefits from de Man's version of deconstruction, tropological deconstruction which consists of two steps to reveal the points where a text can be misread by critics. Second, Spivak disobeys de Man's instructions and goes further: after revealing the points that may lead to misreading the text, she uses these very points to deliberately misread the text. She describes this deliberate misreading as a "mistaken" reading.[31] In the following paragraphs, the relationship between Spivak's work and de Man's will be explained because describing this relationship is essential for an understanding of her reading of Kant and the first three texts tackled in this book.

De Man's tropological deconstruction

The first influence of de Man's approach on Spivak is his version of deconstruction. For de Man, all texts including philosophical ones are figural texts that contain figures of speech or tropes. He explains that "the paradigm of all texts consists of a figure (or a system of figures) and its deconstruction."[32] Spivak calls de Man's version "tropological deconstruction."[33] Tropological deconstruction can be defined as that which deconstructs the text by revealing how the tropes cause the interruption of the understanding of the text. This interruption leads to the deconstruction of the text and, as a result, it leads the reader to misread the text. In light of de Man's explanation, misreading happens unintentionally due to the interruption produced by the tropes of the text. Spivak expresses her specific interest in de Man's explanation of parabasis.

Parabasis comes originally from Greek comedy and can be defined as "the moment when the continuity of the dramatic narrative is disrupted by

---

[30] Simon Swift, "The Lesson of Gayatri Spivak," *Parallax* 17:3 (2011): 88.

[31] Spivak, *Critique,* 9.

[32] Paul de Man, *Allegories of Reading: Figural Language in Rousseau, Nietzsche, Rilke and Proust* (London: Yale University Press, 1979), 205.

[33] Spivak, *Critique,* 23

the sudden intrusion of the playwright."[34] Spivak says that in Greek drama, parabasis is the moment when the Chorus steps out "to tell the public how to respond to the main text of the Old Comedy."[35] As for de Man, he takes 'parabasis' from the German poet and critic Friedrich Schlegel (1772-1829). Schlegel said that irony is a 'permanent parabasis' and, consequently, stability and continuity are always interrupted.[36] De Man, being a deconstructionist, takes this to denote that "irony as the radically diachronic operation of permanent parabasis is a proto-form of Jacques Derrida's principle of *différance,* which always already interrupts—or differs and defers—any purportedly synchronic claim to sheer immediacy or self-presence."[37] Textually speaking, for de Man, parabasis is "the interruption of a discourse by a shift in the rhetorical register."[38] Therefore, for Spivak, parabasis is a proper tool for deconstructing great western texts to interrupt them and produce a counter-narrative in the interest of the subaltern. It is the part of the text which is interrupted by all reminders of discontinuity, Spivak argues, "that has become for me the description of the resistance fitting our time."[39] In Spivak's reading of Kant, parabasis as the interruption of the text is based on the 'native informant.'

Spivak uses tropological deconstruction in her reading of Kant's third critique and she declares her "attempt to read the anthropological moment in Kant as consonant with Paul de Man's version of deconstruction."[40] She applies this deconstructionist approach following the example of de Man's discussion of the allegory of reading in Jean Jacques Rousseau's *profession de foi* (The profession of faith), which is a section of Book IV in Rousseau's *Emile, or On Education* (1762). In his *Allegories of Reading: Figural Language in Rousseau, Nietzsche, Rilke and Proust* (1979), de Man deconstructs Rousseau's text following two steps. The first is the tropological step according to which de Man shows how the text reveals that what is claimed as truth in the text is only a trope. The

---

[34] Ayon Roy, "Hegel contra Schlegel; Kierkegaard contra de Man," *PMLA* 124:1(2009): 107.

[35] Gayatri Chakravorty Spivak, "From Haverstock Hill Flat to U.S. Classroom," in *What's Left of Theory: New York on the Politics of Literary Theory,* edited by Judith Butler *et al* (London: Routledge, 2000), 31.

[36] Roy, "Hegel contra Schlegel," 107.

[37] Roy, "Hegel contra Schlegel," 108.

[38] Paul de Man, "The Concept of Irony," in *Aesthetic Ideology,* edited by Andrzej Warminski (Minneapolis: Univ. of Minnesota Press, 1996), 178

[39] Spivak, "Learning from de Man," 28.

[40] Spivak, *Critique,* 1.

second is the performative step according to which de Man reveals how the text offers a substitute truth-claim in order to offer the corrected version of truth. In other words, de Man shows that a philosopher, like Rousseau, may face a gap, a truth-claim, while reasoning. To fill such a gap, the philosopher introduces another truth-claim and it is here where the text deconstructs itself and it is these interruptions in the text that lead readers to misread. When the deconstructionist reads such a text, s/he must follow two steps. The first is finding the gap in the text and the second is revealing the truth-claim used to fill this gap.

Spivak benefits from this two-step deconstruction in her reading of philosophy and literature. Spivak does use the term 'truth-claims' in dealing with literary texts. For example, in "Imperialism and Sexual Difference" where she analyses Baudelaire's "Le cygne" and Kipling's "William the Conqueror," Spivak says:

> My theoretical model is taken from Paul de Man. De Man suggests that a critical philosopher initially discovers that the basis of a truth-claim is no more than a trope. In the case of academic feminism the discovery is that to take the privileged male of the white race as a norm for universal humanity is no more than a politically interested figuration. It is a trope that passes itself off as truth, and claims that man or the racial other is merely a kind of troping of that truth of man – in the sense that they must be understood as unlike (non-identical with) it and yet with reference to it.[41]

Spivak implies that a dominant discourse uses a trope on the first side of the binary as if it were a truth. Then, everything placed on the other side of the binary is only a troping of this claimed truth. Accordingly, in the patriarchal discourse the man is the truth and the woman is the trope. However, Spivak understands from de Man that what is claimed as true, the man, is only a trope and, consequently, what is claimed as a trope of the truth is a trope of the trope. Hence, the binary can be deconstructed. A critic must first reveal this troping structure and then reveal the truth-claim.

As explained above, for Spivak a truth-claim in philosophy is a maxim, or an intended 'mistake' used by the philosopher to fill a gap in his theory. However, one may wonder what a truth-claim in literature may mean, especially fiction – since the texts tackled in this book are fictional ones. We can explain Spivak's use of the concept 'truth-claim' in fiction in the following manner: since Spivak applies de Man's tropological deconstruction

---

[41] Gayatri Chakravorty Spivak, "Imperialism and Sexual Difference," *Oxford Literary Review* 8 (1986): 225.

to both literature and philosophy, this means that, like de Man, Spivak believes that all texts, whether philosophical or literary, do not present the truth. De Man thinks that all texts use the medium of language which is interrupted by the tropes to produce knowledge. According to Spivak, what happens is that philosophy presupposes and literature represents and in both cases truth-claims are used.[42] This is clear in Spivak's book: *A Critique of Postcolonial Reason* where she discusses philosophy, literature, culture and history as all equally producers of a structure of knowledge which foreclosed the 'native subaltern female.' It may occur to Spivak's readers that she is stating the obvious since it is known that literature does not offer the truth. However, it must be clarified that the problem for Spivak is that although literature does not present the truth, literary truth-claims, like the savagery of the Other, at certain stages were consolidated as the truth to justify political decisions and actions like colonialism. In addition, literary truth-claims passed themselves as truth in education and this constructed the colonial subjects as was the case in India. Although she, as a critic, is aware that these are only truth-claims, Spivak did not have the same awareness when she was a student. She says:

> [W]e were brought up in an education system in India where the name of the hero of that philosophical system was the universal human being, and we were taught that if we could begin to approach that universal human being, then we would be human.[43]

Spivak follows the two-step tropological deconstruction in reading Kant's third critique. According to Spivak's understanding of it, *Critique of Judgment* deconstructs itself first by showing that what it presents as freedom, achieved when reason defeats the fear resulting from encountering the sublime, is only a trope because it happens through a programmed process to which we are obliged to attune our mind and this attunement happens through western culture. This freedom, construed by Spivak in this manner, is not accessed by the 'native informants' since they are not prepared by western culture. The second step in the text's deconstruction of itself is clear when Kant is troubled by finding out the purpose of the existence of the New Hollanders and the Fuegians. In order to resolve this problem and supplement his theory, Kant needs to exclude them from the Name of Man. One can understand from Spivak's analysis that the exclusion

---

[42] Spivak, *Critique,* xi.
[43] Gayatri Chakravorty Spivak, *The Postcolonial Critic: Interviews, Strategies, Dialogues,* ed. Sarah Harasym (London: Routledge, 1990), 7.

of the 'native informant' as the trope of the western male is the truth-claim that helps Kant prove the rational man as a universal truth.

After she has deconstructed Kant's critique in the de Manian way, Spivak exploits the tropes that make Kant's text open to misreading. Heedless to de Man's warning against reading Kant empirically, Spivak misreads Kant on purpose and describes her misreading as a 'mistaken reading.' She makes use of the interruption in Kant's text caused by the New Hollander and intervenes claiming that this figure stands for the 'native informant.' Thus, the new Hollander is the figure of interruption that allows Spivak to use the resulting parabasis to draw her own conclusions producing her own truth-claim: the foreclosure of the 'native informant.' Kant's truth-claim, Spivak emphasises, belongs to the axiomatics of imperialism. For example, she makes clear that by concluding that there is an author of the world, God, Kant fills the lack in the human mind which cannot recognise the final purpose of existence. However, Kant undermines how other cultures filled the same gap. Spivak infers that though there is no clear discussion of racial and cultural difference, it is implicitly present. She also infers that for Kant the best supplementation of the lack in the human mind comes through Christianity. All these inferences serve the aim of Spivak's travesty of Kant's text because they lead to the conclusion that in order to correct the mistake committed by the 'native informant' and offer a corrected version of truth, Christianity should be spread and this leads to the civilising mission of imperialism.

De Man's influence on Spivak is also represented by his critique of Kant and the German philosopher, poet and playwright Friedrich Schiller which drew Spivak's attention to the philosophical mistake against which de Man warns. Spivak proposes a new method for reading great western texts. This method consists of two stages. The first is the two-step tropological deconstruction advocated by de Man and the second is the philosophical 'mistake' that is rejected by de Man. A better understanding of this deviation from de Man's warning against the philosophical mistake can be achieved by explaining the context of this warning and Spivak's attitude to it.

De Man's criticism of Schiller and Spivak's 'mistaken' reading of Kant

Undoubtedly, Spivak's reading of Kant was informed by the lectures which de Man delivered between 1981 and 1983 and which were published in *Aesthetic Ideology* in 1996. In his lecture "Kant and Schiller," which he delivered in 1983, de Man criticises Schiller for introducing the empirical into Kant's purely epistemological *Critique of Judgment*.

De Man's reading is concerned with showing that the way Schiller approaches Kant's mathematical sublime – the absolutely huge that our imagination cannot grasp – and the dynamic sublime – that is to be found in nature like tempests – is a philosophical mistake or a misreading. In a lecture preceding "Schiller and Kant," de Man tries to prove that Kant's third critique contains figures of speech that can lead to misreadings of the text. He reads the experience of the sublime as a story in which imagination, unable to judge the sublime, sacrifices itself and its freedom for the sake of reason. Then, de Man wonders how the faculties of the mind which are supposed to be discussed as transcendental concepts in the service of a philosophical text can act like conscious human beings capable of sacrifice. As a result, de Man maintains that the faculties of the mind in Kant's explanation of the sublime are tropes not mental categories and they are governed by the laws of figural language not those of the mind. The trope around which the dynamic sublime revolves in de Man's understanding is anthropomorphism, attributing human behaviour or characteristics to things or natural phenomena. De Man emphasises this by saying: "instead of being an argument, it [the experience of the sublime] is a story, a dramatized scene of the mind in action. The faculties of reason and imagination are personified or anthropomorphized."[44] In his opinion, this figurality in the third critique makes the text open to misreading and, as an example, de Man explains Schiller's reading of Kant which introduced an empirical aspect into a philosophical text.

Schiller, de Man argues, re-inscribes Kant's theory of the sublime by viewing the mathematical sublime and the dynamic sublime as antitheses, or two drives: the drive to know and represent the sublime and the drive to maintain the body when encountering the sublime in nature. De Man observes that Schiller introduces the psychological discourse, an intervention which is justified by the latter's career as a playwright. Moreover, Schiller adds concrete elements to the experience of the sublime when he, for example, argues that it is not sublime that man, encountering a natural sublime like a tempest, puts up a fence to protect his body from danger, since man in this case uses tools from nature as a means of protection. However, it is sublime that, contrary to the body, man's reason can still be extremely free even when a tempest threatens man's safety. De Man's problem with Schiller's reading is related to the first part which is the example of putting up a fence because, as de Man

---

[44] De Man, "Phenomenality and Materiality in Kant," in *Aesthetic Ideology,* 86.

insists, "this notion of physical danger, of a threatening physical Nature, in an empirical sense – highly empirical, we are threatened concretely by fire, or by a tempest – you will find no trace of that whatsoever in Kant."[45] In Kant, the element of danger, as read by de Man, serves only to introduce the element of shock at realising the failure of imagination to represent the sublime. It is merely an epistemological issue related to developing a certain state of mind rather than practical self-preservation like putting up a fence. Kant explains that the human mind cannot achieve freedom from the fear of the sublime when danger is real. This freedom is only possible when man is safe and can imagine being threatened by the obstacles of nature. Thus, for de Man, Kant did not speak about danger as reality but as a trope. What we can understand from de Man's criticism is that the fact that danger is only a trope in Kant's text is what causes Schiller's misreading of it. De Man advocates:

> Kant was dealing with a strictly philosophical concern, with a strictly philosophical, epistemological problem, which he chose to state for reasons of his own in interpersonal, dramatic terms, thus telling dramatically and interpersonally something which was purely epistemological and which had nothing to do with the pragmata of the relationship between human beings. Here, in Schiller's case, the explanation is entirely empirical, psychological without any concern for epistemological implications. And for that reason, Schiller can then claim that in this negotiation, in this arrangement, where the analogy of danger is substituted for the real danger, where the imagination of danger is substituted for the experience of danger, that by this substitution, this tropological substitution, that the sublime succeeds, that the sublime works out, that the sublime achieves itself, and brings together a new kind of synthesis [...] Schiller appears as the ideology of Kant's critical philosophy.[46]

In brief, accusing him of lacking philosophical concern, de Man insists that Schiller re-inscribes Kant's sublime reasonably when regarding writing a successful play with the purpose of affecting the audience by scenes of terror, rather than when answering Kant's questions about the structure of the faculties of imagination and reason. Hence, Schiller commits a philosophical mistake and offers a misreading of Kant.

Depending on de Man's model, one can argue that Kant's use of 'man in the raw' (the New Hollander and the Fuegian) is also a trope and that it cannot be taken to the world of the real as is the case in Spivak's reading

---

[45] De Man, "Kant and Schiller," *Aesthetic Ideology*, p. 139.
[46] Paul de Man, "Kant and Schiller," 143, 147.

which associates these figures with the real 'native informant' who cannot be represented symbolically. Thus, as Schiller adds a concrete experience of danger to Kant's sublime, Spivak adds the anthropological aspect through insisting on the anthropological 'native informant.' The 'native informant' is an addition which Spivak then valorises considering that without foreclosing this figure, Kant's theory and his introduction of the rational man as a universal cannot be possible.

De Man's emphasis on the purely epistemological interests of Kant's text results in taking all the latter's examples to be only casual points that serve the philosophical concerns of his critiques. Spivak regards this de Manian emphasis on epistemology as giving excuses to Kant, particularly concerning the 'native informant.' For her part, Spivak declares that her aim in reading Kant is "to situate rather than expurgate the anthropomorphic moment in Kant."[47] This addition of the 'native informant' is Spivak's travesty as concerns Kant's third critique. She travesties this addition to lead her readers to the following line of thinking: de Man declares that the reception of Kant led to materialism and empiricism, as shown in his criticism of Schiller; Spivak insists that the materialism and empiricism resulting from Kant's philosophy were exploited by politicians to justify the imperialist project of the civilising mission in other parts of the world, such as the South. Therefore, as politics anthropologised the New Hollander and the Fuegian as figures that must be civilised, Spivak travesties these figures anthropologically to prove that Kant's text needed this foreclosure in order to consolidate his theory.

Whereas de Man supposes that Schiller's misreading is an unintentional one based on a "distant memory" of a passage in Kant's text, Spivak admits that her 'mistaken' reading is a deliberate strategy when she says:

> I will call my reading of Kant 'mistaken.' I believe there are just disciplinary grounds for irritation at my introduction of the 'empirical and the anthropological' into a philosophical text that slowly leads us toward the rational study of morals as such. I rehearse it in the hope that such a reading might take into account that philosophy has been and continues to be travestied in the service of the narrativization of history. My exercise may be called a scrupulous travesty in the interest of producing a counternarrative that will make visible the foreclosure of the subject whose lack of access to the position of narrator is the condition of possibility of the consolidation of Kant's position.[48]

---

[47] Spivak, *Critique,* 16.
[48] Spivak, *Critique,* 9.

She also says: "Schiller did not intend his mistake; he was a Kantian" and "it is on the ground of intended versus unintended mistakes that we can differentiate ourselves from Schiller."[49] By insisting on the deliberate anthropologising of Kant's text, Spivak stresses that she has done this strategically, finding her justification in Derrida. Derrida disapproves of naively anthropologising philosophy but only "outlines doing so strategically" for other non-western nationalities to find a place within philosophical debates to speak from. He justifies this strategic anthropologising of philosophy in "The Ends of Man," a lecture which he delivered in 1968 at an international colloquium tackling the relationship between anthropology and philosophy.[50] Derrida explains that western philosophy till his time revolved around anthropos, the human being as distinguished from other beings. He refers to western philosophers' obsession with defining Being, human truth or the essence of man and describes this obsession as philosophical anthropology. Thus, for Derrida western philosophy was a repetitive failure to define man, and it was a basis for different ideologies such as the spiritualist, atheist, or Marxist. Furthermore, during the search for the meaning of Being, western philosophers like Martin Heidegger, Derrida asserts, privileged self-presence, the being that we are. Discussing Heidegger's texts Derrida says:

> It is this self-presence, this absolute proximity of the (questioning) being to itself [...] which motivates the choice of the exemplary being, of the text, the good text for the hermeneutic of the meaning of Being. It is the proximity to itself of the questioning being which leads it to be chosen as the privileged interrogated being.[51]

This privilege of self-presence implies the exclusion of the Other who lies at the margins of philosophy. In light of this privilege of the self in western philosophy which claims universality, Derrida justifies the attempts of philosophers who come from non-western cultures to anthropologise philosophy until they find the place to speak from. Derrida declares that at the time when "The Ends of Man" was written, philosophical nationalities had been formed in opposition to how philosophy had defined itself as universal, trying to master and interiorise difference. The colloquium at which Derrida delivered this lecture included philosophical nationalities that encountered one another to define their differences and establish relationships among these differences.

---

[49] Spivak, *An Aesthetic Education*, 20.
[50] Spivak, *Critique,* 17.
[51] Jacques Derrida, "The Ends of Man," in *Margins of Philosophy,* translated by Alan Bass (London: Harvester, 1982), 125-126.

This is what Spivak means by Derrida's outline of the strategic anthropologising of philosophy. She quotes:

> [T]he anxious and busy multiplication of colloquia in the West is doubtless an effect of [a] difference [...] of an entirely other order than that of the internal or intra-philosophical differences of opinion [...] that is bearing down, with a mute, growing and menacing pressure, on the enclosure of Western collocution. The latter doubtless makes an effort to interiorize this difference, to master it, [...] by affecting itself with it.[52]

Following Derrida's example, Spivak reads Kant's third critique as attempting to define man as a rational being filling the gap by excluding the 'native informant.' Adding the figure of the 'native informant' to Kant's text is a strategy that gives Spivak the grounds that consolidate her effort to offer a critique of postcolonial reason. Whereas Kant, in Spivak's argument, forecloses the 'native informant' to complete his critique, she herself sheds light on this foreclosure to start her critique and this is her counter-narrative.

Kant and western feminism in Spivak's work

Spivak establishes the relationship between Kant's foreclosure of the 'native informant' and the discourse of western feminism of the twentieth century by quoting the following passage from Kant's third critique:

> There is only one external purposiveness which is connected with the internal purposiveness of organization, and yet serves in the external relation of a means to a purpose, without the question necessarily arising as to what end this being so organized must have existed for. This is the organization of both sexes in their mutual relation for the propagation of their kind [...] Why must such a pair exist? The answer is: This pair first constitutes an organizing whole, though not an organized whole in a single body.[53]

Here, Spivak argues that whereas Kant has no explanation for the existence of the 'native informant' in terms of the theory of purposes, he has an explanation to offer concerning woman's presence in nature. Consequently, Spivak says:

---

[52] Derrida, "The Ends of Man," *Margins of Philosophy,* translated by Allan Bass (Chicago: Univ. of Chicago Press, 1982), 113, quoted in Spivak, *A Critique,* 17 [emphasis in the original]

[53] Kant, *Critique of Judgement,* 275, quoted in Spivak, *A Critique,* 29.

The discontinuity between sex- and race- differentiation is one of the arguments in this book [*A Critique of Postcolonial Reason*]. When the Woman is put outside of Philosophy by the Master Subject, she is argued into that dismissal, not foreclosed as a casual rhetorical gesture. The ruses against the racial other are different.[54]

This discontinuity between the struggle of feminism and that of the 'native informant' governs Spivak's reading of the texts tackled in this book.

Hence, the relationship between Kant's third critique and feminism in Spivak's reading of literature can be discussed in two ways. First, this relationship can be explained in terms of inheritance and similarity. Second, the difference between Kant's approach to the female and that to the 'native informant' drives Spivak to the conclusion that the struggle of feminism and that of the racial Other are discontinuous. The discontinuity between the two struggles re-shapes Spivak's feminist ideas and it is through her study of *Jane Eyre, Wide Sargasso Sea, Frankenstein, Foe* and "Pterodactyl" that she re-emphasises her position within the feminist background dominant at that time. When she discusses 'man in the raw' in Kant's critique, Spivak says:

> As I hope to show, the figure of the "native informant" is, by contrast [to woman], foreclosed. Rhetorically crucial at the most important moment in the argument, it is not part of the argument in any way. Was it in this rift that the seeds of the civilizing mission of today's universalist feminism were sown?[55]

She argues that the discourses of western feminism inherited the foreclosure of the 'native informant' from Kant's philosophy. Consequently, western feminism foreclosed the 'native subaltern female' from the passage to female freedom since this female needs the civilising mission of western feminism before she can pass to freedom. Mentioning some examples, like Sarah Kofman and Beverly Brown, Spivak argues that western feminists traced the exclusion of women in Kant's text without including the 'native subaltern female' who is doubly excluded in Kant, first as a woman and second as a 'native informant.' This neglect and exclusion of the 'native subaltern female' is what led Spivak to re-define her position within western feminism. She does this by rejecting feminist essentialism and by emphasising heterogeneity.

---

[54] Spivak, *Critique,* 30.
[55] Spivak, *Critique,* 13, n. 20.

The shift from the second wave to the third wave of feminism

Spivak is often described as an anti-essentialist feminist because, as Mark Sanders states, she defines herself "against metropolitan feminism and its unquestioned assumptions and agendas."[56] For Spivak, such unquestioned assumptions lead western feminism to the trap of essentialism. One of the explanations of essentialism, especially with regard to Spivak's studies, is offered by Childs and Williams who say:

> One instance would be the belief that language has an essential meaning – that there is a concrete, specific, unchanging meaning for a term such as 'British' or 'West Indian': as opposed to a belief that words take on their meanings through usage and discursive power. Such essentializing becomes the basis for exclusion and exploitation through a rhetoric of verisimilitude and authenticity that asserts what is 'real' or 'true'.[57]

Applied within feminism, Alison Stone vies, essentialism entails that "there are properties essential to women and which all women (therefore) share [...] the properties that are universal and essential to all women might be either natural or socially constructed."[58] That is, women are given a fixed identity and meaning, without paying attention to the differences that distinguish different women's experiences.

The feminist background in relation to which Spivak was trying to position herself can be understood by summarising the differences between what are sometimes referred to as the second and third waves of feminism. Speaking of the three waves of feminism, we must be aware that the history of feminism is long dating back to the early twentieth century and perhaps further. However, reviewing the feminism of the last fifty years, a possible definition of first-wave feminism is the one presented by Barbara Arneil in *Politics and Feminism* when she says:

> The goal for most of the first wave feminists was largely to get white middle- and upper- class women inside the public and cultural world from which they were excluded. In keeping with liberal tenets, they argued that women were rational, differences between men and women were largely social rather than natural in origin and therefore education and training

---

[56] Sanders, *Gayatri Chakravorty Spivak,* 74.

[57] Childs and Williams, *An Introduction,* 159.

[58] Alison Stone, "On the Genealogy of Women: A Defence of Anti-Essentialism," in *Third Wave Feminism: A Critical Exploration,* edited by Stacy Gillis *et al* (Basingstoke: Palgrave Macmillan, 2007), 18.

could make women citizens in the same way men were. The goal was equality.[59]

The first wave, as Linda Nicholson argues, started with two political movements: "the first was the Women's Rights Movement, emerging early in the 1960s. This was a movement composed of largely professional women who began putting pressure on federal and state institutions to end the discrimination that women experienced in entering the paid labor force."[60] The second movement, the Women's Liberation Movement, emerged in the later part of the 1960s and it emerged out of the New Left. The New Left was a movement constituted of activists and educators who focused on marginality and identity politics and it started in the 1960s. This Women's Liberation Movement, Nicholson continues, was the source of the most theoretical writings of second-wave feminism.

Second-wave feminism, as many commentators, like Alison Stone, agree is the feminist generation which replaced the common anatomical features that bring women into a collectivity with common social constructions of women's roles such as domestic duties. The beginning of this idea was Simone de Bouvoir's *The Second Sex* (1949) where she states: "[o]ne is not born, but rather becomes, a woman. No biological, psychological, or economic fate determines the figure that the human female presents in society."[61] Second-wave feminist books and essays were written by French feminists like Julia Kristeva, Hélène Cixous, and Luce Irigaray. In 1981, *New French Feminisms: an Anthology* was published with the aim of beginning an exchange with the United States feminist scholarship because French feminist writings since 1968 had not been known in the United States.[62] In the introduction, the editors of this book try to differentiate between American and French feminisms. American feminists whose "style of reasoning [...] follows the Anglo-American empirical, inductive, anti-speculative tradition" insisted that women were present but invisible, and therefore they tried to resurrect the lost voices. French feminists, most of whom were intellectuals, professors of literature, and psychoanalysts tended to consider that women were absent completely in all patriarchal systems, like language and capitalism.

---

[59] Barbara Arneil, *Politics and Feminism* (Oxford: Blackwell, 1999), 156.

[60] Linda Nicholson, "Introduction," in *The Second Wave: A Reader in Feminist Theory*, edited by Linda Nicholson (New York: Routledge, 1997), 1.

[61] Simone de Bouvoir, *The Second Sex,* translated by H. M. Parshley (London: Jonathan Cape Ltd, 1953), 295.

[62] Elaine Marks and Isabelle de Courtivron, ed., *New French Feminisms: an Anthology* (Brighton: The Harvester Press, 1981), ix.

They tended to theorise about this female absence and the domination of the male discourse.

Spivak read the work of French feminists, inter alia Kristeva, and wrote for the two American journals, *Critical Inquiry* and *Yale French Studies*, which showed an interest in French feminism. However, in 1981 when she was asked to write for these two journals, Spivak decided not to be the spokeswoman for French feminism any longer, as she declared in 1985:

> I thought 'Isn't it strange that I should have become a spokeswoman for French high feminism, what's going on here?' So, to *Critical Inquiry*, I said that what I really wanted to do was to translate a piece of revolutionary Bengali feminist fiction, (my native language is Bengali) [...] and to YFS I suggested talking about my predicament as a spokeswoman for French feminism in the United States.[63]

From this declaration, one can argue that Spivak's dilemma as a feminist during the early 1980s was due to her being a Bengali woman who realised that the 'native subaltern female' did not have a position to speak from and could not participate in the feminist struggle. This relates to Spivak's conclusion that there is no continuity between the struggle of the feminist and that of the racial Other which she reads in Kant's third critique. Spivak's realisation that western feminism did not embrace the 'native subaltern female' led to the shift in her interests, a shift that started with writing "French Feminism in an International Frame" and translating Devi's short story "Draupadi" in 1981.[64] In "French Feminism in an International Frame," Spivak presents her criticism of French feminism for its complicity with the imperialist discourse in that it excludes the 'native subaltern female' from the feminist passage to freedom:

> The complicity of a few French texts in that attempt could be part both of the problem – the "West" out to "know" the "East" determining a "westernized Easterner's" symptomatic attempt to "know her own world"; or of something like a solution-reversing and displacing [...] the ironclad opposition of West and East.[65]

Indicative of her attitude to French feminism is Spivak's argument with respect to Julia Kristeva's book, *About Chinese Women* (1977), that

---

[63] Gayatri Chakravorty Spivak, "Strategies of Vigilance: An Interview with Gayatri Chakravorty Spivak," edited by Angela McRobbie, *Block* 10 (1985), 6.

[64] Spivak, *The Post-colonial Critic*, 167-8.

[65] Spivak, "French feminism in an International Frame," *Yale French Studies* 62 (1981): 155.

Kristeva's interest in Chinese women, like French feminists' interest in what they call 'Third-World' women, stems from a desire to consolidate the self.[66] Spivak contends that when encountering the silent Chinese women, Kristeva asks about her own identity rather than theirs. In seeking the consolidation of the self, the discourse of feminism is similar to that of Kant's third critique where the 'native informant' was needed only to consolidate the presentation of western rational man and was then immediately expelled. Spivak links Kristeva's encounter with the Chinese women to the repeated question she says is asked by western thinkers interested in issues of Otherness: "if we are not what official history and philosophy say we are, who then are we (not), how are we (not)?"[67] Thus, even when French feminism involves the 'Third-World' woman in feminist struggles, Spivak continues, there is no genuine other-directed politics because the real aim is consolidating the self.

Having realised that there is no genuine other-directed politics in French feminism, Spivak proposes the idea of unlearning the privilege as a step that can enable 'First-World' feminists to better approach 'Third-World' women. In other words, she implies, if they want to develop a different readership among 'Third-World' women, French feminists must stop viewing themselves as the universal feminist norm without appreciating the heterogeneity of women. If western feminists continue to feel privileged thinking that they know the 'Third-World' woman and can address her and help her, the exclusion of "millions of illiterate rural and urban Indian women who live 'in the pores of' capitalism, inaccessible to the capitalist dynamics that allow us our shared channels of communication, the definition of common enemies" will persist.[68] In addition, western feminists need to be aware that "[t]he pioneering books that bring First World feminists news from the Third World are written by privileged informants and can only be deciphered by a trained readership."[69] Without taking these recommendations into account, First-World feminism "will not necessarily escape the inbuilt colonialism of First World feminism toward the Third."[70] By stating this, Spivak means that as in colonialism the coloniser was privileged over the colonised, the 'First-World' woman

---

[66] In "French Feminism," Spivak was still using the terms "Third World," "First World" and consequently "Third-World Women." Therefore, in the paragraphs discussing the article, "Third World women" not the 'native subaltern female' will be used.

[67] Spivak, "French Feminism," 158-9.

[68] Spivak, "French Feminism," 156.

[69] Spivak, "French Feminism," 156.

[70] Spivak, "French Feminism," 184.

is privileged over the 'Third-World' woman, and herein feminism's complicity with imperialism is revealed.

Thus, Spivak implies that she was caught up in an institutional feminism which she would later criticise for its essentialism in tackling women's issues. In an interview with Elizabeth Grosz, Spivak said: "the Anglo-US-Western European intellectual – is imprisoned within an institutional discourse which says what is universal is universal without noticing that it is specific too."[71] What Spivak means by specific here is that this presentation of the universal female is based on a specific norm, the western; hence this is a false universal. Being part of this institutional feminism, Spivak herself was an essentialist feminist in her early writings, as she admitted to Ellen Rooney, saying:

> When I began to write as a feminist, the idea of differences being unjustly made and unjustly not recognized needed the presupposition that what was self-same or identical was an essence. It was okay as a strategic presupposition; it certainly allowed me to learn and teach. But it does seem that like most strategies, for me at least, it has served its purpose, and at this point I can't go on beating that horse anymore.[72]

Because the idea of heterogeneity was not acknowledged, the only way to struggle for feminism was by women's bonding to encounter one type of suffering, patriarchal suppression. Spivak, like other feminists, made use of this essentialism and this gave her the opportunity to learn and teach in the American academy until she became a well-known feminist scholar and had the chance to reject this essentialism and support heterogeneity, which is the orientation of third-wave feminism. For instance, Spivak taught *Jane Eyre* for an academic year, and learnt that her previous admiration for the heroine, Jane, had made her inattentive to the fact that the Jamaican Creole, Bertha, is denied the passage to female individualism in some Anglo-American feminist readings of the novel. So, her involvement with essentialist feminism paved Spivak's way towards learning how to pay attention to the heterogeneity of women's experiences and becoming more concerned with the 'native subaltern female.' This strategic essentialism which enabled Spivak to find a place to speak from in order to learn and then expose the exclusion of the 'native subaltern female' reminds us of the strategic anthropologising of philosophy in Derrida's "The Ends of Man." It is in Derrida's work where Spivak finds justification for her strategies.

---

[71] Gayatri Chakravorty Spivak, "Criticism, Feminism and the Institution," edited by Elizabeth Grosz, *Thesis Eleven* 11 (1984/85): 178.
[72] Gayatri Chakravorty Spivak, "In a Word: Interview," in *The Second Wave*, 369.

Spivak's criticism of Anglo-American feminism was narrowed down to cover its literary criticism in "Three Women's Texts" and the first and clearest example of this is her reference to Sandra M. Gilbert and Susan Gubar's reading of *Jane Eyre*. Gilbert and Gubar are usually described as second-wave feminist critics. Their most famous book is *The Madwoman in the Attic: the Woman Writer and the Nineteenth-Century Literary Imagination* which was published in 1979. This book was the result of teaching a course in literature written by women, and it was influenced by Elaine Showalter's *A Literature of Their Own: British Women Novelists from Brontë to Lessing*. In the preface to their book, Gilbert and Gubar admit that Showalter was very useful to their project because she demonstrated that nineteenth-century female writers did have a literary tradition. Indeed, Showalter argues that during the nineteenth century "women themselves have constituted a subculture within the framework of a larger society, and have been unified by values, conventions, experiences and behaviors impinging on each individual."[73] In 1979, Showalter used the term 'gynocriticism' to refer to this interest in women as writers. Having the same concerns as Showalter's and having nineteenth-century women writers as the subject of their study, Gilbert and Gubar declare: "we were surprised by the coherence of theme and imagery that we encountered in the works of writers who were often geographically, historically, and psychologically distant from each other."[74]

This gave Gilbert and Gubar the hope of discovering a "distinctively female literary tradition" which should be studied in its entirety.[75] Gilbert and Gubar wanted to explore and understand the anxieties that must have produced this female writing tradition. They were mainly interested in the fact that those women suffered from men's domination not only of mansions but also of the literary traditions. Gilbert and Gubar summarised women's suffering under the patriarchal suppression, being the suffering of the western female characters in the novels they studied, disregarding by this the different types of oppressing female characters of other races. For instance, to find out the anxieties that affected female writers, Gilbert and Gubar studied a female character like Jane Eyre on a journey towards

---

[73] Elaine Showalter, *A Literature of Their Own: British Women Novelists from Brontë to Lessing,* quoted in Mary Eagleton, ed., *Feminist Literary Theory: a Reader* (Malden, MA: Blackwell Publishing Ltd, 2011), 11.

[74] Sandra Gilbert and Susan Gubar, *The Madwoman in the Attic: The Woman Writer and the Nineteenth-Century Literary Imagination* (New Haven: Yale University Press, 1979), xi.

[75] Gilbert and Gubar, *The Mad Woman,* xi.

female individualism, but they also rendered subaltern female characters like Bertha Mason as the western heroines' dark doubles.

In her argument about the complicity between western feminism and imperialism, Spivak borrows from Chandra Talpade Mohanty, as Childs and Williams propose: "[s]everal of Spivak's points pick up from those of Chandra Talpade Mohanty who has argued against the discursive production within the social sciences of a composite entity she calls the 'Third World Woman.'"[76] In 1984, one year before "Three Women's Texts," Mohanty wrote "Under Western Eyes: Feminist Scholarship and Colonial Discourse." In this article, Mohanty is concerned with the representation of the 'Third-World' woman in the writings of western, particularly American, feminists during the late 1970s and early 1980s. She believes that as colonisation "almost invariably implies a relation of structural domination, and a suppression – often violent – of the heterogeneity of the subject(s) in question,"[77] western feminism colonises the heterogeneity of the lives of 'Third-World' women by producing the monolithic subject, 'Third-World' woman. For Mohanty, western feminism appropriates knowledge about women in the 'Third World' by taking western feminist interests as the referent. Mohanty thinks that this homogenising of 'Third-World' women is a political and purposeful practice because of the feminist desire for intervention into particular hegemonic discourses like anthropology, sociology, and literary criticism. Western feminism summarises the oppression of 'Third-World' Women in patriarchy and forgets about the complexities of race, religion, class and caste. One of the effects of the dominant representations of western feminism is its conflation with imperialism in the eyes of particular 'Third-World' women. The average 'Third-World' woman is represented as ignorant, poor, uneducated, tradition-bound, domestic, family-oriented, and victimised. This is in contrast with the implicit self-representation of western women as educated, modern, and free physically and intellectually. Borrowing the term from Michelle Rosaldo, Mohanty adds that some western feminists describe 'Third-World' women as "ourselves undressed."[78] By this, western feminists construct themselves as the referent. Mohanty concludes that associating feminism with imperialism is

---

[76] Childs and Williams, *An Introduction,* 167.

[77] Chandra Talpade Mohanty, "Under Western Eyes: Feminist Scholarship and Colonial Discourse," *Boundary 2* 12:13 (1984): 333.

[78] M.Z. Rosaldo, "The Use and Abuse of Anthropology: Reflections on Feminism and Cross-Cultural Understanding," *Signs*, 5:3 (1980), 389-417, esp. 392, quoted in Mohanty, "Under Western Eyes: Feminist Scholarship and Colonial Discourse," 337.

attributable to western feminists' self-representation as the true subjects while reducing 'Third-World' women to a homogenised object of knowledge.

"Three Women's Texts" concentrates on the exclusion of 'native subaltern female' characters in nineteenth-century western texts. By highlighting the heterogeneity of women's struggles in her readings of literature, Spivak positions herself as one of the third-wave feminists. In "On the Genealogy of Women: A Defence of Anti-Essentialism," Alison Stone defines third-wave feminists who emerged in the late 1980s and 1990s as those who "object, in particular to, exclusive tendencies within the dominant feminist theories of the 1970s and 1980s, theories that emerged more or less directly from second wave feminism."[79] In *Politics and Feminism,* Arneil defines third-wave feminism as embracing "the diversity and differences in perspectives among 'women,' ultimately straddling both 'one' and the 'other'"[80] As Shelley Budgeon explains, third-wave feminists can be defined by a "deconstructive impulse" to start from multiple differences among women instead of dealing with the categories 'man' and 'woman.'[81] Second-wave feminists wrote about women as a universalised or homogenised sisterhood, a homogeneity that is refused by third-wave feminists – usually described as anti-essentialist feminists. Like other third-wave feminists, Spivak jettisons essentialism because in her opinion "[w]ithin mainstream U.S. feminism the good insistence that 'the personal is political' often transformed itself into something like '*only* the personal is political.' The strategic use of essentialism can turn into an alibi for proselytizing academic essentialisms."[82] Thus, Spivak moved chronologically through the two waves of feminism during her career. Later, she would explain her affiliations with second-wave feminism as a politically useful strategy for maintaining the possibility of women's collectivity and consequently political activism. However, this strategic essentialism should be forsaken when the aim of forming a collectivity is achieved, and the following step should be paying attention to differences. Abandoning essentialism entails forsaking the idea of the representation of, with the meaning of speaking for, heterogeneous women. What is needed now is not the political representation of women but the ethical encounter which will be explained in later parts of this book.

---

[79] Alison Stone, "On the Genealogy of Women," 16.

[80] Arneil, *Politics and Feminism,* 186.

[81] Shelley Budgeon, *Third Wave Feminism and the Politics of Gender in Late Modernity* (Basingstoke: Palgrave Macmillan, 2011), 4.

[82] Spivak, "In a Word: Interview," 358.

To sum up, Kant's *Critique of Judgement* is important for Spivak's critique in two ways. First, she uses de Man's two-step deconstruction to demonstrate that Kant's argument deconstructs itself when it denies the 'native informant' the freedom available for western Christian man. In the third critique, Kant concludes that everything in nature is in accordance with man's faculties of mind. However, he is puzzled by the presence of the 'native informant.' Spivak explains that facing this figure of interruption, the 'native informant,' Kant resolves the problem by recourse to a truth-claim that excludes the 'native informant' from the Name of Man. The result of this truth-claim is the construction of an image of the 'native informant' as uncivilised and incapable of reasoning. Second, since Kant finds logic in the female's existence by arguing that she is necessary for propagation, this means that the struggles of the racial Other and that of western feminism are discontinuous. It is this discontinuity that she traces in her approach to the three canonical texts she studies in "Three Women's Texts." In this book, "Three Women's Texts" will be tackled in light of what has been discussed in this chapter. The next three chapters will demonstrate how Spivak's readings of *Jane Eyre, Wide Sargasso Sea,* and *Frankenstein* depend on her understanding of Kant's foreclosure of the 'native informant' and of feminism's exclusion of the 'native subaltern female.' Moreover, as is the case in her reading of Kant, Spivak applies de Man's tropological deconstruction to reveal the complicity between Anglo-American feminism and imperialism in foreclosing the 'native subaltern female.'

CHAPTER TWO

SPIVAK'S TROPOLOGICAL DECONSTRUCTION OF *JANE EYRE*

Spivak's study of *Jane Eyre* first appeared in "Three Women's Texts and a Critique of Imperialism" published in *Critical Inquiry* in 1985. Many critics testify to the undeniable influence of this article which inaugurated postcolonial readings of different nineteenth-century novels. The critic Carl Plasa describes it as "the catalyst to the postcolonial reassessment of Brontë."[1] Sangeeta Ray also admits that any study of Spivak as "a postcolonial literary reader par excellence" must begin with this article.[2] "Three Women's Texts," like other Spivakian articles, is complicated in its evocation of many intellectuals and ideas. Spivak's seven pages on *Jane Eyre* introduce critics such as Elizabeth Fox-Genovese, Terry Eagleton, Sandra M. Gilbert and Susan Gubar, Louis Althusser, Michel Foucault and Kant as well as analysing the characters of Jane, Bertha and St. John Rivers. This complexity is far from surprising since density and diversity are collateral features in Spivak's writing.

Although Spivak does not say that she is applying tropological deconstruction to her reading of *Jane Eyre,* reading *A Critique of Postcolonial Reason* one can argue that tropological deconstruction was exactly what Spivak was doing while analysing *Jane Eyre*, as this chapter will explain. In addition, although she does not use the term 'parabasis' in the body of the article, Spivak's method of reading the three texts under discussion shows that her analysis depends on a certain parabasis or interruption that is at work in each text. The first part of this chapter will explain the significance of literature for Spivak's thought in general and will list some elements that make *Jane Eyre* a specifically important text for her. To explain why Spivak believes that the novel was read as a text about female individualism excluding the 'native subaltern female,' the second part will present the main points of the literary feminist critics,

---

[1] Carl Plasa, *Charlotte Brontë* (Basingsto: Palgrave Macmillan, 2004), x.
[2] Ray, *Gayatri Chakravorty Spivak: In Other Words* (Sussex: Wiley-Blackwell, 2009), 27.

Sandra Gilbert and Susan Gubar's 1979 reading of *Jane Eyre*, since this reading is the example emphasised by Spivak herself. Then, the two steps of Spivak's deconstruction will be explicated. Female individualism will be shown as the first truth-claim that proves to be a false universal due to the parabasis stemming from Bertha's sudden appearance. The second truth-claim, which replaces the first, will be revealed by relating the register of St. John Rivers, who goes to India as a missionary, with Kant's categorical imperative of civilising the 'native informant.'

The significance of literature and specifically *Jane Eyre* for Spivak

Literature, for Spivak, is significant because it is the domain where the reader can be constituted as subject as she herself was constituted by reading *Jane Eyre*. Spivak claims that: "[l]iterature buys your assent in an almost clandestine way, and therefore it is an excellent instrument for a slow transformation of the mind, for good or for ill."[3] She also argues that the aim of teaching literature is "at least to shape the mind of the student so that it can resemble the mind of the so-called implied reader of the literary text, even when that is a historically distanced cultural fiction."[4] In this respect, Stephen Morton relates Spivak's focus on literature to her awareness of the role of English studies in India. He says:

> Spivak emphasizes how English studies played an important role in reinforcing the political authority of the British Empire by persuading the Indian middle class that there was a moral and intellectual purpose behind colonialism [...] this colonial rhetoric is particularly apparent for Spivak in the figurative language and geographical metaphors of such nineteenth-century British novels as *Jane Eyre*.[5]

Spivak reads literature in a way that, she hopes, will enable her to slowly produce a counter-narrative that changes the way in which the 'native subaltern female' has been represented in western literary texts like *Jane Eyre*. Reading literature with this purpose is a step which will later lead Spivak to the aesthetics of education as will be discussed towards the end of this book.

"Three Women's Texts" starts with a warning against reading nineteenth-century British novels without attending to two important

---

[3] Spivak, "The Burden," 137.
[4] Spivak, "The Burden," 135.
[5] Morton, *Gayatri Spivak*, 18.

"obvious" but "disregarded" facts about the ideological relationship between imperialism and literature: "imperialism, understood as England's social mission, was a crucial part of the cultural representation of England to the English. The role of literature in the production of cultural representation should not be ignored."[6] In other words, the relationship between imperialism and literature is reciprocal. On the one hand, imperialism was part of the image of England as the civiliser of other parts of the world and this image was consolidated and stressed in the literature of the nineteenth century. An example of this image of England as civiliser is the British ban on the Hindu practice of sati in India as will be explained later in this chapter. On the other hand, authors benefitted from the axiomatics of imperialism in the structures of their novels and the movement of the fictional action.[7] Depending on Kant, Spivak presents a definition of the axiomatics of imperialism as the maxims – truth-claims or subjective principles – used by the philosopher to support his theories. Consequently, she implies that the axiomatics of imperialism were used in order to fill gaps in the literary text and support the fictional plot. Such axiomatics enable authors to assume a system of signs that they can use to support the plot of their work. The axiomatic that Spivak refers to in "Three Women's Texts" is provided by the philosophy of Enlightenment, namely Kant's. It is the axiomatic that represented the 'native informant' as savage and unable to pass to freedom and aesthetic judgment without being civilised by the white Christian man first. The use of such axiomatics in literature, in Spivak's opinion, constructed a particular image of the "Third World."[8] This fact indicates that Spivak believes the 'Third World,' the 'native informant' and the 'Third-World' female are all constructions based on the subjective principles, or maxims, which philosophers and novelists created to support their writings. By the warning with which Spivak starts, she leads us to understand that it was imperialism that offered these constructions and, eventually, consolidating them in literature was in the interest of the imperialist project because such constructions of the Other as savage justified colonialism and its violence.

As Spivak reads the New Hollander as an example of the 'native informant' in Kant's third critique, she reads Bertha as an example of the 'native subaltern female' in *Jane Eyre*. There are many elements that justify Spivak's choice of this novel as an example of the foreclosure of the 'native subaltern female.' First, the novel presents a silent Other in the representation of Bertha. Second, the novel enacts a scene of self-

---

[6] Spivak, "Three Women's Texts," 243.
[7] Spivak, "Three Women's Texts," 27.
[8] Spivak, "Three Women's Texts," 243.

immolation which reminds Spivak of the Hindu practice of sati, the widow sacrifice which was banned by the British during their rule of India. Third, the novel ends with an account of the heroism of St. John Rivers as a missionary in Calcutta. Spivak declares that realising the power of her suggestion to read "the self-immolation of Bertha Mason as 'good wife' [...] remains unclear if we remain insufficiently knowledgeable about the history of the legal manipulation of widow-sacrifice in the entitlement of the British government in India."[9] Obviously, Spivak believes that sati was one of the practices that were emphasised by the British government in India in order to justify its interference in Hindu culture and law. An idea about how Spivak construes the British manipulation of sati can be obtained from her essay: "Can the Subaltern Speak? Speculations on Widow Sacrifice" which was first given as a lecture in the summer of 1983 and was published in Cary Nelson and Lawrence Grossberg's *Marxism and the Interpretation of Culture* in 1988. In "Can the Subaltern Speak?" Spivak strives to prove through the example of sati that the subaltern female cannot speak for herself, proposing that this category of the subaltern was marginalised by both the coloniser and the colonised: "[b]etween patriarchy and imperialism, subject-constitution and object-formation, the figure of the woman disappears, not into a pristine nothingness, but into a violent shuttling which is the displaced figuration of the 'third-world woman' caught between tradition and modernization."[10]

Spivak explains that sati from the Hindu perspective expresses the female's loyalty to her husband. The Indian woman's free will is associated with her desire for or refusal of self-immolation and under the "ideological production of the sexed subject," the female takes her sanctioned suicide as a "signifier" of her desire.[11] Thus, a female who immolates her body after her husband's death is promised to receive the heavenly rewards, while she who does not, will remain the prisoner of her body. The British perception of sati was different and Spivak offers an example of how sati was viewed by the British in India. The example is *Suttee: A Historical and Philosophical Enquiry into the Hindu Rite of Widow Burning* (1928) by the British poet, translator, historian, and novelist Edward John Thompson (1886-1946), who became a missionary in Bengal in 1909. Spivak quotes Thompson's statement that "the victims of suttee were punished for no offense but the physical weakness which

---

[9] Spivak, "Three Women's Texts," 259.

[10] Gayatri Chakravorty Spivak, "Can the Subaltern Speak? Speculations on Widow Sacrifice" in *Marxism and the Interpretation of Culture*, ed. Cary Nelson and Lawrence Grossberg (Basingstoke: Macmillan Education, 1988), p. 306.

[11] Spivak, "Can the Subaltern Speak?" 300.

had placed them at man's mercy. The rite seemed to prove a depravity and arrogance such as no other human offense had brought to light."[12] The British, Spivak claims, always boasted that they did not interfere in the Hindu law. However, she argues that they did interfere in the case of sati by banning the practice. They related the protection of widows to the establishment of a good society in India even after independence. Spivak quotes the following statement: "[t]he recurrence of *sati* in independent India is probably an obscurantist revival which cannot long survive even in a very backward part of the country."[13] She argues that banning sati was construed as: white men saving brown women from brown men.[14] By redefining sati as a crime after it was tolerated by the Hindu as a ritual, Spivak continues, the British government entitled itself to be the legislator with the duty of establishing the good society; therefore, Spivak stresses that this is an example of how "[i]mperialism's image as the establisher of the good society is marked by the espousal of the woman as *object* of protection from her own kind."[15] Furthermore, Spivak implies that this interference in Hindu culture and law was introduced as goodwill from the "benevolent and enlightened males" who knew what is best for Hindu widows. Hindu men claimed that widows were satisfied with the practice and that they freely chose to be burnt and the British claimed the opposite, but no one listened to the widows' voice at that time and now this voice cannot be revived. Therefore, Spivak would emphasise in her later writings that the responsibility towards the 'native subaltern female' should not be based on the benevolence which makes her an object of knowledge whose identity and interests can be defined and decided for her.

While the history of the British manipulation of sati is not the point here, it is important to understand that Spivak's reading of *Jane Eyre* is based on three assumptions. At the level of history, Spivak assumes that the British rule in India judged sati as an uncivilised practice, thereby justifying their rule of India for civilising purposes. At the level of literature, Spivak assumes that Bertha, although a Jamaican Creole rather

---

[12] Edward Thompson, *Suttee: A Historical and Philosophical Enquiry into the Hindu Rite of Widow Burning* (London: George Allen and Unwin, 1928), quoted in Spivak, "Can the Subaltern Speak?" 301.

[13] J. M. Derret, *Hindu Law Past and Present: Being an Account of the Controvercy which Preceded the Enactment of the Hindu Code, and Text of the Code as Enacted, and Some Comments Thereon* (Calcutta: A. Mukherjee and Co. 1957), 46, quoted in Spivak, "Can the Subaltern Speak?" 298.

[14] Spivak, "Can the Subaltern Speak?" 297.

[15] Spivak, "Can the Subaltern Speak?" 299.

than an Indian widow, can stand for the Indian sati because the text enacts her self-immolation and because the text ends with an account of a missionary in Calcutta. As for the role of philosophy, in this regard, Spivak assumes that the philosophy of Enlightenment, with specific reference to Kant, provides both politicians and literature with the axiom that the Other needs to be civilised in order to become a rational subject. In terms of technique Spivak's reading of *Jane Eyre* follows two steps in the tropological deconstruction of the text. First, she reveals female individualism as the first truth-claim in the novel. Spivak's reading shows that the presence of the 'native subaltern female,' represented by Bertha, is the gap which raises doubts about this truth-claim. Then, Spivak shows how this gap is filled with an axiomatic of imperialism which is at work in the role of St. John, the role which Spivak interprets in the light of Kant's categorical imperative. However, before illustrating Spivak's tropological deconstruction of the novel, one must have an idea of Gilbert and Gubar's analysis. Spivak takes Gilbert and Gubar's study as the example of *Jane Eyre* being read as a text about female individualism excluding the 'native subaltern female.'

Sandra Gilbert and Susan Gubar: an isolationist admiration for Jane

Gilbert and Gubar analyse *Jane Eyre* in their book *The Madwoman in the Attic*. The reading offered by Gilbert and Gubar seems to be the source of Spivak's introductory claim that "the emergent perspective of feminist criticism reproduces the axioms of imperialism. A basically isolationist admiration for the literature of the female subject in Europe and Anglo-America produces the high feminist norm."[16] By the 'isolationist admiration' for the literature of the European female, Spivak denotes the essentialism of twentieth-century Anglo-American feminist criticism and the exclusion of the 'native subaltern female.' What Spivak implies is that by privileging Jane as the norm of the free individualist female and depriving Bertha of the same freedom, Gilbert and Gubar's reading repeats the imperialist privilege of coloniser over colonised and self over the Other. Comparing Jane's story to John Bunyan's *Pilgrim's Progress*, Gilbert and Gubar see Jane's story as a *bildungsroman*. In other words, it is a journey from Jane the child to Jane the individualist adult. The difficulties that she faces in this journey are the same that all women face in a patriarchal society. Then, Gilbert and Gubar discuss Jane's journey to

---

[16] Spivak, "Three Women's Texts," 243.

achieve individualism step by step until they reach the most important encounter in the novel, the one between Jane and Bertha. Their fundamental point about Bertha is her madness, which they read as an emblem of Jane's anger. They discuss this through the theme of doubleness. Doubleness for Gilbert and Gubar starts in the red room, where Mrs. Reed imprisoned the child, Jane. Left alone and angry in that room, Jane looks at her angry face in the mirror. The doubleness reappears in an intensified manner in the days before Jane's marriage to Rochester when she views Bertha's face in the mirror. Doubleness even becomes clearer when Jane speaks about her two dreams which precede her encounter with Bertha. In the first she finds herself carrying a little child and unable to call Rochester's name. In the second she sees Thornfield destroyed and inhabited by owls and bats, Rochester leaves her and the child rolls from her knee. Gilbert and Gubar consider this child to be Jane, the orphan. Jane will not be liberated from this orphan until she is equal to Rochester. This will be achieved only when Jane gets her wealth from her uncle and returns to Rochester to find that Thornfield has been burnt down by Bertha.

Consequently, Gilbert and Gubar conclude that: "on a figurative and psychological level it seems suspiciously clear that the spectre of Bertha is still another – indeed the most threatening – avatar of Jane. What Bertha now *does* [tearing Jane's wedding veil], for instance, is what Jane wants to do."[17] They add: "Bertha is Jane's truest and darkest double: she is the angry aspect of the orphan child."[18] In their opinion, this doubleness is lucid not only in the oppositions between Jane and Bertha but also in the similarity or the 'monitory' relationship:

> The imprisoned Bertha, running 'backwards and forwards' on all fours in the attic, for instance, recalls not only Jane the governess, whose only relief from mental pain was to pace 'backwards and forwards' in the third story, but also that 'bad animal' who was ten-year-old Jane, imprisoned in the red-room, howling and mad.[19]

So, having only gender issues in mind, Gilbert and Gubar are not concerned with Bertha's description as Creole. They want Bertha to be the "Invisible Woman" who cries out in all women's pain.[20] Carolyn Vellenga Berman justifies this: "Brontë's categorization of the Creole *as* Creole is

---

[17] Gilbert and Gubar, *The Madwoman*, 359.
[18] Gilbert and Gubar, *The Madwoman,* 360.
[19] Gilbert and Gubar, *The Madwoman,* 361.
[20] Laura E. Donaldson, *Decolonizing Feminisms: Race, Gender & Empire Building* (London: Routledge, 1993), 14.

unimportant to [Gilbert and Gubar's] analysis, since it indicates neither gender nor sexuality, and it designates the lunatic's race and nationality only in the most oblique fashion."[21] Gilbert and Gubar also quote Claire Rosenfeld, who speaks about novelists using psychological doubles by two characters "one socially acceptable or conventional personality, the other externalizing the free, uninhabited, often criminal self."[22]

There are important points in Gilbert and Gubar's analysis that relate it to what Spivak discusses in "French Feminism in an International Frame." The first is that Gilbert and Gubar unite all women's problems into one type, the patriarchal oppression from which Jane suffers. By disregarding Bertha as the Other woman who suffers from a different kind of oppression, the racial, they marginalise her. In their reading, Bertha does not have access to female individualism because she is only Jane's dark double. The second point is that Gilbert and Gubar make the encounter with Bertha an encounter that serves the knowing of the self, Jane's in this case, rather than an encounter to know the Other – similar to Spivak's reading of Kristeva's encounter with the silent Chinese women. So, Spivak finds no genuine other-directed politics either in French feminism or in Gilbert and Gubar's reading of *Jane Eyre*.

The tropological deconstruction of the novel

The first step of Spivak's tropological deconstruction of *Jane Eyre* is revealing female individualism as the first truth-claim represented by the text and approached by Gilbert and Gubar. She implies that the discourse of Anglo-American feminism which is used by Gilbert and Gubar approaches the text in the following manner: the truth – or the real subject – in this text is Jane who is represented as the able subject of female individualism. The trope is Bertha who is viewed as Jane's dark double, an incomplete copy of Jane. Thus, as she explains the troping underlying the binary man/woman in "Imperialism and Sexual Difference," she implies that Bertha is understood with reference to Jane. The truth-claim of female individualism which Jane can access is based on this troping of Bertha. This female individualism can be refuted for two reasons. First, Jane's freedom is ascribed to her being ideologically limited by sexual

---

[21] Carolyn Vellenga Berman, *Creole Crossings: Domestic Fiction and the Reform of Colonial Slavery* (New York: Cornell University Press, 2006), 8.
[22] Claire Rosenfeld, "The Shadow Within: the Conscious and Unconscious Use of the Double," in *Stories of the Double,* ed. Albert J. Guerard (Philadelphia: J. B. Lippincott, 1967), 314, quoted in Gilbert and Gubar, *The Mad Woman in the Attic,* 360.

reproduction and excluded from participating in the project of soul-making. Second, the presence of Bertha complicates the concept of female individualism since this individualism cannot be universal if there is still an Other woman who cannot achieve it. In other words, Bertha is used by Spivak as the parabasis, the figure of interruption in her reading of *Jane Eyre.*

As far as Jane's female individualism is concerned, Spivak emphasises the need to differentiate between the interpellation of the subject as individual and as an individualist. She says that what is at stake for "feminist individualism in the age of imperialism, is precisely the making of human beings, the constitution and 'interpellation' of the subject not only as individual but as 'individualist.'"[23] To understand this statement, one needs to take into consideration Spivak's evocation of the French Marxist Louis Althusser by her use of the concept of 'interpellation.' However, the evocation of Althusser here does not necessarily mean that Spivak's approach to the novel is strictly Althusserian. Spivak repeatedly points out that she is a bricoleur, using whatever concepts can serve her ideas. For example, she proclaims: "I'm a very eclectic person. I use what comes to hand. I'm not a fundamentalist. And I'm not an Althusserian in the strict sense. I'm more interested in opening up texts than in establishing, like some medieval scholar, the authenticity of a text."[24]

Althusser explains interpellation in his essay "Ideology and Ideological State Apparatus (Notes Towards an Investigation)." The concept of interpellation refers to how the subject is constituted by ideology. Althusser says that individuals in ideology live "in a determinate (religious, ethical, etc.), representation of the world whose imaginary distortion depends on their imaginary relation to their conditions of existence, in other words, in the last instance, to the relations of production and to class relations."[25] Ideology calls the individual into being as "a subject endowed with a consciousness in which he freely forms or freely recognizes ideas in which he believes."[26] Ideology has practices and rituals; that is, the individual behaves in certain ways and adopts certain practical attitudes. The individual, interpellated as a subject, believes that his/her practices are freely chosen by him/her, but in reality they are those of the ideological apparatus on which his/her consciousness depends.

---

[23] Spivak, "Three Women's Texts," 244.
[24] Spivak, *The Post-colonial Critic,* 55.
[25] Louis Althusser, *Lenin and Philosophy and Other Essays*, trans. Ben Brewster (New York: Monthly Review Press, 2001), 113.
[26] Louis Althusser, *Lenin and Philosophy and Other Essays*, 113.

Spivak evokes interpellation in order to show that though Jane in the
novel is interpellated as an individualist, she is not so. For Spivak,
imperialist ideology restricts Jane to the role of sexual reproduction and
gives her equality with the man, Rochester, only within the frame of
family life. Through her marriage based on her equality with Rochester in
terms of wealth, Jane moves to the centre of social relations: this is how
Gilbert and Gubar think she achieved her individualism. However, for
Spivak there is a gap here that puts Jane's individualism at stake because
the great mission of civilising the Other, or soul-making, is confined to the
male, St. John, whose plan is to marry Jane and go to Calcutta to spread
Christianity. Spivak views the tasks assigned to Jane and St. John in the
text as two forms of ideological interpellation: childbearing and soul-
making. For Spivak, Gilbert and Gubar's description of the novel as 'Plain
Jane's Progress' is "simply replacing the male protagonist with the
female."[27] This shows, she argues, that they do not distinguish between
"sexual reproduction and soul making, both actualised by the unquestioned
idiom of imperialist presuppositions evident in the last part of *Jane
Eyre*."[28] Spivak tries to show that nineteenth-century female individualism
was confined to the woman moving to the centre of the family and that this
individualism was dictated by the imperialist ideology that kept the
woman confined to sexual reproduction. Spivak starts from the first scene
of the novel where family and individualism play an important role in
determining the division of spaces in the opening of *Jane Eyre*. Spivak
quotes only one line of the passage that clarifies the role of family in the
novel; however, for more clarity, one can quote the whole passage
reading:

> There was no possibility of taking a walk that day [...] Eliza, John, and
> Georgiana were now clustered round their mamma in the drawing-room:
> she lay reclined on a sofa by the fireside, and with her darlings about her
> looked perfectly happy. Me, she had dispensed from joining the group [...]
> A small break-fast room adjoined the drawing-room, I slipped in there.[29]

Reading this passage, one can notice that it depicts a family enjoying their
gathering in the drawing room and an orphan girl dismissed from this
gathering. A mother surrounded by her children illustrates the role
ascribed to women during that age. It is the role of sexual reproduction to

---

[27] Spivak, "Three Women's Texts," 249.
[28] Spivak, "Three Women's Texts," 249.
[29] Charlotte Brontë, *Jane Eyre* (London: Penguin Books, 1994), pp. 1-2. All
subsequent references to this edition will be reflected as page numbers within
parentheses.

which Jane will return at the end of the novel when she marries Rochester. As for Spivak, she sees in this passage a scene of the "marginalization and privatization" of Jane.[30] It depicts Jane's withdrawal to the margin which is a room adjoined to the "sanctioned architectural space of the withdrawing room or drawing room."[31] Spivak also stresses the fact that Jane does not even withdraw to the dining room or the library. These are both sanctioned spaces when speaking of "the domestic inscription of space within the upwardly mobilizing currents of the eighteenth- and nineteenth-century bourgeoisie in England and France."[32]

Having shed light on Jane's withdrawal, Spivak describes her as the marginal individualist. Though she does not quote Terry Eagleton directly, Spivak refers to his study of *Jane Eyre* and here is a point – withdrawal from family as a step towards individualism – where her study and Eagleton's meet. Eagleton explains the role of the freedom from family in the progress of Brontë's female protagonists:

> At the centre of all Charlotte's novels, I am arguing, is a figure who either lacks or deliberately cuts the bonds of kinship. This leaves the self a free, blank, 'pre-social' atom: free to be injured and exploited, but free also to progress, move through the class structure, choose and forge relationships, strenuously utilise its talents in scorn of autocracy and paternalism.[33]

Further, Spivak argues that Jane chooses a double marginalisation by mounting the window-seat and closing the moreen curtains. Now that Jane is free from the oppressing familial space, she picks up a book and resorts to creative imagination. She is contented: "I was then happy: happy at least in my way" (4). Looking at the pictures in the book, Jane forms ideas of her own. This scene, Spivak implies, shows that Jane is escaping from an ideologically dictated space and, as Laura Chrisman observes, Spivak "views spatial representation as dictated by ideology" to illustrate how female individualism was imagined in the eighteenth and nineteenth centuries.[34] Spivak's analysis of this scene in terms of ideology comes from Elizabeth Fox-Genovese's article, "Placing Women's History in History" (1982). Fox-Genovese's article relates the success of feminism to the ability of women to achieve their individualism. She explains the change in the social construction of gender, through which men dominated

---

[30] Spivak, "Three Women's Texts," 246.

[31] Spivak, "Three Women's Texts," 246.

[32] Spivak, "Three Women's Texts," 246.

[33] Eagleton, *Myths of Power: A Marxist Study of the Brontës*, 2nd edn. (London: Macmillan, 1988), 26.

[34] Chrisman, *Postcolonial Contraventions*, 60.

women, starting from medieval until modern times, arguing that gender
systems always allocated specific tasks and responsibilities to men and
others to women within the family. Fox-Genovese argues that the family
was a unit of governance and occupied a central place in the gender
system which enabled monarchs to rule both men and women. Therefore
any change of women's status should happen at the level of the family
which "has constituted the primary arena in which gender systems have
been reproduced and transformed."[35] What Spivak implies by raising Fox-
Genovese's argument is that confining women to the role of sexual
reproduction was necessary in the eighteenth and nineteenth century as a
part of the ideology used for monarchs to rule both men and women.
Therefore, Spivak reads the opening scene of Mrs. Reed and her children
as dictated by this very ideology and the withdrawal of Jane as an escape
from this ideology. Hence, the opening passage prefigures Jane
undertaking the journey towards individualism by her withdrawal from the
space of the family. Although at this stage of the novel, Spivak renders
Jane as the marginal individualist, Spivak is adamant to illustrate that the
end of the novel raises doubts about Jane's achievement of this
individualism. Whereas, Jane is to be eventually satisfied with the
woman's position in the family through her marriage to Rochester, the
project of soul-making remains confined to the male missionary whose
important journey is given the privilege of concluding the novel.

Spivak does not stop at the role of the ideological interpellation of the
woman in terms of childbearing as shown in the opening of the novel, but
continues to show how this ideological interpellation is manifested in
Jane's marrying Rochester rather than St. John. Spivak discusses the two
proposals Jane receives through the concept of *pouvoir-savoir* or
power/knowledge. An explanation of *pouvoir/savoir* appears in Spivak's
"More on Power/Knowledge" where she clarifies that she takes the
concept from the French philosopher Michel Foucault and explains that
while *savoir* can be translated as 'knowing' in English, *pouvoir* does not
have a precise equivalent. It can be translated as 'power,' but in this case it
may lose the aspect of 'can-do'ness which Foucault's doublet connotes in
Spivak's reading. She gives the example of marriage to elucidate this
doublet further, arguing that it is what a woman knows about marriage that
determines her everyday behaviour and her ability to preserve this
marriage. For example, if marriage for the woman is her movement from
the father's protection to that of a husband, then she will behave in a way

---

[35] Elizabeth Fox-Genovese, "Placing Women's History in History," *New Left Review* 133 (1982), 17.

that keeps this marriage stable regardless her sexual desires. Again, this brings into play Althusser's theory of the rituals and practices of an ideology. In the last example, the ideology of a patriarchal society interpellates the woman as an individual and makes her behave in the ways which she thinks stem from her self-determination and freedom.

Spivak discusses two types of marriage in *Jane Eyre*. The first is Jane's marriage to Rochester that belongs to the register of "domestic-society-through-sexual-reproduction cathected as 'compassionate love.'"[36] This is connected with the bourgeois politics of the family. In this respect, to make Spivak's idea clearer, one can refer to Ann Laura Stoler who reads Foucault's *History of Sexuality* by focusing on race in the history of nineteenth-century European sexuality. Concerning European families, Stoler explains:

> European women and men won respectability by steering their desires to legitimate paternity and intensive maternal care, to family and conjugal love [...] To be truly European was to cultivate a bourgeois self in which familial and national obligations were the priority and sex was held in check.[37]

The second type of marriage is St. John's offer to marry Jane and to embark together on a social mission to spread Christianity in Calcutta. This belongs to soul-making or "the imperialist project cathected as civil-society-through-social-mission."[38] The pressure that Jane feels under St. John's proposal leads her to want to return to Rochester. When she goes back to Rochester, Jane discovers that Bertha has immolated herself; this self-immolation makes Jane's marriage to Rochester possible. Spivak's reading indicates that it is here where the author's deployment of the imperialist axiomatic at hand to support the structure of the text is revealed. What Spivak means is that Jane's marriage and movement to the centre of the family would not have been possible without St. John offering her the chance to go with him as a missionary, which led her to run away from him to Rochester, and without Bertha's self-immolation which Spivak sees as a representation of sati. Both St. John's offer and Bertha's self-immolation belong to the register of the imperialist discourse since, as Spivak discusses in "Can the Subaltern Speak [?]," the British banned the practice of sati in India.

---

[36] Spivak, "Three Women's Texts," 244.

[37] Ann Laura Stoler, *Race and the Education of Desire: Foucault's History of Sexuality and the Colonial Order of Things* (Durham: Duke University Press, 1995), 182.

[38] Spivak, "Three Women's Texts," 244.

Depending on Jane's choice of the sexual-reproduction register of marriage, Spivak argues that the text denies Jane the participation in soul-making as a social mission, meaning that she has not accessed the register allowed for men, which indicates, for Spivak, that nineteenth-century female individualism was still limited. In Spivak's opinion, this "marks the inaccessibility of the imperialist project as such to the nascent 'feminist' scenario."[39] By highlighting that the novel confines the woman's success to achieving equality with the man within the scope of the nuclear family, Spivak's reading indicates that this female individualism is only a truth-claim that is at stake because the woman is still understood with reference to man. Thus, even when a feminist reading of literature, like Gilbert and Gubar's, tries to prove the western woman's female individualism, it keeps her freedom defined by her equality to man. This maintains the dichotomy man/woman with man as the true subject and woman as the trope. Above all, an attempt like Gilbert and Gubar's produces another binary, western woman (Jane) / 'native subaltern female' (Bertha), claiming that the first part is the true subject and the second is the trope. Spivak interrupts the text powerfully through shifting the attention from Jane to Bertha as the parabasis which Spivak deploys to deconstruct the general understanding of the novel as a text about female individualism.

The Parabasis of *Jane Eyre*: Bertha Mason and sati

Like the New Hollanders and Fuegians in Kant's third critique, Bertha is introduced into *Jane Eyre* as Rochester's mad Creole wife who is later to be sacrificed so that Jane can marry Rochester. Therefore, Bertha's self-immolation becomes the parabasis which Spivak exploits in order to intervene in and deconstruct the text. Spivak presents Bertha as an example of the 'native subaltern female' who has no history and she laments the "imperialist narrativization of history, that it should produce so abject a script for her [Bertha]."[40] For Spivak, Bertha is "a figure produced by the axiomatic of imperialism. Through Bertha, the white Jamaican Creole, Brontë renders the human/animal frontier as acceptably indeterminate, so that a good greater than the letter of the Law can be broached."[41] By the 'letter of the Law,' Spivak here refers to Bertha and Rochester's marriage. When Spivak declares that Bertha's presentation in the novel opens the way for 'a good greater than the letter of the Law,' she

---

[39] Spivak, "Three Women's Texts," 249.
[40] Spivak, "Three Women's Texts," 244.
[41] Spivak, "Three Women's Texts," 247.

alludes to the fact that the novel suggests the civilising mission as a better solution than the legal marriage for the uncivilised Other. In other words, Bertha's position between human and animal can be seen as a justification for the project of soul-making with which the novel ends. Hence, although Bertha has a colonial past, Spivak puts her in a margin similar to that of the colonised woman. Moreover, Spivak uses the term 'native' to describe Bertha and, in *A Critique of Postcolonial Reason,* she includes her analysis of Bertha as part of the critique of constructing the 'native subaltern female' in eighteenth- and nineteenth- century British literature. Before further discussion of Spivak's debatable association of Bertha with the 'native subaltern female,' it is useful to trace Bertha's appearances and representation in the novel, so that one gives context to Spivak's argument.

The novel presents Bertha only in Chapter 26, although her actions precede her appearance: her laugh and murmurs, her attempt to burn Rochester in his bed, her cutting of Jane's wedding veil. She is introduced as a Creole and an amalgamation of madness, drunkenness and bestiality; however the text leaves her racial features ambiguous. To prevent Jane and Rochester's marriage, Bertha's brother appears to reveal the marriage of Rochester and Bertha, "daughter of Jonas Mason, merchant, and of Antoinetta Mason, his wife, a Creole" (408). The document that testifies to this marriage declares that Bertha's mother was a Creole. It concentrates on the mother – being a Creole – but does not mention anything about the father except his being a merchant. Jane presents two accounts of Bertha. Readers come across the first before both Jane and the reader realise Bertha's presence and the second when Jane encounters Bertha in her prison at Thornfield. In the first account of Bertha's face, Jane tries to visualise it to Rochester:

> Fearful and ghastly to me – oh, sir, I never saw a face like it! It was a discoloured face – it was a savage face. I wish I could forget the roll of the red eyes and the fearful blackened inflation of the lineaments! […] This, sir, was purple: the lips swelled and dark; the brow furrowed: the black eyebrows widely raised over the bloodshot eyes. Shall I tell you of what it reminded me? […] Of the foul German spectre – the vampire (399).

Jane sees Bertha's features through the 'dark oblong glass.' Consequently, her description fails to define Bertha's colour clearly, but it succeeds in showing how Jane sees it in a way that emphasises Bertha's Otherness, which is more obvious. Bertha's face is discoloured or purple and it is also savage. It is a face the like of which Jane has never seen before. When Jane encounters Bertha as Rochester's wife, she again sees her in the dark because the room is without a window and Bertha is in the deep shade as described in the following passage:

> In the deep shade, at the farther end of the room, a figure ran backwards and forwards. What it was, whether beast or human being, one could not, at first sight tell: it grovelled, seemingly on all fours; it snatched and growled like some strange wild animal: but it was covered with clothing, and a quantity of dark, grizzled hair, wild as a mane, hid its head and face (412).

Apart from these two passages, Bertha's Otherness is emphasised in Rochester's account of his life with her. He always refers to her as 'monster,' 'goblin,' 'beast,' etc. Further, there is an allusion to cannibalism when he says: "when my wife is prompted by her familiar to burn people in their beds at night, to stab them, to bite their flesh from their bones, and so on (424)." All the accounts of Bertha in the text blur the line that separates animal from human. It is the colonial domination of other parts of the world during the eighteenth century which provided Brontë with a Bertha whose function in the novel is to blur this line and who refuses to be educated. This makes Gilbert and Gubar also exclude her from the journey to individualism, as Mcleod puts it:

> Bertha is robbed of human selfhood; she has no voice in the novel other than the demoniac laughter and the discomforting noises that Jane reports. Her [Bertha's] animalistic character disqualifies her [Bertha] from the journey of human self-determination for which Jane is celebrated by Anglo-American feminist critics.[42]

Now that the textual context of Bertha's appearances has been presented, Spivak's categorisation of her as a 'native subaltern female' can be discussed. The first issue to be discussed with regard to this categorisation is Spivak's description of Bertha as 'native.' Criticising Gilbert and Gubar's approach to Bertha, Spivak says: "[h]ere the native 'subject' is not almost an animal but rather the object of what might be termed the terrorism of the categorical imperative."[43] The literary critic Peter Hulme contends that Spivak's "use of 'native' suggests an underlying difficulty: in the West Indies the 'native' is either for the most part absent – if what is meant is indigenous – or 'creole' – if what is meant is 'born in the West

---

[42] John McLeod, *Beginning Postcolonialism* (Manchester: Manchester University Press, 2000), 152-3.

[43] Spivak, "Three Women's Texts," 248.

Indies.'"[44] The term covers Indian and African natives, in addition to its failure to draw a line between black and white Creoles. In a similar vein, Firdous Azim stresses the importance of the differentiation between the 'authentic native' and the Creole. She believes that as "a Creole, she [Bertha] is differentiated from the 'authentic' native, and represents multiple points of dislocation that the colonising venture had brought in its wake."[45] Both Hulme's and Azim's conclusions reveal the need to be more specific in using the term 'native.' Above all, Laura Chrisman highlights Bertha's colonial past, emphasising that Spivak "unwittingly implies that the Caribbean, colonial origin of the Mason family is unlikely to carry any such discursive resonance of its own."[46] Thus, if Bertha's past is based on colonising the Caribbean, it will be confusing that Spivak considers her subaltern.

The second point is that even the element of colour has no significance as far as Spivak's categorisation of Bertha is concerned. Many critics read Jane's accounts trying to highlight the issue of colour in the representation of Bertha. For example, Susan Meyer argues that Bertha can easily be imagined as white: being the daughter of a West Indian planter and the sister of the yellow-skinned Mason, and most importantly being considered for marriage by a British aristocratic young man.[47] Though Bertha is of a white origin, the actual colour of her skin may be dark due to the climate of the West Indies as some critics argue. For instance, Berman contends that "folk theories of climatic and cultural contaminations blamed the torrid West Indies for 'burnt' Creole skin."[48] However, colour is important only because it may be a mark of Otherness, but when dealing with a Creole character, debates about colour become of less importance since 'Creole' with its derogatory implications is a term that includes both whites and blacks:

---

[44] Peter Hulme, "The Locked Heart: The Creole Family Romance of *Wide Sargasso Sea*," in *Colonial Discourse/Postcolonial Theory*, edited by Francis Barker et al (Manchester: Manchester University Press, 1996), 75.

[45] Firdous Azim, *The Colonial Rise of the Novel* (London: Routledge, 1993), 182.

[46] Laura Chrisman, "The Imperial Unconscious Representations of Imperial Discourse," *Critical Quarterly* 1990 (32:3): 39.

[47] Susan Meyer, "Colonialism and the Figurative Strategy of *Jane Eyre*" in *Macro-politics of Nineteenth Century Literature: Nationalism, Exoticism, Imperialism*, ed. Jonathan Arac and Harriet Ritvo (Philadelphia: University of Pennsylvania Press, 1991), 163-164.

[48] Carolyn Vellenga Berman, *Creole Crossings: Domestic Fiction and the Reform of Colonial Slavery* (London: Cornell University Press, 2006), 133.

From the seventeenth century to the nineteenth, however, the most common use of the term in English was to mean 'born in the West Indies', whether white or negro. Although, therefore, the term had 'no connotation of colour' (*OED*), it increasingly conjured, in European eyes, the 'threat' of colonial miscegenation.[49]

This means that, as advocated by both Berman and Azim, we need not deal with Creole as a racial categorisation. Berman tends to treat the Creole in *Jane Eyre* in a way that makes the term cover all the West Indies classes, colonisers and colonised. Berman makes use of textual evidence, namely of Rochester's admission that he sought many European mistresses and finally wanted to have an English wife in his search for "the antipodes of the Creole (438)." This leads Berman to view Creole as a "geographical [not racial] type."[50] Azim also comments on the geographical aspect of the Creole, contending that the "racial classification is based not on colour alone but on displacement from the place of origin. The Creole is geographically displaced."[51]

Spivak is certainly aware of the insignificance of colour and race in any discussion of a Creole character. She says: "[i]t is crucial that we extend our analysis of this example [Bertha] beyond the minimal diagnosis of 'racism.'"[52] She also describes Bertha as "the white Jamaican Creole."[53] If Bertha cannot be described as native for the reasons given by Hulme and Azim, and if her colour is not significant in light of Spivak's purposes, the question that arises here would be: on what basis does Spivak establish her theory of the foreclosure of the 'native subaltern female' in *Jane Eyre?* The answer to this question can be found in Moore-Gilbert's analysis of Spivak's reading when he argues that Spivak reads Bertha only within the text, disregarding her colonial past:

> While recognizing that Bertha is in fact a white Creole and a member of the plantocracy which built its wealth on slavery, Spivak reads her 'catachrestically' as occupying the position of the colonized subject [...] a reading partly invited by the insistence in Brontë's novel not only on Bertha's origins in the West Indies, but on her dark features and 'animal' qualities.[54]

---

[49] Ashcroft et al, *Key Concepts*, 57.
[50] Berman, *Creole Crossings,*123.
[51] Azim, *The Colonial Rise of the Novel*, 182.
[52] Spivak, "Three Women's Texts," 247.
[53] Spivak, "Three Women's Texts," 247.
[54] Moore-Gilbert, *Postcolonial Theory*, 95.

Undoubtedly, Moore-Gilbert's remark that Spivak reads Bertha catachrestically as the colonised subject is significant. He explains that "[c]atachresis is a more local, tactical manoeuvre, which involves wrenching particular images, ideas or rhetorical strategies out of their place within a particular narrative and using them to open up new arenas of meaning (often in direct contrast to their conventionally understood meanings and functions.)"[55] Spivak herself uses the term catachresis in many of her writings, though not in "Three Women's Texts." She defines catachresis as "a concept-metaphor without an adequate referent."[56] One can argue that apart from the self-immolation and outside the limits of the text, a white Jamaican Creole like Bertha is not the right referent when thinking of the 'native subaltern female.' It is the textual representation of Bertha that helps Spivak to a great extent to read catachrestically. On the one hand, the text presents Bertha as having all the qualities that are ascribed to the term native, as for example in *Key Concepts in Post-Colonial Studies*:

> The root sense of the term as those who were 'born to the land' was, in colonial contexts, overtaken by a pejorative usage in which the term 'native' was employed to categorize those who were regarded as inferior to the colonial settlers or the colonial administrators who ruled the colonies. 'Native' quickly became associated with such pejorative concepts as savage, uncivilised or child-like in class nouns such as the natives.[57]

This definition can be used to figure out Spivak's reasons for using the term 'native' catachrestically. Bertha – according to Jane and Rochester's accounts – has the pejorative properties associated with the term 'native'. Bertha is even inferior to them because white Creoles like Bertha's family were looked down on by the British abolitionists who found Otherness even in whiteness:

> [T]he figure of the white West Indian slaveholder also occupied an important place. Often represented particularly by abolitionists, as profit-obsessed, degenerate creoles, who brutalised their sable victims, the 'un-English' West Indian was a stock figure of antislavery discourse and a white 'other' against which metropolitan British identity was formulated.[58]

---

[55] Moore-Gilbert, *Postcolonial Theory,* 84.
[56] Gayatri Chakravorty Spivak, *Outside in the Teaching Machine* (London: Routledge, 1993), 60.
[57] Ashcroft, *Key Concepts*, 158.
[58] David Lambert, *White Creole Culture: Politics and Identity During the Age of Abolition* (Cambridge: Cambridge University Press, 2005), 15-16.

Moreover, McLeod argues that the representation of Bertha reveals the "slippage [which] repeats a frequent assumption in colonial discourses that those born of parents not from the same 'race' are degenerate beings, perhaps not fully human, closer to animals."[59]

Bertha is represented as the uncivilised Other. However, it is Bertha's self-immolation which mainly contributes to Spivak's categorisation of her as a 'native subaltern female.' Spivak intentionally brings sati to the foreground. In brief, in order to interrupt and deconstruct the text, Spivak travesties the parabasis resulting from Bertha's self-immolation to say that Bertha is the 'native subaltern female' who is excluded from the freedom which is offered to Jane. This exclusion happens both in the text and in feminist criticism such as Gilbert and Gubar's. Hence, Bertha's presence in the text complicates the truth-claim of female individualism as a universal represented in Jane's journey exactly as the New Hollanders and Fuegians complicate Kant's introduction of the universal rational man. Bertha is banished from the text, so that the universal female individualist can be consolidated as the universal norm of the woman who succeeds in breaking the chains of patriarchy. However, by analogy with Spivak's approach to the 'native informant' in Kant, Bertha disappears from the symbolic order only to return as the unrepresentable 'native subaltern female' about whom Spivak is speaking. In Kant's critique, the gap caused by the presence of the 'native informant' is resolved by excluding this figure from the kind of man and also by arguing that judging the sublime requires culture. As for *Jane Eyre,* resolving the gap caused by Bertha's madness comes at the end of the novel via the heroic words that describe St. John's mission in India.

The second step: St. John and civilising the 'native informant' as the new truth-claim

In her analysis of Jane and Bertha, Spivak shows that female individualism is the first truth-claim of the text. This truth-claim must be corrected since there is a 'native subaltern female' who does not have access to this freedom due to her savagery. In analysing St. John, Spivak's reading shows that the previous truth-claim is replaced with another: that the 'native subaltern female' must be civilised as the following paragraphs will explain through the role of St. John in relation to Kant's categorical imperative.

---

[59] McLeod, *Beginning Postcolonialism,* 152.

First of all, Spivak is adamant to highlight Rochester's view of Europe in contrast to the West Indies, a view which led him to the decision to leave for England. In this quotation, Spivak argues, "[t]he field of imperial conquest is here inscribed as Hell."[60] Here is the passage as it appears in Spivak's article:

> "One night I had been awakened by her yells...it was a fiery West Indian night.
> "'This life', said I at last, 'is hell! – this is the air – those are the sounds of the bottomless pit! I have a right to deliver myself from it if I can ... Let me break away, and go home to God!'...
> "A wind fresh from Europe blew over the ocean and rushed through the open casement: the storm broke, streamed, thundered, blazed, and the air grew pure...It was true Wisdom that consoled me in that hour, and showed me the right path....
> "The sweet wind from Europe was still whispering in the refreshed leaves, and the Atlantic was thundering in glorious liberty....
> "'Go,' said Hope, 'and live again in Europe ...You have done all that God and Humanity require of you.'"[61]

This passage, in Spivak's opinion, shifts the imperative from the human motive towards the divine injunction. By using the term 'imperative', Spivak brings to the surface Kant's categorical imperative which he explains in his *Critique of Pure Reason* where he clarifies that the categorical imperative is the moral law that depends on pure reason and is independent of any empirical aspect; it "expresses a species of necessity and a connection with grounds which does not occur anywhere else in the whole nature."[62] In other words, whereas we understand what is in nature depending on existence and appearance, ethical and moral commands are understood as a must without depending on sensibility or appearances. A categorical imperative depends on "nothing other than a mere concept."[63] In the scope of Spivak's reading of Kant and *Jane Eyre*, the categorical imperative is the civilising mission, the soul-making of the racial Other and it stemmed from nothing but a concept, that the Other is uncivilised. Again, in light of Spivak's ideas, the itinerary of this concept is as follows: colonialists met the racial Others and constructed them as savage, the

---

[60] Spivak, "Three Women's Texts," 247.
[61] Brontë, *Jane Eyre* (New York: n.p., 1960), 455, quoted in "Three Women's Texts," 247.
[62] Kant, *Critique of Pure Reason,* trans. Paul Guyer and Allen W. Wood (Cambridge: Cambridge University Press, 1998), 540.
[63] Kant, *Critique of Pure Reason,* 540.

philosophy of the Enlightenment used this construction to consolidate its theories, and finally eighteenth-century British literature inherited the technique of filling the gap with this construction of the Other. Eventually, philosophical and literary representations of the Other supported politicians in their justification of colonial practices.

In her reading of Kant's third critique, Spivak explains that Kant considers man as a purpose of nature because everything in nature is designed to please his mind. However, Kant cannot explain the presence of the New Hollanders and Fuegians as a purpose of nature because they view the sublime as fearful. Further, Spivak emphasises that Kant proposes that judging the sublime requires culture which prepares man to receive moral ideas and that the Christian faith in God is the best way to fill the gap when man thinks about why nature itself exists. In her reading of *Jane Eyre*, Spivak quotes Kant's statement that "[i]n all creation every thing one chooses and over which one has any power, may be used as means; man alone, and with him every rational creature, is an end of himself."[64] Yet, she indicates that if man is not prepared by western culture and Christian faith, he cannot be an end in himself. Therefore, she considers that if Kant's categorical imperative is to be travestied to justify imperialism it can be formulated in the following manner: "*make* the heathen into a human so that he can be treated as an end in himself."[65] Spivak quotes the above passage, where Rochester raises God's demands as regards Europe's Other, to determine the moment when the text prepares readers for the next truth-claim. This shift leads Spivak to discuss the imperialist register in *Jane Eyre* not only in terms of the marriage between Bertha and Rochester and Bertha's self-immolation, but also in terms of the "greater good than the letter of the Law."[66] This greater good can be understood through attending to the implications of the novel's ending with St. John's mission, a conclusion which Spivak finds strange. If Jane is the heroine throughout the novel, why should the novel end with an account of St. John's mission in India?

While discussing the opening passage of *Jane Eyre,* Spivak emphasises the fact that Jane withdraws from the space of the Reed family. Then, she observes that Jane's creative imagination is activated while she is reading a book. In other words, the whole novel is narrated using Jane's words that belong to a different register than that of St. John except the penultimate paragraph of the novel which Spivak quotes:

---

[64] Kant, *Critique of Practical Reason,* trans. J. M. D. Meiklejohn et al (Chicago, 1952), 326, 328, quoted in Spivak, "Three Women's Texts," 248.

[65] Spivak, "Three Women's Texts," 248.

[66] Spivak, "Three Women's Texts," 247.

Firm, faithful, and devoted, full of enery, and zeal and truth [St. John Rivers] labours for his race […] His is the sternness of the warrior Greatheart, who guards his pilgrim convoy from the onslaught of Apollyon […] His is the ambition of the high master-spirit[s] […] who stand without fault before the throne of God; who share the last mighty victories of the Lamb; who are called, and chosen, and faithful (642).

Spivak finds this conclusion a source of discomfiture. She probably draws on Eagleton's study of *Jane Eyre* where he argues that "the fact that the novel allows him [St. John] the last word reflects its uneasiness about the victory to which it brings Jane."[67] Hence, Spivak also stresses the fact that St. John is "granted the important task of concluding the text."[68] Concluding the novel in this manner is not only confusing because it raises questions about Jane's individualism. Spivak takes the argument a step further, suggesting that this concluding paragraph shows "the unquestioned idiom of imperialist presuppositions."[69] The implication of Spivak drawing our attention to this conclusion is that the text produces the truth-claim that replaces the claim of the individualism of the woman. In other words, the new truth-claim is the following: in order for the 'native subaltern female' to pass to freedom and for the universal feminist individualist to be introduced, the 'native subaltern female' must be civilised by western culture and Christianity. The new truth-claim is evident in St. John's words, which Spivak quotes to show how he justifies his mission:

[M]y vocation? My great work? […] My hopes of being numbered in the band who have merged all ambitions in the glorious one of bettering their race – of carrying knowledge into the realms of ignorance – of substituting peace for war, freedom for bondage , religion for superstition, the hope of heaven for the fear of hell? (529-30)

To conclude this chapter, one can argue that although written after "Three Women's Texts", Spivak's reading of Kant published in 1999 explains the technique used by Spivak to deconstruct *Jane Eyre*. Spivak deconstructs the novel tropologically depending on the two steps which de Man proposed in his lectures between 1981 and 1983. The first truth-claim of the novel is female individualism which is complicated by the gap resulting from the presence of Bertha and her self-immolation posing limits to this freedom. This gap is filled with St. John's project of soul-

---

[67] Eagleton, *Myths of Power*, 23.
[68] Spivak, "Three Women's Texts," 249.
[69] Spivak, "Three Women's Texts," 249.

making according to which the 'native subaltern female,' who cannot access the western woman's freedom, must be civilised through Christianity.

CHAPTER THREE

WIDE SARGASSO SEA AND THE RE-INSCRIPTION OF *JANE EYRE*

The second part of "Three Women's Texts" is Spivak's study of Jean Rhys's *Wide Sargasso Sea* (1966). The relationship between this novel and *Jane Eyre* is deep-rooted as clear in Rhys's following statement:

> So reading "Jane Eyre" one's swept along regardless. But I, reading it later, and often, was vexed at her portrait of the 'paper tiger' lunatic, the all wrong creole scenes, and above all by the real cruelty of Mr. Rochester. After all, he was a very wealthy man and there were many kinder ways of disposing of (or hiding) an unwanted wife.[1]

She also says: "I thought I'd try to write her [Bertha] a life."[2] So, *Wide Sargasso Sea* is the prequel of *Jane Eyre*.[3] As Shakti Jaising argues, Rhys's novel is routinely "invoked for its anti-imperialist rewriting of the English classic *Jane Eyre*" and, therefore, it "is a staple text in courses on modern and postcolonial literature across the Anglophone world."[4] Spivak's reading of this novel is powerful and significant due to the fact that after this reading, new perspectives emerged within the criticism of Rhys's writing. Jaising contends that Spivak's is "an insightful reading" which led "Anglo-American criticism [...] to expand beyond exploring the novel's self-created relationship with *Jane Eyre*, emphasising also the white West Indian protagonist's connection with her black maid and former slave, Christophine."[5]

---

[1] Jean Rhys, *Jean Rhys Letters, 1931-1966,* ed. Francis Wyndham and Diana Melly (London: Deutsch, 1984), 262.

[2] Jean Rhys, "Jean Rhys Interviewed by Elizabeth Vreeland," in *The Paris Review,* 76 (1979), 234.

[3] Morton, *Gayatri Spivak,* 23.

[4] Shakti Jaising, "Who is Christophine? The Good Black Servant and the Contradictions of (Racial) Liberalism," in *MFS Modern Fiction Studies,* 56:4 (2010), 816.

[5] Jaising, "Who is Christophine[?]," 816.

There are four important points that must be taken into account when discussing Spivak's reading of this novel. First, Spivak reads this novel as a re-inscription of *Jane Eyre*. This means that although the novel is an attempt to rescue the silent Bertha of *Jane Eyre,* named Antoinette in Rhys's text, from marginalisation, it can still be seen as buttressing the imperialist desire for the domestication of the 'native subaltern female' through Antoinette's relationship with Tia and Christophine. Second, as discussed in the previous chapter, Spivak reads Bertha in *Jane Eyre* catachrestically as a 'native subaltern female' but this does not mean that this applies to Antoinette since in *Wide Sargasso Sea* Bertha, as Antoinette, is represented in the context of her belonging to the plantocracy and her desire to see the 'native subaltern female' as her mirror image. Thus, Antoinette here is redeemed not as a 'native subaltern female'/sati but as the white Creole who, Spivak thinks, "is caught between the English imperialist and the black native."[6] This means that Antoinette is not the parabasis in Rhys's text as was Bertha in Brontë's text. Third, Spivak uses tropological deconstruction in approaching Rhys's text and the parabasis is possible through the representation of Tia and the good black servant, previously a slave, Christophine. Spivak deconstructs Rhys's presentation of Antoinette, Rochester and Christophine and this deconstruction leads to the conclusion that, though it has some points of strength in tackling the issue of the 'native subaltern female,' *Wide Sargasso Sea* re-inscribes *Jane Eyre* with its imperialist discourse.

The following paragraphs attempt to explain Spivak's deconstruction of *Wide Sargasso Sea*. The chapter demonstrates that Spivak reveals the first truth-claim of the text which is vindicating Antoinette and "Rochester" as victims and eliminating the possibility of their complicity with imperialism.[7] Spivak's deconstruction of this idea will be presented in two parts. The first is her reading of the thematics of Narcissus as regards Antoinette. This part illustrates Antoinette's search for an image for herself in the black natives with the aim of consolidating the self. The second part is Spivak's deconstruction of Rhys's claim that "Rochester" is a victim of the oedipal relationship with his father and for this aim Spivak

---

[6] Spivak, "Three Women's Texts," 250.

[7] Rhys does not give this man a name although she makes clear references to Brontë's Rochester. Spivak does not discuss the man by calling him Rochester. Instead, she refers to him as 'the Rochester figure,' 'the Rochester character' or 'the Man.' Following the example of Nancy Harrison in her book: *Jean Rhys and the Novel as Women's Text* (Chapel Hill: University of North Carolina Press, c1988), and in order to avoid any confusion, this character will be referred to as "Rochester" in this chapter.

resorts to the deconstruction of the thematics of Oedipus she detects in the text. Then, the chapter will move to explain Spivak's reading of Christophine whose withdrawal at the end of the novel leaves a new silencing of the 'native subaltern female.' Through her emphasis on Christophine's withdrawal and Antoinette and "Rochester's" return to the fictional world of *Jane Eyre*, Spivak stresses her conviction that Rhys re-inscribes Brontë's text.

The first truth-claim in the novel:
Antoinette and "Rochester" are victims

Antoinette

Spivak's reading implies that the novel is an attempt to vindicate Antoinette who associates herself with the blacks not with the English settlers. Yet, Spivak's argument tries to prove that Antoinette only associates herself with the black natives for the sake of consolidating herself. Spivak attempts to explain her idea by recourse to the thematics of Narcissus. Her argument is based on two pivotal points. First, she shows how Antoinette is vindicated in this novel by illustrating the demarcation between Brontë's Bertha and Rhys's Antoinette in terms of function. She discusses this through the textual analysis of Rhys's rewriting of the scene in which Bertha attacks her brother, Richard Mason, in *Jane Eyre*. Second, she shows that the novel re-inscribes the imperialist epistemic violence through Antoinette's attempts to 'self' the Other in order to consolidate the image of herself. This re-inscription of the imperialist desire to 'self' the Other will be explained depending on Spivak's deconstructive understanding of the thematics of Narcissus.

Starting from the first point which is the vindication of Antoinette, Spivak emphasises that while Bertha is a figure that blurs the line separating human from animal, Antoinette's humanity and sanity remain intact. To prove this, Spivak contrasts the scene of Bertha's biting her brother in the two novels. In *Jane Eyre*, Jane reports a conversation between "Rochester" and Richard Mason from which we get the following account: Richard comes to visit Bertha in her prison in the third floor at Thornfield. "Rochester" advises him not to come near her, but Bertha looks so quiet at first. Then, contrary to Richard's expectations, she attacks him with a knife. When "Rochester" takes the knife, she attacks like a tigress and bites Richard. Of course, in light of this account, there is no explanation offered for Bertha's fierce attack except her bestial madness. In *Wide Sargasso Sea*, the scene is recounted by Grace Poole, Antoinette's guardian, who declares that it is when Richard said: "I cannot interfere legally between yourself and your husband,"[8] namely when he uttered the word 'legally,' that Bertha attacked him. As rewritten by Rhys, the scene leads Spivak to the conclusion that "it is the dissimulation that Bertha discerns in the word 'legally' – not an innate bestiality – that prompts her violent *re*action."[9] We can understand Spivak's italicisation of 're' as stressing the fact that Bertha's behaviour is caused by the fact that 'legally' justifies Antoinette's husband owning her through legal marriage. As Morton says, legal marriage "defines Bertha as Rochester's private property."[10] Morton also argues that "[l]ike Hindu Law, an ideology of good wifely conduct was also prevalent in British society, under the terms of English common law. For Spivak, this ideology is covered over in *Jane Eyre*, but it is foregrounded in *Wide Sargasso Sea*."[11]

Furthermore, Spivak regards the legal marriage as tantamount to a kind of epistemic violence practised on Bertha by her husband. She proposes that Rhys's novel shows the way in which the politics of imperialism determines even the personal and human through "Rochester's" insistence on calling Antoinette by her mother's name, Bertha. Howells adds evidence that supports Spivak's argument by saying that the significance of "Rochester's" summoning of this name "is underlined as Antoinette begins to show signs of violent behaviour from this point on."[12] Spivak's interest in drawing attention to Rochester's renaming of Antoinette is similar to her commentary on the British misrepresentation of Indian women who performed sati. In "Can the Subaltern Speak?" Spivak refers to Edward Thompson who, inter alia, was concerned with the practice of sati and wrote about it. In *Suttee: A Historical and Philosophical Enquiry into the Hindu Rite of Widow-Burning* (1928), Thompson mentions General Charles Robert West Hervey who was in the British Army in India and who made efforts to deal with the issue of sati. Hervey obtained names of some satis of Bikanir, a district in the state of Rajasthan in Northern India. According to Thompson, these names included: "Ray Queen, Sun-ray, Love's Delight, Garland, Virtue Found, Echo, Soft Eye, Comfort, Moonbeam, Love-lorn, Dear Heart, Eye-play, Arbour-born,

---

[8] Jean Rhys, *Wide Sargasso Sea*, ed. Angela Smith (London: Penguin Books, 1997), 120. Subsequent references in the novel will be to this edition and will be reflected as page numbers within parentheses.

[9] Spivak, "Three Women's Texts," 250.

[10] Stephen Morton, *Gayatri Chakravorty Spivak* (London: Routledge, 2003), 89.

[11] Morton, *Gayatri Chakravorty Spivak*, 89.

[12] Coral Ann Howells, *Jean Rhys* (Hemel Hempstead: Harvester Wheatsheaf, 1991), 118.

Smile, Love-bud, Glad Omen, Mist-clad or Cloud-sprung."[13] Spivak comments:

> Once again, imposing the upper-class Victorian typical demands upon 'his woman' (his preferred phrase), Thompson appropriates the Hindu woman as his to save against the 'system.' [...] There is no more dangerous pastime than transporting proper names into common nouns, translating them, and using them as sociological evidence. I attempted to reconstruct the names on that list and began to feel the [colonial administrator's] arrogance. What, for instance, might 'Comfort' have been? Was it 'Shanti'?[14]

Behind these translated names, hide the women whose stories are now inaccessible. Their names are translated into English by the British colonial authority and this is an example of imperial interference with the personal and human. Again, in this passage Spivak refers to ownership when she says that Thompson refers to these Hindu women as his own and this explains his and Hervey's misnaming of them in the same way "Rochester" misnames Antoinette to inscribe her as Bertha and justify how he treats her.

Spivak goes on to say that Antoinette's anger raised by the word 'legally' shows the latter as a critic of imperialism and this is how Brontë's Bertha is vindicated in Rhys's text. Antoinette is caught between the English imperialist and the black native because she is a white Creole girl growing up during emancipation. Many critics study this situation in more detail than Spivak does. One example is Coral Ann Howells who says that Antoinette and her mother, Annette, were "[h]ated by the blacks and despised for their poverty by both blacks and other whites."[15] Howells gives a clearer example of this dilemma by showing two different types of alliance sought by Antoinette and her mother. Annette favours the alliance with new colonialism by her marriage to the English Mr. Mason while Antoinette seeks alliance with Tia after the burning of their estate by the ex-slaves.[16] Then, Howells continues, Antoinette becomes "a displaced person in her own country, entirely dependent on a dowry supplied by her English stepfather and at the mercy of an arranged marriage with an Englishman who has been sent to the West Indies to seek his fortune."[17] However, when she is taken to England, Antoinette tries to associate

---

[13] Spivak, "Can the Subaltern Speak?" 305.
[14] Spivak, "Can the Subaltern Speak?" 305-6.
[15] Howells, *Jean Rhys,* 110.
[16] Howells, *Jean Rhys,* 111.
[17] Howells, *Jean Rhys,* 111.

herself with Tia again. By arguing that Antoinette is a critic of imperialism, Spivak illustrates that Brontë's Bertha has been saved from the margin in the character of Antoinette. Thus, we can argue now that Antoinette is not an emblem of the 'native subaltern female' in *Wide Sargasso Sea*. The rest of Spivak's analysis of Antoinette proves that the latter is vindicated as a colonialist and this can be demonstrated in her attempts to 'self' the Other. 'Selfing' the Other, in Spivak's opinion, is a strategy that was used by the imperialist discourses which collapsed the Other into the self, as clarified in this book's introduction. This collapsing resulted in the colonialist claim of knowing the Other, a claim which, in turn, gave colonialists the right to represent the Other by constructing him/her as the savage who needs to be civilised. 'Selfing' the Other in Rhys's text is demonstrated in Antoinette's attempts to associate herself with the slaves and servants. To unfold these attempts, Spivak resorts to the deconstruction of the thematics of Narcissus which she offered for the first time in her essay "Echo," a study which draws on "Narcissus in the Text" (1976) by John Brenkman.

The Thematics of Narcissus

The myth of Narcissus is presented in Book III of the Latin narrative poem *Metamorphoses* by Ovid. When Narcissus was born, his mother asked the River-God whether her son will attain a ripe old age. The River-God answered that Narcissus will live a long life as long as he does not know himself. The boy grew up and many girls sought his love, but he was very proud and rejected them. Echo was one of the nymphs who loved Narcissus. However, Echo was not able to speak her own words; she was only able to repeat others' words. This was her punishment because she used to distract the goddess Juno with endless tales, distracting Juno, thereby, from the nymphs who had relationships with the god Jove. Echo saw Narcissus and followed him. She could not reveal her love because she could only repeat Narcissus' words. When she tried to embrace Narcissus, he rejected her. Later, Narcissus saw his own reflection on the surface of a tranquil lake in a very calm place. Without knowing that he was looking at his own image, he fell in love with this reflection. He tried to embrace the reflection but he could not and when he spoke, only Echo repeated his words: 'alas,' 'in vain' and 'farewell.' Narcissus was consumed by love and turned into a flower. As for Echo, she hid in the woods until her bones turned into stone. What was left of her was only her voice.[18]

This is the narrative of the Narcissus myth. On face value, the narrative seems to be about Narcissus being punished for his pride and harsh rejection of Echo. It could also be read as a prophecy of Narcissus' early death coming true. Most readings of and references to the myth concentrated on Narcissus, not Echo, especially in psychoanalytic studies such as Sigmund Freud's "On Narcissism: An Introduction" (1914) where Freud depends on the myth of Narcissus in analysing sexual development. Narcissus was associated with self-admiration and making the self as one's object of sexuality. These ideas can also be found in the work of sexologists like Havelock Ellis. However, this is not essential for Spivak who rather concentrates on Echo and depends on John Brenkman's study "Narcissus in the Text." In fact, Brenkman's reading insists that Narcissus is not a collection of stable themes. On the contrary, he believes that the text situates its characters, Narcissus and Echo, in a way that makes the myth open to contradictory interpretations. Then, through philosophical texts by Kant, Heidegger, Husserl and Derrida, he relates "Narcissus" to the philosophical project of protecting the purity of the self from "any primordial relation to what is other."[19]

Among other issues, Brenkman is concerned with repetitions and the difference they produce. Repetition includes Echo's echoing voices and Narcissus' reflected image in the pool. He postulates that although Echo is bound to repeat others' voices, she becomes the agent of her speech through "the changes in meaning produced by partial echoes – that Echo's words emerge as her own and not merely as the repetition of another's."[20] He presents several examples of how Echo's repetitions become proper responses that continue Narcissus' remarks. Spivak takes from Brenkman's study the instance when Narcissus questions Echo: "Why do you fly from me?" and she echoes "fly from me [?]". Echoing 'fly from me' does not maintain the form of the interrogative which is in Narcissus' question and this, Spivak believes, makes Echo the agent of her words though they are repetitions of others' utterances. Spivak believes that the discrepancy between the interrogative and imperative forms of the Latin "fly from me" may imply that Echo's answer to Narcissus question can be interpreted as either "I cannot answer you, or I am not your proper respondent – a deferment independent of, indeed the opposite of, the

---

[18] Ovid, "Narcissus and Echo" in *Metamorphoses,* trans. David Raeburn (London: Penguin Books, 2004), 109-116.
[19] John Brenkman, "Narcissus in the Text," *Georgia Review,* 30 (1976), 314.
[20] Brenkman, "Narcissus in the Text," 303.

sender's intention."[21] This discrepancy for Spivak illustrates that Echo's punishment fails in and also shows the risk of response. Spivak's argument here indicated that even when repeating the exact words of Narcissus, there is something that does not pass between them, which is the interrogative form here. Echo's repetition is not a response to Narcissus' question. At the same time, the change of the form may indicate that Echo, as Other, cannot be an exact copy of the self, Narcissus.

Moving to Narcissus, Brenkman describes the pool as the appropriate place where Narcissus dies for self-knowledge. The pool is tranquil, clear and secluded which makes it in harmony with Narcissus' isolation. Even the sun cannot warm the place because of the trees that surround it. This clear tranquil water reflects his image which he mistakes for another youth. He finds that the reflection smiles when he smiles and cries when he cries but he discovers that it is his reflection only when he realises the impossibility of speech communication between them. Brenkman explicates what happens at this moment, saying:

> Narcissus declares 'iste ego sum' only when, as he speaks, he brings together the silence of the lips he sees and the sound of the voice he hears. His illusion is fractured, that is, only when he articulates the difference between the space of the image and the time of the voice – the space of the other and the time of the self.[22]

As Echo repeats what others say but with a difference that allows her to suspend Juno's punishment, Narcissus' reflection repeats the image but as soon as the verbal difference is revealed between the two images, Narcissus recognises his deception. Spivak takes Narcissus to be "an icon of mortiferous self-knowledge."[23] Repeating Tiresias' line: "he will live as long as he does not know himself," Spivak argues that Narcissus can instantiate "the construction of the self as an object of knowledge."[24] This statement indicates that Spivak views this as an instant when someone looks at the mirror with the aim of knowing the self. Spivak will later analyse the relationship between Antoinette and Tia in terms of this mirroring scene.

By concentrating on Echo, Spivak reads the myth against the grain and highlights the side that cannot speak. She proves that Echo does speak but nobody has paid attention to how Echo's repetitions achieve her agency. By bringing her deconstruction of the myth "Narcissus" to her discussion

---

[21] Spivak, "Echo," in *The Spivak Reader,* 185.

[22] Brenkman, "Narcissus in the Text," 313; "iste ego sum" means: I am that one.

[23] Spivak, "Echo," 181.

[24] Spivak, "Echo," 182.

of Antoinette, Spivak leads us to a clearer idea about what happens in *Wide Sargasso Sea*, associating Antoinette with Narcissus and Tia with Echo. In fact, Spivak focuses on mirror imagery as reproducing the thematics of Narcissus in *Wide Sargasso Sea*. Mirror imagery means splitting the self into a subject and an object, a split that in Spivak's analysis of Antoinette appears in two forms: 'selfing' the Other and othering the self. In order to understand how Spivak associates Antoinette's case with the thematics of Narcissus, it is important to quote the following passage from Brenkman:

> In fact, even as there is no (visual) difference between them, the reflected image and what it reflects are divided by an absolute difference. A difference that inhabits and even constitutes the repetition: the original is corpus, its reflection is but umbra or imago. The other is not another like the self but the other of the self.[25]

Spivak indicates that the representation of Antoinette depends on the thematics of Narcissus and she adds 'the imaginary' between brackets.[26] Using 'the imaginary' here is important because it illustrates the fact that central to Antoinette's mirror imagery is the illusion of self-unity which is explained in Lacan's definition of the imaginary. Lacan explains the imaginary as the mirror stage and it starts when the infant first sees his/her body as a whole unity in the mirror. This image replaces the primordial fragmented image of the self and leads to a process of realising an inner subjectivity. The image of the whole body constitutes the ego and gives the illusion of coherence both of the image and the inner self.[27]

Spivak explains Antoinette's presentation in terms of her need for this cohesion at the expense of Tia. Spivak comments on the mirror image which appears in the first section of the novel when Antoinette tries to associate herself with Tia, the black servant girl. While her family's house is being burnt in the incident of the slaves' rebellion, Antoinette expresses her wish to live with Tia and to be like her since they ate the same food and bathed in the same river. Tia, for her part, carries a stone and throws it at Antoinette who viewed herself and Tia as identical saying:

---

[25] Brenkman, "Narcissus in the Text," 306.
[26] Spivak, "Three Women's Texts," 251.
[27] Jacques Lacan, "The Mirror Stage as formative of the function of the I as revealed in psychoanalytic experience." (1949), in *Écrits: A Selection*, trans. Alan Sheridan, (New York: W. W. Norton & Company, 1977), 1-7.

> We had eaten the same food, slept side by side, bathed in the same river. As I ran, I thought, I will live with Tia and I will be like her.... When I was close I saw the jagged stone in her hand but I did not see her throw it....We stared at each other, blood on my face, tears on hers. It was as if I saw myself. Like in a looking glass. (24)

It is here where Spivak's approach to Narcissus and Echo meets with her reading of Antoinette. Echo repeats the words with difference and Tia repeats all Antoinette's movements with a difference. Thus, Antoinette wants to see and is actually convinced that Tia is her mirror image because the former is shattered inside and wants to be in control of her self-unity. However, Tia repeats the movement but she also produces difference first by throwing the stone which results in another difference; blood on one face and tears on the other. By this, Tia interrupts the understanding of the text and illustrates that the 'native subaltern female' cannot be a copy of the self. Spivak does not say that Tia is an example of the 'native subaltern female.' However, because Spivak's reading focuses on how Tia does not speak for herself and is only represented by Antoinette's narration, she can be read as an example of the 'native subaltern female.' One can explain Spivak's belief that the novel re-inscribes the imperialist discourse through the thematics of Narcissus in the following manner: Antoinette's attempt to see Tia as her mirror image is an attempt to domesticate the 'native subaltern female,' to see her as a copy of the self. This attempt is motivated by Antoinette's dilemma as a white Creole caught between the English imperialist and the black native. Antoinette's face-to-face encounter with Tia is for the aim of knowing and consolidating Antoinette's self and not for the aim of communicating with Tia. Like in *Jane Eyre,* the 'native subaltern female' here is put in the service of the white Creole female who is searching for an identity or individualism. Nonetheless, Spivak continues, Antoinette's imperialist maneuver fails because, unlike Narcissus, she is not looking at her reflection on the surface of water. The division separating her from Tia is the imperialist division between coloniser and colonised. Spivak describes Tia as "the Other that could not be selfed, because the fracture of imperialism rather than the Ovidian pool intervened."[28]

Then, Spivak's argument shows that failing to associate herself with Tia, Antoinette in her dreams in England is forced to associate herself with Brontë's Bertha through the second mirror image presented in the last section of the novel as Antoinette's third dream. Antoinette sees herself entering the hall of her husband's house in England with a candle and then

---

[28] Spivak, "Three Women's Texts," 250.

she sees the ghost: "I saw her – the ghost. The woman with streaming hair. She was surrounded by a gilt frame but I knew her" (123), and the dream ends with Antoinette calling Tia again. Then, Antoinette wakes up and says: "[n]ow at last I know why I was brought here and what I have to do" (124). Here, Spivak finds Antoinette acting out the conclusion of *Jane Eyre* and identifying "herself as the so-called ghost in Thornfield Hall."[29] Further, this end is read by Spivak as an awareness of Antoinette's role for which she has been transplanted in England fictively through *Jane Eyre*. Spivak links Antoinette's statement: "[t]his cardboard house where I walk at night is not England" (118) to a book between cardboard covers and contends that Antoinette has to transform her 'self' into the fictive Other of *Jane Eyre*'s England and cause the destruction of Thornfield and finally kill herself, so that Jane becomes the female individualist. By illustrating Antoinette's failure to associate herself with Tia and her return to Brontë's narrative in the end, Spivak makes a very important and complicated point. She reveals that *Wide Sargasso Sea* deconstructs itself in that Rhys could not offer Antoinette more than this role of being sacrificed for the sake of Jane. Spivak's reading of Rhys's delineation of Antoinette leaves us with two implications. First, throughout the novel, Antoinette is the white woman who tries to domesticate the 'native subaltern female' to serve the former's search for herself. Therefore, the novel cannot be acquitted from the charge of complicity with the imperialist discourse. Second, the end of the novel returns Antoinette to the role of the 'native subaltern female' through taking her again to the fictional world of *Jane Eyre* to be self-immolated for Jane's sake. The difference between the two novels now for Spivak is that "the woman in the colonies is not sacrificed as an insane animal for her sister's consolation."[30] In Spivak's opinion, Rhys's text offers a different explanation of Bertha's madness by replacing the factors of heredity and race in Brontë's text with the trauma caused by the disempowerment of the white Creoles in Jamaica as Moore-Gilbert says: "in Spivak's view, *Wide Sargasso Sea* provides a quite different aetiology of Bertha's crisis from the biologically determined (because of factors related to heredity/racial mixing in her family) 'madness' into which Brontë's Bertha descends."[31]

Hence, Spivak's reading of Antoinette is de Manian and it consists of two steps. First, she reveals that though facing a dilemma and though a critic of the imperialist discourse that uses legality to interfere in the personal, Antoinette herself acts out this imperialist discourse by trying to

[29] Spivak, "Three Women's Texts," 250.
[30] Spivak, "Three Women's Texts," 251.
[31] Moore-Gilbert, *Postcolonial Theory,* 95.

see Tia as her own image. Tia in this part of Spivak's analysis is the parabasis because when she throws the stone at Antoinette, Tia interrupts the text and makes it clear that the claim of 'selfing' the Other is only a truth-claim that is deconstructed. The second step in Spivak's analysis of Antoinette is the return of this character to her role as in *Jane Eyre*, a return which also supports Spivak's stress that the text cannot escape the imperialist discourse.

"Rochester"

The second point which makes Spivak believe that Rhys's text is a re-inscription of *Jane Eyre* with its imperialist discourse is the representation of "Rochester." Spivak's reading of Rhys's "Rochester" implies that the novel re-inscribes the imperialist division between the female and male not by using the registers of sexual reproduction and the social mission as was the case in Brontë's text. In *Wide Sargasso Sea*, the register is different as Spivak clarifies saying: "[i]f in the nineteenth century, subject-constitution is represented as childbearing and soul making, in the twentieth century psychoanalysis allows Northwestern Europe to plot the itinerary of the subject from Narcissus [the "imaginary"] to Oedipus [the "symbolic"] This subject, however is the normative male subject."[32] In *Jane Eyre*, the female subject is assigned the mission of child-bearing, and the male subject is given the mission of soul-making. Again, in *Wide Sargasso Sea*, the two subjects are divided in terms of psychoanalysis. Whereas the female subject, Antoinette, is presented as stuck in the mirror stage looking for a coherent consolidated self, the male subject, "Rochester," is presented in light of Oedipus in an attempt to present him as a victim of patriarchy.

Rhys's text palpably indicates that "Rochester" is actually made a victim of a patriarchal law of inheritance by which the property is entailed to the eldest son forcing the younger son to "buy an heiress" from the colonies.[33] Thus, Spivak maintains that Rhys uses the thematics of Oedipus in presenting "Rochester" as a victim. In her discussion of *Jane Eyre*, Spivak makes clear that the justification for Rochester's treatment of Bertha was based on presenting Bertha as occupying the position that separates human from animal. As for "Rochester" in *Wide Sargasso Sea*, Rhys needed a pretext other than the imperialist construction of Bertha as savage. Therefore, Spivak suggests that presenting "Rochester" as a victim

---

[32] Spivak, "Three Women's Texts," 251.
[33] Spivak, "Three Women's Texts," 251.

of the oedipal relationship between him and his father is the new pretext to justify the way he treated his Creole wife. Yet, the idea is not that simple because although Spivak resorts to psychoanalysis to analyse Rhys's presentation of "Rochester," she eventually deconstructs Rhys's attempt to vindicate him.

The psychoanalytic version which Spivak is using here is Lacanian rather than Freudian and this can be concluded from her use of the terms 'imaginary' and 'symbolic.' The key term necessary for understanding Spivak's analysis of "Rochester" in the psychoanalytic context is the "Name of the Father" which was developed by Jacques Lacan. The itinerary of this term started with Freud's reference to Sophocles' *King Oedipus* where Oedipus cannot escape the oracle of killing his father and marrying his mother. For example, in *The Interpretation of Dreams* (1899) Freud explains that children may have loving wishes for one parent and hostile wishes for the other. He tells us about a male patient who had murderous impulses towards his severe father.[34] Freud goes on to explain through the example of Oedipus the relationships between son, mother, and father showing that the oedipal exchange between father and son is based on rivalry. The son perceives his father as the source of all authority and desire. Aware of this authority, the son becomes afraid of castration by his father and decides to identify himself with the father with a belief that one day he can occupy such a position. Fear from castration which prevents incest makes the Name of the Father the source of prohibition and law.

Lacan's treatment of the oedipal relationship is different from Freud's in that Lacan takes the argument to the level of language and signification. He emphasises that all signification starts with the signifier 'Name of the Father.' He says: "[b]efore the Name of the Father, there was no father, there were all sorts of other things."[35] For Lacan, this signifier allows signification to proceed normally by giving identity to the subject, and signifies the oedipal prohibition of incest. Consequently, the Name of the Father is the signifier which allows the law to start. If this signifier is foreclosed, in the sense of being excluded from the symbolic order, the result is that this signifier will return in the real but it will be impossible for it to be written as a text.[36] Spivak's argument is that Rhys uses the

---

[34] Sigmund Freud, *The Interpretation of Dreams,* trans. Joyce Crick (Oxford: Oxford University Press, 1999), 200-204.

[35] Jacques Lacan, *The Psychoses: The Seminar of Jacques Lacan,* ed. Jacques-Alain Miller, trans. Russell Grigg (London: Routledge, 1981), 306.

[36] The idea of foreclosing a concept by exclusion from the symbolic order has been explained in Chapter One of this book.

Oedipus thematics to vindicate "Rochester" but she denies him the Name of the Father. This forecloses the first symbol of "Rochester's" story and therefore the whole story is foreclosed. It is thus how Spivak deconstructs "Rochester's" vindication.

Spivak elucidates her opinion of the oedipal exchange in *Wide Sargasso Sea* through her discussion of "Rochester's" letters to his father. She illustrates the replacement of the passage in which Brontë's Rochester speaks about the fresh wind that saves him and leads him to return to England. Instead, Spivak argues, "Rochester" in *Wide Sargasso Sea* thinks about a letter he should have written to his father: "I thought about the letter which should have been written to England a week ago. Dear Father [...]" (40). Spivak's argument can be clarified by contextualising this scene. "Rochester" thinks about the unwritten letter immediately after watching Antoinette critically, as he himself says, and observing her Otherness: "[l]ong, sad, dark alien eyes. Creole of pure English descent she may be, but they are not English or European either. And when did I begin to notice all this about my wife Antoinette?" (40). That Antoinette is busy talking in patois with Carolina while the rain is dripping down "Rochester's" neck adds to his "feeling of discomfort and melancholy" (40). Under the pressure of this feeling, he remembers the letter. Shortly after this, "Rochester" describes the natural world of the West Indies, revealing his distress because everything is too much for him, "too much blue, too much purple, too much green [...] And the woman is a stranger" (42). Suddenly he directs us again to the unwritten letter which Spivak quotes:

> Dear Father. The thirty thousand pounds have been paid to me without question or condition. No provision made for her (that must be seen to)....I will never be a disgrace to you or to my dear brother the son you love. No begging letters, no mean requests. None of the furtive shabby manoeuvres of a younger son. I have sold my soul or you have sold it, and after all is it such a bad bargain? The girl is thought to be beautiful, she is beautiful. (42)

Spivak describes this passage as the suppressed letter to a father and purports that this letter provides the correct explanation of the tragedy of the novel. However, it is unwritten.

Then, Spivak refers to the letter which Rochester actually writes but which does not reach its destination:

> Dear Father, we have arrived from Jamaica after an uncomfortable few days. This little estate in the Windward Islands is part of the family property and Antoinette is much attached to it....All is well and has gone

according to your plans and wishes. I dealt of course with Richard
Mason….He seemed to become attached to me and trusted me completely.
(46)

Spivak asserts that this letter is uninteresting. Yet, she continues, its
importance lies in the fact that we do not know whether the letter reached
"Rochester's" father because "Rochester" – wondering how people send
their letters there – puts his in the drawer. Spivak concludes that "Rhys's
version of the oedipal exchange is ironic, not a closed circle," and that
"Rochester's" "writing of the final version of the letter to his father is
supervised, in the strictest possible sense, by an image of the *loss* of the
patronymic."[37] Spivak insists on this patronymic loss because: "Rhys
denies "Rochester" the one thing that is supposed to be secured in the
oedipal relay: the Name of the Father. In *Wide Sargasso Sea*, the character
corresponding to Rochester has no name."[38] Spivak does not explain the
idea further but one can conclude the implication depending on her
approach to the Name of Man in her reading of Kant which is explained in
Chapter One of this book. Depending on Lacan's concept of foreclosure,
Spivak says that even though the 'native informant' is excluded from the
Name of Man in Kant's third critique, this 'native informant' returns in the
real as the impossible that cannot be symbolically represented or written.
Again here, Spivak implies that when "Rochester" is deprived of the Name
of the Father, he loses his position within the symbolic order and,
consequently, he does not have a text of his own. If Rhys denies
"Rochester" the ownership of his text by depriving him of the patronymic,
then the claim that he is a victim of the oedipal exchange is also
foreclosed.

To further explain Spivak's refutation of the novel's claim that
"Rochester" is a victim of his father's patriarchy, we need to follow
Spivak's notes and refer to her essay "The Letter as Cutting Edge" (1977)
in which she approaches Chapters Twelve and Thirteen of Samuel
Coleridge's *Biographia Literaria* through the application of Lacan's
psychoanalysis. Spivak is concerned with Coleridge's claim that he
received a letter from a friend of his asking him to suppress the
argumentation of the original Chapter Thirteen of his *Biographia*. She
quotes Coleridge saying:

> Thus far had the work been transcribed for the press, when I received the
> following letter from a friend, whose practical judgment I have had ample

---

[37] Spivak, "Three Women's Texts," 252.
[38] Spivak, "Three Women's Texts," 252.

reason to estimate and revere [...] In consequence of this very judicious
letter, [...] I shall content myself for the present with stating the main
result of the Chapter, which I have reserved for that future publication, a
detailed prospectus of which the reader will find at the close of the second
volume.[39]

Spivak argues that this friend is known to be created by Coleridge's
imagination. Since Coleridge's friend is invented by his imagination, the
letter is then from Coleridge to himself. Therefore, Spivak describes it as
"a written message to oneself represented as being an external
interruption."[40] Spivak means that it is Coleridge who wanted to suppress
the chapter but he created the other, his imaginary friend, to justify this
suppression and this imaginary friend's letter stands for the legislation
which justifies the suppression. Thus, Coleridge disowns his name as
author by declaring the presence of a greater power although his aim in the
Biographia is the unity of the self. The letter is the slippage that
deconstructs the unity of the self which Coleridge was trying to prove.
Spivak explains that the letter becomes the signifier of Coleridge's desire
for the Name of the Father which will be united with law. She describes
this as a desire "that Lacan will analyze into the desire of the other and the
desire to produce the other as well as to appropriate the other, the object,
the object substitute as well as the image of the subject or subjects – a play
of all that masquerades as the 'real.'"[41] In other words, Coleridge's friend
and the letter as well as the suppressed chapter are all inaccessible. They
act as the real which has been excluded from the symbolic order so that
they become the impossible that cannot be inscribed symbolically.

By analogy, what happens with "Rochester" in Rhys's text is that the
letter which he does not send is a desire for the 'Name of the Father' to
justify the way he treats his Creole wife. His letters to his father reveal his
desire for a text dictated by the law of the father or, as Spivak describes
Coleridge's imaginary friend, legislator. What Spivak says in "The Letter
as Cutting Edge" can be linked with the situation of "Rochester" as the
latter invokes the letters to his father because – like the boy in Freud's
study – he wants to identify himself with the father. As Coleridge disowns
his own name as author, "Rochester" is denied the Name of the Father and
this is the point which Spivak uses to deconstruct the claim that Rochester
is a victim in Rhys's text. Symbolically, "Rochester's" father and letters

---

[39] Samuel Coleridge, *Biographia Literaria,* pp. 198, 201-202, quoted in Spivak,
"The Letter as Cutting Edge," in *In Other Worlds: Essays in Cultural Politics,* 4.
[40] Spivak, "The Letter," 5.
[41] Spivak, "The Letter," 7.

are inaccessible because there is no patronymic and because the letters do not reach their destination. The novel fails to vindicate "Rochester" as the victim of his father. To support that Spivak's argument leads to this implication, one can resort to the psychoanalytic study of "Rochester" offered by Nancy R. Harrison in her book *Jean Rhys and the Novel as Women's Text* (1988). In fact, Spivak had read Harrison's book when it was still forthcoming as shown in the endnotes of "Three Women's Texts." Harrison herself, in her acknowledgement page, thanks Spivak for her scrupulous readings of the book in its early stages. Harrison presents "Rochester's" dilemma as a nameless man who is searching for his origins, arguing that "Rochester" is trying to construct himself narratively and his attempt provides the "testing ground for the real combatants, the mother-text and the father-text."[42] In Harrison's opinion, "Rochester" prefers the father-text and does not want to give himself to the mother-text which may bastardise his own text. That is why he invokes the father as a figure who can provide him with his mirror image. Yet, Harrison then contends that "Rochester" eventually capitulates to a mother-text, Brontë's, when he decides to return to England. Consequently, the oedipal complex remains unresolved. Spivak's argument, given more detail from Harrison's study, leads to an important conclusion about Spivak's deconstruction of Rhys's claim that "Rochester" is a victim of the oedipal relationship. Since "Rochester" is denied the Name of the Father and a text of his own, and since he capitulates to Brontë's text by his return to England, then it is Brontë's text that is re-inscribed again with its imperialist discourse. Thus, Spivak implies that Rhys fails to avoid the discourse of imperialism by her inability to resolve the oedipal exchange in the novel.

As in her reading of Antoinette, Spivak uses de Manian deconstruction in analysing "Rochester." First, she reveals that the text claims that he is a victim of the oedipal exchange. Then, the text encounters its gap which is caused by the loss of the patronymic and the substitute claim is provided by "Rochester's" return to England and to Brontë's text. Hence, Spivak is able to argue that *Wide Sargasso Sea* re-inscribes the imperialist discourse of Brontë's text.

---

[42] Nancy R. Harrison, *Jean Rhys and the Novel as Women's Text* (London: The University of North Carolina Press, 1988), 195.

Christophine

As Keith A. Russell II wrote in 2007, "[i]t is difficult to find an analysis of Christophine since 1985 that does not use Spivak as a point of entry."[43] In *Wide Sargasso Sea*, Christophine is Antoinette's black servant who was brought from Martinique as a wedding present for her mother. Berman declares that "Christophine is a favorite of anti-imperialist critics, who often cite her as a voice resisting or even contesting the limits of Rhys's white Creole project."[44] As for many critics, again for Spivak Christophine is "a powerfully suggestive figure."[45] There are two dimensions to Spivak's study of this character because she regards Christophine as both a limit to the discourse of the novel and simultaneously a source of strength in it.

That she credits the novel for producing a character like Christophine is clear in Spivak's following statement: "Christophine is the first interpreter and named speaking subject in the text."[46] Spivak's evidence is taken from the first lines of the novel in which Antoinette recalls Christophine explaining why her mother was not approved by Jamaican ladies, saying in patois: "because she pretty like pretty self" (5). This function is one of the issues that make Christophine an attractive Other figure and, as Ray observes, Spivak wants to emphasise this point. Ray contends: "Spivak's argument about radical alterity hinges on the figure of Christophine, who does not occupy the savage space assigned to Bertha Mason in *Jane Eyre* and who functions as the voice of reason and reprimand to both Antoinette and Rochester."[47] However, a careful reading of Spivak's analysis of Christophine leads to the conclusion that Christophine is not to be seen as an example of the 'native subaltern female' throughout the novel. Christophine occupies the subject position of the 'native subaltern female' only towards the end of the text as will be explained later in this section.

Although Christophine is treated as a commodity – wedding present – in the text, Spivak offers two examples that demonstrate Christophine's critical functions. First, Christophine comments on the "black ritual practices as culture-specific and cannot be used by whites as cheap

---

[43] Keith A. Russell II, "Now every word she said was echoed, echoed loudly in my head": Christophine's Language and Refractive Space in Jean Rhys's *Wide Sargasso Sea*" in *Journal of Narrative Theory*, 37:1 (Winter 2007), 87.
[44] Berman, *Creole Crossings*, 180.
[45] Spivak, "Three Women's Texts," 252.
[46] Spivak "Three Women's Texts," 252.
[47] Ray, *Gayatri Chakravorty Spivak*," 33.

remedies for social evils."[48] Spivak does not refer to the textual evidence, but she is most probably speaking about the following passage in which Christophine narrates what happened when Antoinette sought her help:

> She come to me and ask me for something to make you love her again and I tell her no I don't meddle in that for béké [white]. I tell her it's foolishness [...]And even if it's no foolishness, it's too strong for béké. (99)

Second, Christophine is allowed to challenge "Rochester" face to face and to offer a complicated analysis of his actions when she says:

> She is Creole girl, and she have the sun in her. Tell the truth now. She don't come to your house in this place England they tell me about, [...] No, it's you come all the long way to her house – it's you beg her to marry. And she love you and she give you all she have. Now you say you don't love her and you break her up. What you do with her money, eh? (102)

This encounter makes Rochester not only "dazed, tired, half hypnotized, but alert and wary, ready to defend [himself]" (102). Thus, while her reading of *Jane Eyre* reveals disappointment with Brontë's presentation of Bertha abjectly, her reading of Rhys's text finds that Christophine is blessed with possible subjectivity – however limited. Until this encounter between her and "Rochester," Christophine cannot be read as the 'native subaltern female' since, at least, Spivak has so far ascribed agency to Christophine as the first interpreter in the text along with the defiance of "Rochester."

The second dimension to Spivak's analysis of Christophine concerns her role in exposing the limits of the novel's attempt at vindicating a marginal character from Brontë's text. Spivak catachrestically reads Christophine as the 'native subaltern female' only towards the end of the novel when "Rochester" drives Christophine to withdraw after which he takes Antoinette to England. It is here where Spivak reads Christophine catachrestically as the 'native subaltern female' because Spivak herself admits that the limitation of her reading is the lack of the historical context of the black servant in Jamaica before and during emancipation. When Spivak reproduces her reading of Rhys's text in *A Critique of Postcolonial Reason,* she refers to another reading of *Wide Sargasso Sea* that appeared after "Three Women's Texts," Mary Lou Emery's *Jean Rhys at "World's End": Novels of Colonial and Sexual Exile* (1990). Spivak admits that other critics "have subsequently fleshed out the West Indian background

---

[48] Spivak, "Three Women's Texts," 252-3.

much more thoroughly than I have been able to."[49] Also, commenting on Emery's reading, Spivak adds:

> Mary Lou Emery's contextually richer opinion is somewhat different. I cannot, of course, be 'responsible' within Christophine's text (in terms of available psychobiographies), as I have tried to be with Bhubaneswari Bhaduri [...] And one would need to be thus 'responsible' in order to venture a judgment about the representation of Christophine. These are the limits and openings of a non-locationist cultural studies, one that does not keep itself confined to national origin.[50]

Although Spivak considers the lack of historical detail as a limitation, she also finds it an opening because, as she declares in "Theory in the Margin," "a merely historically contextualized interpretation might produce closures that are problematic even as they are reasonable and satisfactory."[51] It is an opening because it allows Spivak to read this character catachrestically. Obviously, if Spivak would have read Christophine according to the historical background, she might not have reached the same conclusions about Christophine's non-containment in the novel. Regardless of the historical background against which Rhys may have constructed Christophine's black agency, what is important for a postcolonial reading is that Christophine is eventually dismissed from the text, so that her story remains unfinished. Spivak states: "Christophine's unfinished story is the tangent to the latter narrative [*Wide Sargasso Sea*], as St. John Rivers' story is to the former [*Jane Eyre*]."[52] As for Spivak's shift to the catachrestic reading of Christophine as the 'native subaltern female,' it can be explained by returning to the moment when Christophine challenges Rochester with her explanation of his actions in terms of his desire for Antoinette's money.

Spivak argues that after being encountered by Christophine, Rochester gets rid of her by conjuring up Law and Order. As a black Creole accused of practising obeah, a kind of folk magic which is banned by English law, Christophine is aware of the power of these two terms. The paradox for Spivak is that just before Rochester threatens her, Christophine shows her confidence in her freedom, saying: "[n]o chain gang, no tread machine, no dark jail either. This is a free country and I am free woman" (103). Spivak deploys this paradox in order to reveal the text's "exposure of civil

---

[49] Spivak, *Critique*, p.125, n. 23.
[50] Spivak, *Critique*, p.131, n. 30.
[51] Spivak, "Theory in the Margin," 158.
[52] Spivak, "Three Women's Texts," 252.

inequality."[53] Rochester's threat achieves the desired end and Christophine is driven away from the text without justice or explanation. She leaves without looking back after saying: "[r]ead and write I don't know. Other things I know" (104). Stressing this statement, Spivak illustrates that she is interested in the fact that Christophine withdraws with the other things she knows, which Spivak seems to take as Christophine's native knowledge and culture that cannot be inscribed in a text which aims at vindicating the white Creole female.

The first implication of this withdrawal for Spivak is that it underscores the limits of any possible subjectivity of the 'native subaltern female.' Though Spivak credits Rhys with avoiding the romanticisation of the individual heroics of the oppressed, she also re-emphasises the fact that the 'native subaltern female' here is used to consolidate the self.[54] Spivak's belief that Christophine is a domesticated Other figure can be explicated by arguing that when Christophine interprets things to Antoinette and supports her defying Rochester, Christophine acts as "the good servant rather than the pure native" who is there to consolidate her mistress's self-image.[55] To further develop Spivak's argument about Christophine's role as consolidating Antoinette and then Christophine's withdrawal, Mary Lou Emery's study is useful. Emery vies: "Jean Rhys uses specifically Caribbean stylistic strategies that enrich the reading of the book. I find most persuasive her explication of such details as 'being marooned.'"[56] Actually, Emery overcomes the problem of identity and belonging by asserting that Antoinette only needs a place to speak from. When her mother says that they are marooned, she means that they are abandoned but Antoinette's imagination takes 'marooned' to have another meaning. She understands it in relation to Christophine and the places to which she can escape. Of course, to show the significance of 'marooned' in her concentration on place rather than identity as Antoinette's dilemma, Emery explains the term 'maroon' in the context of different peoples. It becomes clear through the itinerary of 'maroon' presented by Emery that the common meaning is '*marronage*' or flight of Indians and Africans to wild or inaccessible places to avoid being exterminated or to escape slavery. Accordingly, Emery considers that Antoinette's death is not defeat but a type of flight which associates her with the black slaves and their tactics of survival.

---

[53] Spivak, "Three Women's Texts," 253.
[54] Spivak, "Three Women's Texts," 253.
[55] Spivak, "Three Women's Texts," 252.
[56] Spivak, *Critique,* 132.

Spivak continues: "[Emery's] bolder suggestion – that the textual practices of *Wide Sargasso Sea* borrow from and enact the technique of obeah – complicates my conviction that the other cannot be fully selfed."[57] This needs to be explained in light of Emery's study. The centrepiece of Emery's study is the 'elsewhere' which Antoinette badly needs in order to speak. This is provided by Christophine's obeah practice which she offers after Antoinette's appeal. The first element of the successful workings of obeah in the text is the positioning of the obeah scene. This scene interrupts the section in which "Rochester" is the narrator. The function of this interruption is "rupturing the 'realism' of [the] narrative point of view" of Rochester's section and makes Antoinette feel at home in Jamaica.[58] Christophine helps Antoinette to sleep and the result is her ability to let "Rochester" hear her voice – written in italics – though she is absent from the argument between him and Christophine. Emery concludes:

> The sleep Christophine has imposed on Antoinette is dangerous to Rochester, for it places Antoinette somewhere else where she can speak on her behalf even when she is absent from the scene. Her voice, too, has begun to possess Rochester's mind, and we see that the battle taking place previously in Antoinette's imagination now plays itself out in full force in Rochester's.[59]

So, supported by Christophine's obeah, Antoinette's struggle with "Rochester" happens on the ground of imagination. This is demonstrated not only through obeah but also through Antoinette's dreams. They disrupt the conventions of realism to "assert the possibility of another kind of knowledge" in a way that enables Antoinette to "rewrite her own myth."[60] Emery goes on to argue that in her last dream, Antoinette returns to the Caribbean: "I turned round and saw the sky. It was red and all my life was in it. I saw the grandfather clock and Aunt Cora's patchwork, all colours, I saw the orchids and stephanotis and the jasmine and the tree of life in flames" (123). This return in Emery's estimation "unites her with all of its [the Caribbean] peoples – the transported English and white Creoles of her family, but also the older native races, and finally the blacks from whom her 'real' life had inevitably estranged her."[61]

[57] Spivak, *Critique,* 132.
[58] Mary Lou Emery, *Jean Rhys at "World's End": Novels of Colonial and Sexual Exile* (Austin: University of Texas Press, 1990), 45.
[59] Emery, *Jean Rhys,* 52.
[60] Emery, *Jean Rhys,* 56.
[61] Emery, *Jean Rhys,* 59.

Emery's argument does add details that support Spivak's claim that Christophine is there to consolidate the self-image of Antoinette and that when it comes to Christophine's practice of obeah and her native knowledge, she is easily dismissed from the text threatened by the English law, as Spivak claims, without justification. Thus, despite her confession that Emery's reading is more historically informed, Spivak still insists: "I can only see this [Emery's argument] as a mark of the limits of the desire to self the other, a desire that is reflected in Rhys's own poem 'Obeah Night.'"[62] Spivak's evocation of the poem here is ambiguous. Emery took the title of her chapter on *Wide Sargasso Sea*, which is "Obeah Nights," from the poem and probably Spivak wants to emphasise that she discovered the desire of 'selfing' the Other even in the source of Emery's title. Spivak does not explain where exactly and how 'selfing' the Other is reflected in the poem, but most likely it can be found in the following part of the poem:

> Lost, lovely Antoinette
> How can I forget you
>   When the spring comes?
> (Spring is cold and furtive here
> There's a different rain)
>   Where did you hide yourself
> After the obeah nights?
>   (What did you send instead?
> Hating and hated?) [63]

In her letters, Rhys states that "Antoinette runs away after the 'Obeah Nights' and that the creature who comes back is not the one who ran away."[64] Possibly, Spivak finds in this poem and in the novel as explained by Emery that Antoinette tries to act like the Other, the marooned blacks, as if she viewed their suffering as a mirror of her own suffering. It is this claim of viewing the Other as a copy of the self that is the basis of the imperialist collapse of the Other into the self in Spivak's opinion.

Like in her reading of Antoinette, Spivak detects a difference in the use of the imperialist discourse between Rhys's text and Brontë's in the case of Christophine. In *A Critique of Postcolonial Reason,* Spivak adds two sentences to her revised version of the article concerning Christophine's withdrawal, illustrating that although Christophine's non-containment

---

[62] Spivak, *Critique,* 132.
[63] Rhys, *Letters,* 266.
[64] Rhys, *Letters,* 263.

reveals the limitations of the text, it can also be viewed as a point of strength. First, she calls Christophine's withdrawal a "proud message of textual – 'read-and-write' – abdication."[65] Christophine is used by the text for the aim of consolidating the self, but when her function has been done, she is dismissed, but she is dismissed as a guardian of otherness and marginality rather than being dismissed as a savage, like Bertha Mason in *Jane Eyre*. Second, Spivak insists on the strength of Christophine's departure by saying: "I must see the staging of the departure of Christophine as a move to guard the margin."[66] The margin – as Ray insists – "eludes the readers' tendency to recuperate the other in a particular cultural, historical, philosophical discourse."[67]

In "Theory in the Margin: Coetzee's *Foe* Reading Defoe's *Crusoe/Roxana*" Spivak says that the critic must ignore or marginalise the inability to start from firm grounding "at the margins, at the beginning and end."[68] Because philosophy hangs out in the margins, Spivak continues, the critics' work from beginning to end is haunted by these margins as "curious guardians."[69] However, Spivak still sees it fruitless to make these margins the centre of attention because this will sabotage their guardianship which is the source of the productive unease attending to what the critic does so carefully. If this unease which results from the awareness of being judged by the margins disappears from the field of studying and teaching literature, the privileged will be established as the disenfranchised or as the liberator of the disenfranchised. Moore-Gilbert explains what Spivak presumably means by this as follows: "[Spivak] seems nevertheless to regard Rhys as redeeming herself precisely through not giving Christophine a larger or more directly oppositional role, since this would fall into the trap of 'selfing' her as 'the intending subject of resistance' with a coherent and unproblematically accessible subjectivity."[70]

Spivak and Parry

Examining Spivak's study of Christophine and her role in the novel, one cannot ignore a central point that is raised by Benita Parry in her article:

---

[65] Spivak, *Critique*, 131.

[66] Spivak, *Critique,* 132.

[67] Ray, *Gayatri Chakravorty Spivak,* 45.

[68] Gayatri Chakravorty Spivak, "Theory in the Margin: Coetzee's *Foe* Reading Defoe's *Crusoe/Roxan*," in *Consequences of Theory*, ed. Jonathan Arac and Barbara Johnson (London: Johns Hopkins University Press, 1991), 158

[69] Spivak, "Theory in the Margin", 158.

[70] Moore-Gilbert, *Postcolonial Theory,* 96.

"Problems in Current Theories of Colonial Discourse" (1987). In this article, Parry challenges postcolonial scholarship, especially the practices of deconstructive critics like Spivak, by revealing the limitations of such practices which restrain the "development of an anti-imperialist critique."[71] Taking Spivak's reading of *Wide Sargasso Sea* as one of her examples, Parry animadverts this reading by accusing Spivak of "deliberated deafness to the native voice where it is to be heard."[72]

Parry insists that Christophine disrupts the text's discourse and rather than simply marking its limits as Spivak presumes. For Parry, Christophine successfully defies patriarchy by refusing her sons' fathers and challenges imperialism by deriding post-emancipation rhetoric, being a "native in command of the invaders' language" which she appropriates with the native idiom to challenge imperialism.[73] Moreover, Parry considers that Christophine can be read as "challenging imperialism's authorized system of knowledge" with the local knowledge she has. Consequently, Parry believes that Christophine's withdrawal with this knowledge is logical since her alternative system of knowledge is prohibited in England.[74] Nonetheless, in her apparent disagreement with Spivak, Parry unintentionally agrees with her because she admits that Christophine's system of knowledge is suppressed in the conclusion of the novel. This shows that what Spivak says of the limits of the novel's discourse is convincing. Christophine does take a certain story with her when she leaves in order to guard the margin, as Spivak insists.

Parry is mainly critical of Spivak's opposition to hegemonic nativism and ethnocentrism because this divests natives of a place where they can move against imperialism. She describes Spivak's theory as "a theory whose axioms deny to the native the ground from which to utter or reply to imperialism's ideological aggression or to enunciate a different self."[75] Parry's argument can be refuted for two reasons. First, as is clear in Spivak's reading, it is only when Christophine withdraws at the end of the text that Spivak considers her as a 'native subaltern female.' Spivak does not turn a deaf ear to Christophine's voice when she criticises imperialism. On the contrary, Spivak admits that Christophine is a powerful critic of imperialism and she credits Rhys for this aspect of Christophine's

---

[71] Benita Parry, "Problems in Current Theories of Colonial Discourse," *Oxford Literary Review* 9 (1987): 34.
[72] Parry, "Problems," p. 39.
[73] Parry, "Problems," p. 38.
[74] Parry, "Problems," p. 39.
[75] Parry, "Problems," 36.

delineation, but for Spivak, when Christophine argues against imperialism, the latter is not a 'native subaltern female.'

In *Outside in the Teaching Machine*, Spivak replies to Parry's argument by drawing a comparison between the postcolonial intellectual and Defoe's Friday who is taught English and given the teachings of Christianity by Robinson Crusoe. Friday then uses what he has learned and helps Crusoe in enlightening Others. Similarly, Spivak maintains that although the postcolonial critic speaks much better than Friday, he/she is like Friday speaking within imperialism:

> Whatever the identitarian ethnicist claims of native or fundamental origin (implicit for example, in Parry's exhortation to hear the voice of the native), the political claims that are most urgent in decolonized space are tacitly recognized as coded within the legacy of imperialism: nationhood, constitutionality, citizenship, democracy, even culturalism.[76]

Spivak takes this lesson from literature, namely *Robinson Crusoe*, and applies it to the intellectual. One can follow Spivak's oeuvre and re-apply the idea to Christophine. Christophine lived among white Creoles and learnt their language and their rhetoric of freedom even when she is speaking of her own freedom. Rhys herself considered that there was a mistake in her presentation of this character: "[t]he most seriously wrong thing with part II is that I've made the obeah woman, the nurse, too articulate," but then she justifies this mistake saying: "there is no reason why one particular negro woman shouldn't be articulate enough, especially as she's spent most of her life in a white household."[77] Though Spivak does not refer to this quotation, it reveals two things that corroborate Spivak's opinions about Christophine. First, Christophine's articulate voice – which makes her "the native, female, individual Self" in Parry's study – has been formed within imperialism when Christophine has been a slave and then a good servant in a white household.[78] Second, Rhys in this quotation refers to Christophine as '*one* particular negro woman' with a voice, implying that she does not represent *all* black Creoles.[79] Like Defoe's Friday, she is one black Creole capable of using white language and concepts of freedom, not the story of slavery which remains at the margin.

---

[76] Spivak, *Outside*, 60.

[77] Rhys, *Letters*, 297.

[78] Parry describes Christophine as "the native, female, individual Self" in Parry, "Problems in Current Theories of Colonial Discourse," 38.

[79] Emphasis added.

In conclusion, reading *Wide Sargasso Sea,* Spivak depends also on de Man's two-step deconstruction, though not mentioning this. First, she reveals the truth-claim which is vindicating Brontë's Bertha in the presentation of Antoinette as a sane human who is a critic of imperialism. The novel also attempts to vindicate Rochester by presenting him as a victim of the oedipal exchange. However, Spivak deconstructs both attempts. First, she reveals through Antoinette's Narcissistic search for her image in the Other, whether Tia or the marooned blacks, that Antoinette repeats the imperialist claim of knowing the Other and collapses this Other into the self. Second, Spivak deconstructs "Rochester's" representation as a victim through proving that he is not the owner of his text, which in turn implies his confinement to Brontë's text. Most importantly, the central figure of parabasis in the text is Christophine. Throughout the text, Christophine criticises imperialist practices but she uses the language and logic she acquired while serving the plantocracy. However, when it comes to what Spivak sees as her native knowledge, the text can no longer contain her. The text succeeds in freeing Bertha from the animalistic image but it re-inscribes the imperialist domestication of the 'native subaltern female.' When the text fails to show that "Rochester" is a victim, the new truth-claim is that Christophine's obeah changed Antoinette into a mad woman and he raises the law to threaten Christophine who is then dismissed from the text. Although it is a positive point that Rhys does not represent Christophine, Spivak also finds it a limitation because when the text tries to rescue Bertha from marginalisation, it causes another marginalisation, that of Christophine. Then, both "Rochester" and Antoinette return to the fictional world of Brontë's text which is re-inscribed by this final move.

It can be concluded that Christophine becomes the appropriate figure of interruption for Spivak only when she is dismissed under the threat of the English law for her cultural practice of obeah. The text uses obeah only for Antoinette to find her mirror image in Tia and the blacks and to escape her dilemma. Thus, Christophine is introduced for Antoinette to consolidate herself. Then Christophine, as the obeah woman, not as the good black servant, is foreclosed from the text to become the impossible that cannot be inscribed as a text. Spivak wishes to see this as a positive point since Christophine is withdrawn to guard the margin against being represented in a text that is still dependent on the domestication of the 'native subaltern female.' Now that Spivak finished her argument about *Wide Sargasso Sea* as a re-inscription of *Jane Eyre,* she moves to *Frankenstein.* She argues that reading *Frankenstein* provides a deconstruction of the worlding of the so-called 'Third World' of *Jane*

Eyre. The next chapter will attempt to explicate how Spivak approaches the final text in "Three Women's Texts."

CHAPTER FOUR

FRANKENSTEIN:
A DECONSTRUCTION OF THE KANTIAN
AND FEMINIST SUBJECTS

After offering her reading of *Jane Eyre* and *Wide Sargasso Sea*, Spivak moves to Mary Shelley's *Frankenstein*, which is written in the form of letters sent to Mrs. Saville from her brother Walton, an obsessed explorer. The letters recount the story of the Genevese Dr. Victor Frankenstein, who, with the aim of renewing life in dead bodies, becomes obsessed with natural philosophy, especially the structure of the human frame. His toils result in making a creature of parts of dead human bodies that will be described as 'monster' or 'fiend' throughout the novel. This part of Spivak's article is not much criticised or referred to by other critics and readers of *Frankenstein*. It is also neglected by some critics of Spivak as compared with her readings of the previous two texts. This may be due to the fact that this text is rarely if at all read in terms of the politics of imperialism. Elizabeth A. Bohls stresses this fact by saying: "amid the copious criticism of Mary Shelley's *Frankenstein* before Spivak and since, very little attention has been paid to Shelley's manifest concern with the political, psychological, moral, and, in particular aesthetics problems occasioned by the fact of empire."[1]

The following paragraphs start with exploring the connections between *Frankenstein* and the previous two texts to clarify Spivak's selection of it. Then, the chapter demonstrates Spivak's identifying the displacement of the male/female roles in Frankenstein's lab as the truth–claim of the novel. This will be followed by explaining how Spivak reads *Frankenstein* as a Kantian allegory which proves the failure of the Kantian rational being. The chapter also shows how Spivak proves this failure by deconstructing this text tropologically resorting to the monster as the parabasis that

---

[1] Elizabeth A. Bohls, "Standards of Taste, Discourses of 'Race,' and the Aesthetic Education of a Monster: Critique of Empire in Frankenstein," *Eighteenth-Century Life* 18 (1994): 23.

interrupts the text. Finally, the chapter differentiates between *Frankenstein's* ending and the endings of the previous two texts.

At first sight, the relationship between *Jane Eyre, Wide Sargasso Sea,* and *Frankenstein* is not clear. Spivak herself is cognizant of the fact that the imperial sentiment is only incidental in the text and this could be a reason why only few critics read it within the frame of imperialism. Most readings of *Frankenstein* before and during the time Spivak wrote "Three Women's Texts" had been related to feminism and feminist autobiography. Inter alia one can mention the 1979 reading of Gilbert and Gubar that appeared in their book *The Madwoman in the Attic.* They view the novel as a feminist reading of John Milton's *Paradise Lost,* and argue that the monster can be a female. In *Literary Women* (1978), Ellen Moers considers the novel to be connected with Shelley's life as a mother who experienced many miscarriages and who lost many of her infants. Another important analysis can be found in "Is there a Woman in this Text?" written by Mary Jacobus in 1980. Jacobus discusses how *Frankenstein* eliminates the female and prefers monstrosity to a corrupt female body. Moreover, in 1982, Barbara Johnson's "My Monster/Myself" provides a reading of *Frankenstein* as a woman's autobiography.

Spivak considers these studies to belong to a hegemonic readership and declares: "I propose to take *Frankenstein* out of this arena [feminist autobiography] and focus on it in terms of that sense of English cultural identity which I invoked at the opening of this essay."[2] In other words, she wants to read the text in terms of the self/Other dichotomy which is crucial to the imperialist discourse. For this aim, Spivak, as Moore-Gilbert argues, "engenders a postcolonial perspective by reading 'the monster,' allegorically, like Bertha Mason, as a symbol of the colonized subject."[3] Thus, as in her reading of *Jane Eyre,* Spivak uses catachresis here which allows her even to associate the monster with the 'native subaltern female' when she places her analysis of *Frankenstein* within the scope of *A Critique of Postcolonial Reason.* Spivak's departure from the hegemonic feminist readings of *Frankenstein* may have led to opinions similar to Moore-Gilbert's in his statement that "[t]his text at first sight seems a surprising choice for comparison with the first two."[4] Yet, a careful reading of Spivak's analysis of this text leads us to discover the different ways in which this text relates to the first two. First, the text contains Clerval's plan of going to India which recalls St. John's in *Jane Eyre.* Second, the text ends with the monster's declared intention of self-

---

[2] Spivak, "Three Women's Texts," 254.
[3] Moore-Gilbert, *Postcolonial Theory,* 96.
[4] Moore-Gilbert, *Postcolonial Theory,* 96.

immolation which recalls Bertha/Antoinette's self-immolation. Third, the monster's departure at the end of the text re-enacts Christophine's withdrawal as happens in *Wide Sargasso Sea.*

However, the most important relationship is the one between *Frankenstein* and *Jane Eyre* as Spivak's statement makes clear: "let us read [...] *Frankenstein* as an analysis – even a deconstruction – of a 'worlding' such as *Jane Eyre*'s."[5] Spivak means that, unlike *Jane Eyre, Frankenstein* does not construct an image of Europe's Other as savage. Also, Spivak painstakingly tries to demonstrate that Shelley's text is different from *Jane Eyre* in that *Frankenstein* does not use the axiomatics of imperialism to support the structure of the narrative; indeed there are two important points which for Spivak deconstruct the axiomatics of imperialism supporting *Jane Eyre.* First, Shelley's text does not employ the language of female individualism, which Spivak has shown to be complicit with imperialism. Second, as Spivak elucidates, *Frankenstein* succeeds in revealing the failure of the project of soul-making through the failure of the Kantian three-part human subject represented by Frankenstein, Clerval and Elizabeth.

Henry Clerval and the incidental imperialist sentiment

Concerning the employment of the imperialist axioms in *Frankenstein,* Spivak says: "My point, within the argument of this essay, is that the discursive field of imperialism does not produce unquestioned ideological correlatives for the narrative structuring of the book. The discourse of imperialism surfaces in a curiously powerful way in Shelley's novel."[6] In reading *Jane Eyre,* Spivak explains how imperialist axiomatics and Bertha's self-immolation help Jane to achieve her female individualism. But in *Frankenstein* Spivak only detects examples of the imperial sentiment. One can attribute Spivak's use of 'sentiment' rather than 'axiom' here to the fact that the imperialist discourse in this text is not used to fill a gap or to move the narrative structure as was the case in *Jane Eyre.* As an example of the imperialist sentiment in the text, Spivak discusses Clerval's plan to go to India. She quotes the passage which shows the motives and reasons for this plan: "in the belief that he had in his knowledge of its various languages, and in the views he had taken of

---

[5] Spivak, *Critique,* 114-5.
[6] Spivak, "Three Women's Texts," 254.

its society, the means of materially assisting the progress of European colonization and trade."[7]

In *Jane Eyre*, St. John wants to go to India for missionary purposes and asks Jane to marry and assist him in spreading Christianity there. Refusing this offer, Jane runs away to Rochester and, finding that Bertha has immolated herself, she marries Rochester. So, the movement of the heroine and the text depends on imperialist axiomatics. In comparison, *Frankenstein* offers another register of imperialism by not using the axiomatics of the barbarism of the Other and the European mission of civilising or as an alibi that hides the economic aims of colonisation. *Frankenstein* overtly expresses the colonial project in India: 'colonization' and 'trade' are the words used by Clerval to justify his plan. Spivak draws her readers' attention even to the distinction between the two texts in terms of the language used by referring to another passage concerning Clerval's plan:

> He came to the university with the design of making himself complete master of the Oriental languages, as thus he should open a field for the plan of life he had marked out for himself. Resolved to pursue no religious career, he turned his eyes towards the East as affording scope for his spirit of enterprise. The Persian, Arabic, and Sanskrit languages engaged his attention (74-5).

For Spivak, the language in this passage is entrepreneurial while Brontë's text uses the heroic missionary language to justify imperialism.

The first truth-claim: the displacement of male/female roles in the laboratory

Spivak says: "*Frankenstein* is not a battleground of male and female individualism articulated in terms of sexual reproduction (family and female) and social subject-production (race and male)."[8] Spivak regards Victor Frankenstein in terms of the holding and withholding of the womb with the aim of supporting her suggestion that male/female functions are deconstructed in Shelley's text. To prove her suggestion, Spivak follows the two de Manian deconstructive steps. She starts with revealing the first truth-claim presented by the text through Frankenstein's laboratory. Then,

---

[7] Mary Shelley, *Frankenstein, or the Modern Prometheus* (London: Penguin Books, 2006), 197. Subsequent references to this edition will be represented as page numbers within parentheses.
[8] Spivak, "Three Women's Texts," 254.

she uses the monster as the parabasis, the interruption that deconstructs this claim and introduces another claim.

In analysing *Jane Eyre,* Spivak reads a celebration of Jane's individualism achieved by moving upward in class structure in eighteenth-century England at the expense of Bertha, read by Spivak catachrestically as the 'native subaltern female.' In Spivak's words, this can be defined as "the fight for individualism in the upwardly class-mobile bourgeois cultural politics of the European nineteenth century."[9] However, the project of soul-making is left for the male, St. John, who will spread Christianity in India. Thus, Spivak implies that feminist readings of *Jane Eyre* remain restricted to the first side of the binary white man/ white woman. This binary is complicit with imperialist axiomatics because in the same way the 'native informant' is defined as different from the white man. Spivak contrasts the feminist celebration which appears in *Jane Eyre* with its absence in *Frankenstein,* an absence which resonates with Spivak's disbelief in the gratification of the female as the best way for changing feminist criticism towards a practice that avoids the "mesmerizing model [of] male and female sparring partners of generalizable or universalizable sexuality who are the chief protagonists in that European context."[10] For Spivak, what is needed is a global sisterhood that includes Asian, African and Arab sisters as well as western women. Accordingly, for Spivak a text which does not present the prototype of the female fighting for her individualism, as opposed to male individualism, evades complicity with the imperialist ideology with its privileging of the white man as a universal human norm. Although Spivak does not see *Frankenstein* as falling into this trap, she admits that there were attempts to rescue the spirit of female individualism in this text.

Spivak offers Johnson's reading of *Frankenstein* with its effort to "rescue this recalcitrant text for the service of feminist autobiography"[11] as an example of this mesmerising model of male and female roles. Three years before Spivak published her article, Johnson had presented her analysis of Shelley's novel. Johnson argues that although *Frankenstein* contains the biographies of three men, Frankenstein, Walton and the monster, the novel can be read as an autobiography of a woman. Also, the story depends on the resemblance between teller and listener, Walton and his sister, Frankenstein and Walton, the monster and Frankenstein. The desire for resemblance that is a characteristic of autobiographies is the transgression in Shelley's text. Then, Johnson refers to the psychoanalytic

[9] Spivak, *Critique,* 148.
[10] Spivak, *Critique,* 148.
[11] Spivak, "Three Women's Texts," 254.

studies that associate Frankenstein's abhorrence of his monster to the divided feelings of Shelley as mother towards her own baby, who died after birth. She conceived this baby from a man who had been married to another woman. What Johnson adds to this parallel is that *Frankenstein* is a description of Shelley's experience of writing the novel. To describe the origin of her story in the preface she added in 1831, Shelley used the same words which Frankenstein used in describing his creation. Shelley says: "[s]wift as light and as cheering was the idea that broke in me" (xi). Frankenstein says: [f]rom the midst of this darkness a sudden light broke in upon me" (52).

Johnson also stresses that Frankenstein's desire to usurp woman's prerogative of giving birth parallels Shelley's competence with the male writers who surrounded her, namely her husband Percy Shelley and their friend Lord Byron, in writing a ghost story:

> On the other hand, the story of Frankenstein is, after all, the story of a man who usurps the female role by physically giving birth to a child. It would be tempting, therefore, to conclude that Mary Shelley, surrounded as she then was by the male poets Byron and Shelley, and mortified for days by her inability to think of a story to contribute to their ghost-story contest, should have fictively transposed her own frustrated female pen envy into a tale of catastrophic male womb envy.[12]

Although Spivak does not agree with Johnson in seeing *Frankenstein* as a woman's autobiography, Spivak's reading seems to be influenced by several points evoked by the former. One of these points is that Shelley identifies with Frankenstein, a point which Spivak also raises very quickly at the end of her reading of *Frankenstein*.[13] However, the central point where Spivak's reading overlaps with Johnson's is related to womb-envy, which Spivak utilises to reveal the first truth-claim: that Frankenstein tries to take up both child-bearing and soul-making.

Spivak contends that Frankenstein's womb is his laboratory where he attempts to fulfill both male and female individualisms – social subject-production/sexual reproduction – at the same time. Frankenstein's artificial womb is the place where he is competing with God as creator and with woman, the womb-holder and the carrier of children. Spivak says: "[i]n Shelley's view, man's hubris as soul maker both usurps the place of God and attempts – vainly – to sublate woman's physiological prerogative."[14] This problematic relationship as described by Spivak "constitutes [the

---

[12] Barbara Johnson, "My Monster/Myself," *Diacritics* 12:2 (Summer 1982): 8.

[13] Spivak, *Critique*, 140.

[14] Spivak, "Three Women's Texts," 255.

novel's] strength" for a postcolonial reader since it evades the complicity between imperialism and female individualism that was clear in *Jane Eyre*.[15] Womb-envy that appeared in Johnson's reading turns into "female-fetish" in Spivak's analysis. Spivak resorts to "a Freudian fantasy" concerning fetishism to develop an argument about a new kind of fetishism presented by Frankenstein's case.[16] In "Fetishism," Freud argues that the fetish of the male depends on the male sexual organ as the normal prototype. Freud believes that the boy believes that his mother has the phallus but then he discovers that she does not. However, the boy does not want to believe that his mother is castrated because such a belief threatens him with castration as well. Therefore, he designs the fetish – which could be the shoes, feet, fur, etc. – to substitute and preserve the woman's phallus.[17] By analogy Spivak says:

> I could urge that if to give and withhold to/from the mother a phallus is the male fetish, then to give and withhold to/from the man a womb might be the female fetish. The icon of the sublimated womb in man is surely his productive brain, the box of the head.[18]

Indirectly, Spivak is evoking Shelley, the named subject, because the passage implies that the author is a female fetishist who gave her male protagonist a productive brain to substitute for the womb. Other critics would not agree with Spivak's notion of female fetishism. A case in point is Mary Ann Doane.

Mary Ann Doane's "Film and Masquerade: Theorising the Female Spectator" whose main concern is with the female spectator being evicted by making her the image in the cinema. This image repeatedly narrativises the female as a pleasurable object. Spivak refers to this article because Doane explains the impossibility of female fetishism saying: "[s]pectatorial desire, in contemporary film theory, is generally delineated as either voyeurism or fetishism, as precisely a pleasure in seeing what is prohibited in relation to the female body."[19] Doane questions the expulsion of the female's desire. Later in her essay, Doane explains that the female "must find it extremely difficult, if not impossible, to assume the position of

---

[15] Spivak, "Three Women's Texts", 259.

[16] Spivak, "Three Women's Texts", 255.

[17] Sigmund Freud, "Fetishism," in *The Standard Edition of the Complete Psychological Works of Sigmund Freud,* vol. XXI, trans. James Starchey (London: The Hogarth Press, 1964), 152-7.

[18] Spivak, "Three Women's Texts," 255.

[19] Mary Ann Doane, "Film and the Masquerade: Theorising the Female Spectator," *Screen* 23 (1982): 76.

fetishist" because she is the image which makes describing her desire possible only in terms of narcissism.[20] The female cannot fetishise because there is no gap between seeing and knowing her body. She sees her genitals and immediately discovers the sexual difference. She is not afraid of disowning what she has but she longs to have what she does not. The male on the other hand sees his mother's lack but later when he is afraid of castration, he revisualises the image and then understands the sexual difference. This distance between seeing and knowing prepares him for fetishism. In Spivak's study, Frankenstein's laboratory is the womb where the male/female functions are deconstructed, and we remain within psychoanalysis because Spivak's first textual reference relates to another psychoanalytic reading of *Frankenstein* by Mary Jacobus.

The first textual incident which Spivak selects to further explain the displacement of the feminine and masculine roles is Frankenstein's nightmare of his dead mother which he has after finishing the making of his monster. Spivak does not quote the passage which describes the nightmare. One can quote the passage for a better understanding of Spivak's argument; the nightmare is the following:

> I thought I saw Elizabeth, in the bloom of health, walking in the streets of Ingolstadt. Delighted and surprised, I embraced her, but as I imprinted the first kiss on her lip, they became livid with the hue of death; her features appeared to change, and I thought that I held the corpse of my dead mother in my arms (60).

Spivak argues that this nightmare along with the actual death of Elizabeth is associated with the "visit of [Frankenstein's] monstrous homoerotic 'son' to his bed."[21] Yet, she does not explain the relationship between the nightmare and the monster's visit. A possible explanation can be found in Mary Jacobus's study to which Spivak refers in a footnote. In Jacobus's study, the nightmare amalgamates eroticism with the horror of the corruption of the female body and the mother's corpse symbolises Frankenstein's unnatural pursuit of nature's secrets in his laboratory. She adds that Frankenstein exchanges the woman for the monster who is described as a mummy, and this means that he prefers monstrosity to corrupt female flesh. Jacobus also argues that from this nightmare, the text starts to eliminate the woman through eliminating both the female monster and Elizabeth, concluding that the "curious thread in the plot focuses not

---

[20] Doane, "Film and the Masquerade," 80.
[21] Spivak, "Three Women's Texts", 255.

on the image of the hostile father (Frankenstein/God) but on that of the dead mother who comes to symbolize to the monster his loveless state."[22]

Hence, it can be argued that the image of the dead mother as diminishing the female function in sexual reproduction which is usurped by Frankenstein himself. In other words, the monster's visit to Frankenstein's bed could be an indication of Frankenstein's role as mother. This could also mean that in this novel it is not the woman who is responsible for the register of sexual reproduction which is the idea Spivak wants to stress. Although Spivak does not use the term 'dead mother', it underlies her discussion especially when she examines the monster's vindictive attitude. In Spivak's opinion, the real reason for the monster's vengefulness is his having been deprived of a childhood: "[n]o father had watched my infant days, no mother had blessed me with smiles and caresses; or if they had, all my past was now a blot, a blind vacancy in which I distinguished nothing" (145). The image of the dead mother also lurks in Spivak's comment on Frankenstein's understanding of the monster's vengefulness, which she regards as both ambiguous and miscued. Frankenstein's interpretation comes towards the end of the novel in an attempt to justify himself for Walton in the following words:

> I created a rational creature and was bound towards him to assure, as far as was in my power, his happiness and well-being. This was my duty, but there was another still paramount to that. My duties towards the beings of my own species had greater claims to my attention because they included a greater proportion of happiness or misery. Urged by this view, I refused, and I did right in refusing, to create a companion for the first creature (271).

For Spivak, this interpretation "reveals [Frankenstein's] own competition with woman as maker."[23] Encouraged by Spivak's argument that Frankenstein's laboratory is his womb and also by her choice of this passage to quote, one can maintain that she implies the following: Frankenstein thinks that the monster is spiteful because his maker has not done his duty towards him as a mother, not a father figure. Such an argument was developed in 1997 by Jane Donawerth in her book *Frankenstein's Daughters: Women Writing Science Fiction.* Donawerth suggests that Shelley imposes a feminine story onto the male protagonist, supposing that this displaced story may belong to the fiction of women bearing children illegitimately that was common during that time. For her,

---

[22] Mary Jacobus, "Is there a Woman in this Text?" *New Literary History* 14 (1982): 132.
[23] Spivak, "Three Woman's Texts", 255.

Frankenstein is like an illegitimate mother when he creates the monster secretly and then avoids his own child. Although Donawerth's analysis takes us in a different direction from Spivak's, she offers a useful explanation of the above passage quoted by Spivak by viewing Frankenstein as taking the role of the mother in understanding the monster's anger. Donawerth says: "Shelley enables male conversion: Victor Frankenstein eventually [felt his duties towards the monster] – not in the form of financial responsibility [...] but in the form of responsibility for the 'happiness' of the creature" like a mother.[24]

The deconstruction of the claim of the novel

Now that Spivak has identified the first claim of the text, she moves to the point where the text itself deconstructs this claim proving Frankenstein's failure to compete with woman as bearer of children. For this aim, Spivak highlights the scene of his destruction of the female monster. This scene demonstrates Frankenstein's failure both in sexual reproduction and in soul-making. In demolishing the experiment of making the monster's female mate, Frankenstein – in Spivak's opinion – is committing a transgression. This action emphasises that Frankenstein, the "hysteric father" is even unable to create the daughter which marks his failure to usurp woman's prerogative despite "his laboratory – the womb of theoretical reason."[25] The rationalisation behind Frankenstein's abstaining from creating the monster's mate:

> [S]he might become ten thousand times more malignant than her mate [...] one of the first results of those sympathies for which the demon thirsted would be children, and a race of devils would be propagated upon the earth who might make the very existence of the species of man a condition precarious and full of terror.[26]

Spivak concludes that what happens in *Frankenstein* is an amalgamation of the language of racism and the hysteria of masculism and the result is a displacement of the feminine and masculine individualists:

> Here the language of racism – the dark side of imperialism understood as social mission – combines with the hysteria of masculism into the idiom of (the withdrawal of) sexual reproduction rather than subject constitution.

---

[24] Jane Donawerth, *Frankenstein's Daughters: Women Writing Science Fiction* (New York: Syracuse University Press, 1997), xxv.
[25] Spivak, "Three Women's Texts," 255.
[26] Spivak, "Three Women's Texts," 256.

The roles of masculine and feminine individualists are hence reversed and displaced.[27]

In other words, his racist view of the monster as the Other leads Frankenstein to refuse the idea of this monster breeding and threatening the human race. One must always remember Spivak's emphasis on the fact that Frankenstein is a representation of the western Christian rational man who was thought to be the norm of society in the eighteenth century as she explains in her reading of Kant's third critique. Frankenstein's racism is combined with his obsession with woman's physiological prerogative as a womb-holder, an obsession which Spivak describes as the hysteria of masculism. Both racism, related to soul-making by viewing the monster as the savage Other, and the hysteria of masculism, viewing the woman in terms of sexual reproduction, lead Frankenstein to the destruction of the female monster. The implication of this destruction is that the western Christian man cannot be the origin of society as Spivak argues saying: "[t]his particular narrative strand also launches a thoroughgoing critique of the eighteenth-century European discourses on the origin of society through (Western Christian) man."[28]

The most important conclusion that can be drawn from Spivak's argument is that the demolished female monster can be seen as the 'native subaltern female.' There are many points in Spivak's argument that lead to this conclusion. The first reason is Spivak's emphasis on Frankenstein's belief that the female monster may be more malignant than the original monster and the immediate result would be breeding children who may threaten the human race. Spivak implies that Frankenstein views this female as savage, as was the case in the representation of Bertha in Brontë's text. He also views her in terms of sexual reproduction only, which is relevant to the imperialist division of male/female functions discussed in Chapter Two of this book. Second, this female monster is excluded from the text completely when her body is destroyed by Frankenstein. Spivak says that the monster's need for Frankenstein to listen to him and make a female mate for him "is, as we have seen, for a gendered future, for the colonial female subject."[29] This request, "not-granted" as Spivak says, leads Spivak to think that although Shelley presents an emancipatory vision of the monster, his future can be sought only away from the master, Frankenstein, and his race. Therefore, *Frankenstein* is still limited by the colonial enterprise. The 'native

---

[27] Spivak, "Three Women's Texts," 256.

[28] Spivak, *Critique,* 135.

[29] Spivak, *Critique,* 140.

informant,' the monster, and the 'native subaltern female,' the destroyed
female monster, can only be excluded from the text.

Thus, Frankenstein fails as a mother figure to the monster and also as a
maker of children when he destroys the daughter. As for the monster, his
introduction to the text interrupts it in two ways. First, it proves
Frankenstein's failure as a mother figure as was explained above and
second, it proves Frankenstein's failure in terms of the Kantian three-part-
subject who is able to think rationally to achieve the highest good in this
world. The coming paragraphs will explain how Spivak views the novel in
terms of an allegory of the Kantian subject and how she detects the novel's
deconstruction of this subject. This deconstruction happens only towards
the end of the text when, after the failure of subjecting him to western
culture, the monster withdraws declaring his intention of self-immolation.

Frankenstein and the Kantian rational 'subject'

As has been argued in Chapter One, Spivak presumes that Kant's
categorical imperative forecloses the 'native informant' and that this
foreclosure was exploited to justify imperialism. In studying *Jane Eyre*,
Spivak claims a relationship between Kant and the novel's imperialist
axiomatics by shedding light on St. John's civilising mission in India.
Spivak supposes that an example like St. John appears in literature due to
Kant's motto that man should be an end in himself and from this premise,
she presumes, emerges the mission of civilising the savage to make
him/her a human who can be an end in himself. For Spivak, Kant's
philosophy presents the western Christian man as the norm of the rational
being who is capable of judging the sublime and receiving moral ideas.

Here, Spivak suggests that *Frankenstein* can be read as a Kantian
allegory and yet by foregrounding the 'native informant' – represented by
the monster – the text is in an aporetic relationship with Kant's
philosophy. The Kantian allegory in *Frankenstein* works in the following
way according to Spivak:

> [Shelley] presents in the first part of her deliberately schematic story three
> characters, childhood friends, who seem to represent Kant's three-part
> conception of the human subject: Victor Frankenstein, the forces of
> theoretical reason or 'natural philosophy'; Henry Clerval, the forces of
> practical reason or 'the mortal relations of things'; and Elizabeth Lavenza,
> that aesthetic judgement – 'the aerial creation of the poets'.[30]

---

[30] Spivak, "Three Women's Texts," 256.

Thus, Frankenstein stands for Kant's first critique, the critique of pure reason in which Kant offers an explanation of the relationship between human beings as knowing minds and the objects of their sense experience. Space and time in which the objects exist depend on the properties of the human mind and the dynamics and laws that govern these objects also depend on concepts already existing in the mind like the concept of causality. Since these objects can give sense experiences that conform to the faculties of the mind, judgments about them can be proved. However, metaphysical judgements like the immortality of the soul and belief in God, which are necessary for securing morality, cannot be proved or disproved because they depend on theoretical reason and, unlike other objects, cannot be experienced by the senses.[31]

In *Frankenstein*, Spivak argues, there is no harmony in the performance of the three parts of the Kantian human subject. One example of this lack of harmony is Clerval's plan to go to India. Yet, it is obvious that Frankenstein is the part that strongly demonstrates the manifold dimensions of the failure of a harmonious cooperation among the three parts when he "creates a putative human subject out of natural philosophy alone."[32] It is clear in the text – though Spivak does not use textual references here – that Frankenstein is obsessed only with theoretical reason. After meeting M. Waldman, who advised Frankenstein to take into consideration every branch of natural philosophy, the latter declares:

> From this day natural philosophy, and particularly chemistry, in the most comprehensive sense of the term, became nearly my sole occupation [...] One of the phenomena which had peculiarly attracted my attention was the structure of the human frame [...] Whence, I often asked myself, did the principle of life proceed? (50-1)

Frankenstein's act of making the monster takes place within the framework of theoretical reason alone, and without consideration for the moral validity of his action. By so doing, Frankenstein introduces the 'native informant.' Spivak's argument of the novel as a Kantian allegory leads to important implications and parallels. First, from Spivak's reading we can conclude that Frankenstein's dependence on pure reason only repeats the example of a philosopher, like Kant; a western Christian rational man depending on pure reason to present to the world a norm of the rational human being. This rational man, the philosopher, introduces

---

[31] Andrew Ward, *Kant: The Three Critiques* (Cambridge: Polity Press, 2006), 3-104.

[32] Spivak, "Three Women's Texts", 256.

the 'native informants' representing them in an ugly way in order to immediately dismiss them from the race of man. Spivak has already shown this in Kant's third critique and she also reveals it in *Frankenstein* as will be explained later with regard to the monster's withdrawal at the end.

So, another truth-claim that Spivak's reading reveals in Shelley's novel is that Frankenstein, the western Christian man, can use pure reason, natural philosophy, to create another rational being. However, Spivak illustrates certain points that enable us to draw the conclusion that this truth-claim is interrupted by the monster and then the parabasis starts. She illustrates that Frankenstein rejects the monster and that the monster's vindictiveness is a consequence of Frankenstein's abandonment of his duties as mother. The monster, as a result, kills Elizabeth. Frankenstein refuses to make the female monster because he feels that such an action will endanger the human race. This fear of the breeding of the monster is what leads Spivak to regard the text in terms of the cultural identity which Spivak invokes at the beginning of "Three Women's Texts." By stressing these points Spivak implies that after introducing the 'native informant' to his society, Frankenstein realises his failure, represented by the threat he thinks he has exposed humanity to. For her, the monster offers an example of the failure of the Kantian subject "if woman and native informant are allowed into the enclosure."[33] Spivak explains the reasons for the failure of Frankenstein as a Kantian subject. First, she quotes what she describes as Frankenstein's miscued explanation of his achievement: "[i]n a fit of madness I created a rational creature" (271). She comments on this quotation illustrating that Frankenstein's summation shows how Kant's hypothetical imperative is mistaken for the categorical imperative as a result of replacing practical reason with natural philosophy.

Natural philosophy relates to the critique of pure reason where, unlike abstract things, objects can be known depending on experiencing them sensibly. As for practical reason, Kant contends that reason can be practical since it motivates humans to obey moral laws and to achieve the highest good. He argues that if the being has a will, defined as the ability of using reason to act on the consciousness of rules, no desire precedes reason in deciding whether a moral law is universal. Since reason spontaneously acts when encountering a law, will is free. Further, practical reason which motivates our free will to obey law presupposes the presence of a creator who founded the moral laws which human reason accepts. Because the highest good needs an eternity to be achieved, then our souls

---

[33] Spivak, *Critique,* 136.

are immortal.[34] In other words, this critique tackles morality and presupposes a human ability to decide whether an action is moral or not. Frankenstein resorts only to natural philosophy disregarding practical reason and does not use his reason to decide on the morality of his plan of creating a rational being.

By so doing, Spivak argues, Frankenstein confuses the categorical imperative with the hypothetical imperative. For Kant, unlike categorical imperatives which entail doing the thing for its own sake, hypothetical imperatives "declare a possible action to be practically necessary as a means to the attainment of something else that one wants (or that one may want)."[35] We are morally obliged to perform the action only if we are sure that the goal is legitimate and that performing the action achieves the desired goal. For a rational being, this would be analytic. Given the general limitations of human knowledge, satisfying the conditions of this imperative is difficult. Spivak rewrites the hypothetical imperative in the following statement: "a command to ground in cognitive comprehension what can be apprehended only by moral will."[36] Frankenstein does not achieve what is commanded by the hypothetical imperative because he does not ask himself whether his goal is moral and whether the way he follows, creating the monster, will achieve this moral goal. What he does is congruent with the categorical imperative – the unconditional demand of performing an action for its own sake. Spivak suggests that such confusion between the two imperatives can easily occur. She wants to lead her readers to the important conclusion that as the monster is the result of this confusion here, the savage image of the 'native subaltern female' was the result of the same kind of confusion in the imperialist project. The monster in Spivak's reading forms the interruption of the Kantian allegory and marks the failure of the claim that the western rational man can create a copy of himself. This failure is explained in the coming paragraphs.

The parabasis: the monster that cannot be 'selfed'

Spivak indicates that the monster interrupts the novel's claim in that he remains a figure of Otherness that cannot be turned into a copy of the self. She clarifies this through showing the difference between the monster and Safie, another figure of Otherness, by resorting to a certain Caliban/Ariel

---

[34] Ward, *Kant,* 141-179.

[35] Immanuel Kant, *Groundwork for the Metaphysics of Morals,* trans. Arnulf Zweig, ed. Thomas E. Hill, JR. And Arnulf Zweig (Oxford: Oxford University Press, 2002), 216.

[36] Spivak, "Three Women's Texts", 257.

symbolism. The most important point that leads Spivak to the conclusion that the monster cannot be selfed and, consequently, deconstructs the claims of the novel is Frankenstein's failure to subject the monster to western education and law. This failure is even later shown in the novel's failure to contain the monster.

There are two types of Other in *Frankenstein:* the monster and Safie, whose father is a Muslim Turk and mother a Christian Arab. Spivak compares them to two characters in Shakespeare's *The Tempest:* Caliban and Ariel. Accordingly, the monster is a Caliban, or the absolutely Other in Spivak's terms, and Safie is an Ariel. As emphasised in the introduction to this book, the absolutely Other in Spivak's thought is the type of Other that cannot be domesticated. Shakespeare's Caliban is described by the characters of the play as a very strange fish-like creature whose appearance is abhorred by all his onlookers. Prospero, Caliban's master, enslaved him claiming that the latter attempted to violate the honour of his daughter Miranda. Miranda herself says that Caliban "is a villain, sir/ I do not love to look on."[37] Caliban answers Prospero's accusation saying: "Would't had been done/Thou didst prevent me – I had peopled else/This isle with Calibans."[38] Thus, it can be argued that, like the monster, Caliban is also prevented from procreation. In brief, Caliban is the Other that cannot be domesticated or reconciled with his master and remains a slave till the end of the play. As for Ariel, he is the unearthly creature who is also enslaved by Prospero but who acts the good servant for the purpose of getting his freedom. Of course, analysing the symbolism of Caliban and Ariel is very complicated with regard to the massive literature written on *The Tempest* and here is not the place for such details. What is important for the aims of this book is Spivak's source of the Caliban and Ariel symbolism offered by the Cuban poet, essayist and literary critic, Roberto Fernández Retamar. Many rewritings of Caliban and Ariel appeared in the literature of the so-called "Third World." In this respect, written in 1971, Retamar's "Caliban: Notes towards a Discussion of Culture in Our America" offers an account of the different rewritings of Caliban and Ariel. Spivak read the essay and evoked it at the beginning of "Three Women's Texts" just before discussing the texts of Brontë, Rhys and Shelley.

Retamar argues that rewritings of *The Tempest* started with the French writer, Ernest Renan, who in 1878 published *Caliban: Suite de "La Tempête."* However, it was not until the colonial countries emerged after the Second World War that the new outlook on *The Tempest* started to

---

[37] William Shakespeare, *The Tempest* (Cambridge: Cambridge University Press, 2002), I, ii, 310-11.
[38] Shakespeare, *The Tempest,* I, ii, 349-51.

advance. It was specifically in 1961 when several Caribbean writers – of whom he mentions Aimé Césaire and Edward Brathwaite – related Caliban to colonised people.[39] In Césaire's work *Une tempête: Adaptation de "La Tempête" de Shakespeare pour un théâtre nègre*, for instance, Caliban is a black slave and Ariel is a mulatto, a person of mixed white and black ancestry. Retamar for his part considers that Caliban stands for Latin-American culture:

> Our symbol then is not Ariel [...] but rather Caliban. This is something that we, the *mestizo* inhabitants of these same isles where Caliban lived, see with particular clarity [...] There is no real Ariel-Caliban polarity: both are slaves in the hands of Prospero, the foreign magician. But Caliban is the rude and unconquerable master of the island, while Ariel, a creature of the air, although also a child of the isle, is the intellectual.[40]

He continues in describing the symbolism of Ariel:

> He can choose between serving Prospero – the case with intellectuals of the anti-American persuasion – at which he is apparently unusually adept but for whom he is nothing more than a timorous slave, or allying himself with Caliban in his struggle for true freedom.[41]

Hence, for Spivak, Ariel falls into the category of the good servant and Caliban into that of the untameable Other that according to Spivak cannot be selfed. Before discussing Spivak's detection of the failure of 'selfing' the monster in *Frankenstein*, one needs to understand where it is possible that she finds the attempt of this 'selfing' in the text. The clearest example lurks in Frankenstein's following declaration which is not quoted by Spivak, but which supports her argument about 'selfing' the Other in *Frankenstein*:

> I doubted at first whether I should attempt the creation of a being like myself, or one of simpler organisation; but my imagination was too much exalted by my first success to permit me to doubt of my ability to give life to an animal as complex and wonderful as man (54).

Many critics have paid attention to Frankenstein's attempt at creating a copy of himself but only Spivak deployed it to expose imperialism's failure to 'self' the Other. Among others, Barbara Johnson discusses this

---

[39] Roberto Fernández Retamar, "Caliban," in *Caliban and Other Essays* (Minneapolis : University of Minnesota Press, c1989), 9-13.

[40] Retamar, "Caliban," 14, 16.

[41] Retamar, "Caliban," 39.

idea in relation to autobiography. She proposes that "[w]hat is at stake in Frankenstein's workshop of filthy creation is precisely the possibility of shaping a life in one's own image: Frankenstein's monster can thus be seen as a figure for autobiography as such"[42] and that "the desire for resemblance, the desire to create a being like oneself – which is the autobiographical desire par excellence – is also the central transgression in Mary Shelley's novel."[43] David Marshall continues: "[t]he punishment for this transgression is that Frankenstein ends up creating a being who is both similar to and unlike himself."[44] Marshall also stresses *Frankenstein* as suggesting "that it may be both mad and monstrous to create likenesses: fictions and figures in one's own image."[45] The madness of creating similarity for Spivak marks the failure of soul-making in transforming the other to an identical copy of the self. In her discussion of *Wide Sargasso Sea*, Spivak deals with this issue through introducing the thematics of Narcissus. In her reading of *Frankenstein,* she discusses this impossibility in two points: the monster's education and the validity subordinating him to the law.

Spivak states that the central narrative of the monster is his clandestine learning to be human. She refers to the fact that the monster reads *Paradise Lost* and Plutarch's *Lives.* He reads the first as true history, and compares the second to the patriarchal lives of his protectors, the De Laceys who own the house in whose shed the monster has been hidden peeping on and listening to them. Yet, Spivak concentrates on the fact that "his *education* comes through 'Volney's *Ruins of Empires.*'"[46] Constantin François de Volney's *Ruins of Empires* was intended to be a prefiguration of the French Revolution. Spivak thinks that this book is "an attempt at an enlightened universal secular, rather than a Eurocentric Christian, history, written from the perspective of a narrator 'from below.'"[47] Again, we can understand Spivak's opinion by adding textual details to her argument. The monster explains to Frankenstein that Felix chose this book due to the fact that the "declamatory style was framed in imitation of the eastern authors. Through this work I obtained a cursory knowledge of history and a view of the several empires at present existing in the world [...] I heard of the slothful Asiatics; of stupendous genius and mental activity of the

---

[42] Johnson, "My Monster/Myself," 4.

[43] Johnson, "My Monster/Myself," 3.

[44] David Marshall, *The Surprising Effects of Sympathy* (Chicago: the University of Chicago Press, 1988), 208.

[45] Marshall, *The Surprising Effects of Sympathy,* 210.

[46] Spivak, "Three Women's Texts," 257.

[47] Spivak, "Three Women's Texts," 257.

Grecians" (143). The narrations of this work induce the monster to think about his identity, and it is through this work that he realises he had no parents, no childhood; he realises his otherness and asks: "[w]hat was I?" (145). Thus, it is plausible to argue that since this book is not Eurocentric and since it triggers the monster's question about his identity, the monster's education as a western rational being that privileges the self and excludes the Other from humanity fails.

Spivak highlights the fact that the monster's education in 'universal secular humanism' is possible only through his eavesdropping on Felix's instructions for Safie, the Ariel of this text.[48] Through this education process, Spivak continues to say, "Shelley differentiates the Other, works at the Caliban/Ariel distinction, and *cannot* make the monster identical with the proper recipient of these lessons."[49] This distinction is illustrated in Safie's inability to reciprocate the monster's attachment although the monster, unseen, hears of the discovery of America and cries with Safie for its helpless original inhabitants. Now, one can discover the possible connections between Safie and Ariel that Spivak makes. Perhaps Spivak links Safie with Ariel because she shares with him the desire for freedom but is ready to give up her belonging to her father's country "[h]aving tasted the emancipation of woman."[50] Considering Safie's position in light of Retamar's view of Ariel and which Spivak certainly read, one can say that Safie, like Ariel, is the intellectual who can either ally with the De Laceys/Prospero or with the monster/Caliban. Safie allies with the De Laceys and rejects the monster. As one commentator says, with her escape from her father and her relationship with Felix, "the novel successively strips [Safie] of her Otherness, showing her to be not-Turkish and not-heathen. Presumably, she will be thoroughly domesticated and Westernized; soon, only a 'quaint' or 'exotic' accent will 'mark' her as Other."[51]

The second moment when *Frankenstein* presents an example of the impossibility of 'selfing' the Other relates to the question of the validity of the monster's subordination to law. Spivak refers to the moment of Frankenstein's decision to make an accusation against the monster. She considers that it is at this moment that "Shelley's Frankenstein does try to tame the monster, to humanize him by bringing him within the circuit of

[48] Spivak, "Three Women's Texts," 257.
[49] Spivak, "Three Women's Texts," 258.
[50] Spivak, "Three Women's Texts," 257.
[51] Joseph W. Lew, "The Deceptive Other: Mary Shelley's Critique of Orientalism in *Frankenstein*," *Studies in Romanticism*, 30:2 (Summer 1991), 282.

Law."[52] Spivak continues her argument saying that the Genevan magistrate speaks with absolute social reasonableness:

> I will exert myself, and if it is in my power to seize the monster, be assured that he shall suffer punishment proportionate to his crimes. But I fear, from what you have yourself described to be his properties, that this will prove impracticable; and thus, while every proper measure is pursued, you should make up your mind to disappointment. (250)

Ostensibly, the monster that Frankenstein described to the magistrate cannot be easily captured as he cannot be contained by proper measures. The monster will not be contained by the text, which Spivak regards as a point of strength in *Frankenstein*. Law is always an important element in Spivak's reading because it is through the evocation of law that the 'native informant' is dismissed from the text. In her reading of *Wide Sargasso Sea*, Spivak highlights that there is a legal discrimination against Christophine who is threatened with jail because she is accused of practising obeah. So, evoking the law succeeds in dismissing her from the text. However, in *Frankenstein,* the law fails to threaten the monster who cannot be subject to this law due to his monstrous properties. Thus, by stressing this fact, Spivak illustrates the failure of subjecting the monster to the law and this, in turn, serves her end that the monster's introduction to the European society represented in the novel proves the failure of the western Christian man as a rational being who can civilise or domesticate the Other. Hence, soul-making, which is seen by Spivak as a consequence of the Kantian ethical moment of making the heathen into a Christian, is deconstructed in *Frankenstein.*

Whereas Safie is associated with Antoinette in Spivak's taxonomy of characters, the monster belongs with Christophine. Like Christophine, the monster is the unresolved tangential moment in *Frankenstein*. We are told that he intends to immolate himself far from all human beings but the self-immolation scene is not offered by the text. As Spivak concludes, in terms of narrative logic the monster is "lost in darkness and distance" (279). She credits the text for this ending because she believes that "Shelley gives to the monster the right to refuse the withholding of the master's returned gaze – to refuse an *apartheid* of speculation."[53] She finds this refusal clear in the following words uttered by the monster:

> I will not be tempted to set myself in opposition to thee [...] How can I move thee?' [...] [He] placed his hated hands before my [Frankenstein's]

---

[52] Spivak, "Three Women's Texts," 258.
[53] Spivak, *Critique,* 140.

eyes, which I flung from me with violence; 'thus I take from thee a sight which you abhor. Still thou canst listen to me'" (118-9)

This moment can be paralleled with Christophine's sudden departure after being threatened by the letter of the law evoked by the "Rochester." Moreover, ending the novel with the monster lost in the darkness makes it different from Brontë's *Jane Eyre* because it avoids the "territorializing individual imagination" with which Brontë's text opens, and the "authoritative scenario of Christian psychobiography" with which it ends.[54]

The clearest implication of Spivak's stress on the positive side of this end is that instead of being inscribed by the text, the monster moves towards the future of the 'native informant' and 'native subaltern female' since he was denied his mate. Despite the fact that Shelley grants the monster a chance to reject his master's lack of response, Spivak still sees Shelley's political imagination as deficient. The reason for Spivak's belief is that Shelley still cannot give the Other a pre-history. Only Frankenstein/the master has history and, even when moving towards an individual future away from Frankenstein, the monster remains locked up in relation to the master. This approach to dichotomies like master/slave, coloniser/colonised and man/woman is what Spivak opposes. By understanding the second side of the binaries only in relation to the first, the binaries are entrenched rather than destroyed. Eventually, the monster remains hovering beyond the text.

Spivak asserts that unpacking the Kantian allegory in *Frankenstein* is politically useful. The implications of this assertion are congruent with the ones concluded from her reading of *Jane Eyre*. It can be conclude that because Kant's human subject has no place for the 'native informant,' his philosophy was utilised by imperialist politicians to achieve colonial expansion at the expense of the Other. In other words, Spivak may be suggesting that as Frankenstein uses the categorical imperative instead of the hypothetical, so did the politics of eighteenth-century imperialism in not paying attention to the morality of its cause, the civilising mission. The result of Frankenstein's labour is the monster that is abandoned by its maker, and the result of imperialism is the 'native informant' who was turned into a similar but not the same version of the coloniser. Consequently, the 'native informant,' like the monster, was excluded from western civilisation as happens in the example of Bertha Mason, whom some feminist studies exclude from the fight for individualism. The monster's questions about his identity and rights threaten the moral authority of western reason, which Victor Frankenstein represents. Spivak

---

[54] Spivak, "Three Women's Texts," 259.

indicates that the monster interrupts the text and causes the deconstruction
of the Kantian allegory in the following manner:

> To ask the Monster's questions towards Kant's solution of the antinomy
> [the opposition between a law and another] would be to destroy the
> permissible narrative that allows the system to stand. And indeed the
> system does not stand, also because, as in Kant, the male subject seeks to
> operate it alone.[55]

The monster in Spivak's reading is the 'native informant' who is allowed
into the text and then, proving the failure of the Kantian philosophy, he is
dismissed from it. To explain the monster's withdrawal from the novel,
Spivak resorts to the novel's structure as letters sent to Mrs. Saville.

Spivak suggests that the novel is a frame, but this frame is not closed
by Mrs. Saville. Consequently, the "frame is thus simultaneously not a
frame, and the monster can step 'beyond the text' and be 'lost in
darkness.'"[56] What Spivak means is that since the text is a group of letters
sent to Mrs. Saville, the text only exists if the reader is reading the letters
with her. She remains outside the text and she "does not respond to close
the text as frame."[57] In other words, the text ends with the final letter
telling that the monster decided to immolate himself and then he is lost in
the darkness. The fact that Spivak wants to draw our attention to is that
exactly like Mrs. Saville the monster goes beyond the text because, as we
are reading with her, we reach the same point she reaches, not knowing
what happens in the narrative, if anything, after the last letter. Our reading
stops here with the monster's withdrawal. Thus, Mrs. Saville and the
monster are paralleled because they both remain beyond the text, not
inscribed. Spivak does stress that Mrs. Saville is the occasion of
Frankenstein, not the protagonist, and this adds to her suggestion that the
novel, unlike *Jane Eyre,* does not use the language of female
individualism. Thus, we can also conclude that Spivak credits the novel
for keeping both the feminist struggle and the racial struggle outside the
text, rather than subordinating the racial struggle to that of feminist
freedom as was the case in *Jane Eyre.* Spivak says: "[w]ithin the allegory
of our reading, the place of both the English lady and the unnameable
monster are left open by this great flawed text. It is satisfying for a
postcolonial reader to consider this a noble resolution for a nineteenth-
century English novel."[58]

---

[55] Spivak, *Critique,* 135-6.
[56] Spivak, *Critique,* 140.
[57] Spivak, "Three Women's Texts," 259.
[58] Spivak, "Three Women's Texts," 259.

Although critics have often neglected Spivak's reading of *Frankenstein,* this chapter has attempted to reveal that Spivak's analysis of this text is very important both in terms of approach and theme. As for the approach, Spivak here follows the same two-step deconstruction that she uses in *Jane Eyre* and *Wide Sargasso Sea.* In terms of implications, Spivak's reading shows that Shelley's text deconstructs the first two. How does this happen? In *Jane Eyre,* the heroine is a female individualist whose freedom is dependent on the marginalisation of the silent Jamaican Creole who is constructed as a savage mad woman. In *Wide Sargasso Sea,* Bertha is rescued from this marginalisation in the character of Antoinette, but still it leaves another margin when Christophine is threatened by the law and withdrawn from the text. The imperialist discourse in *Wide Sargasso Sea* appears in Antoinette's desire to self the 'native subaltern female.' *Frankenstein* is the final text and it deconstructs both texts in two ways. First, there is no female individualism and no heroine seeking feminist freedom in opposition to the male. The feminine subject, Mrs. Saville, remains outside the text. The female is not given the role of sexual reproduction as in *Jane Eyre.* Both sexual reproduction and soul-making are undertaken by Frankenstein, the western rational man, and both fail at the end and again the monster withdraws and remains beyond the text. *Frankenstein* departs from *Wide Sargasso Sea* in that the monster's withdrawal does not happen under the threat of law but under the inability of the law to subordinate him. Though Spivak views this withdrawal positively, she still detects a political deficiency because in the end Shelley remains limited to the representation of the mirror separating master from slave with the master's refusal to respond to the slave's call.

However, for Spivak, this representation is not what is needed for a postcolonial critic. Spivak's readings of postcolonial texts attempt to find registers that depart from the representing 'native informant' and, in particular, the withdrawal of the 'native subaltern female.' Spivak finds a different register in *Foe* and "Pterodactyl" but this different register needs an understanding of Spivak's affiliation with Derrida's thought. Therefore, before moving to the discussion of *Foe* and "Pterodactyl," the next chapter will discuss Spivak's affiliation with Derrida which is essential to the understanding of the two texts.

CHAPTER FIVE

SPIVAK'S AFFILIATION
WITH DERRIDA'S THOUGHT

After offering her critique of the imperialist construction of the 'native subaltern female' as manifested in the literary texts she discussed in "Three Women's Texts," Spivak directed her attention to texts coming from the South. This part of the book will deal with this shift in Spivak's interest as demonstrated in her articles: "Theory in the Margin: Coetzee's *Foe* Reading Defoe's *Crusoe/Roxana*" (1988) and "Pterodactyl, Pirtha, and Puran Sahay" (1999). Spivak's reading of *Foe* and "Pterodactyl" shows that both texts offer an ethical approach to the subaltern. Whereas de Man's tropological deconstruction was specifically useful when dealing with the critique of imperialism in canonical texts, Derrida's version of deconstruction is the major influence in Spivak's analysis of texts coming from the periphery like Coetzee's and Devi's. This shift is towards the ethics of reading the 'native subaltern female' in literature.

This chapter will discuss the theoretical background that enabled this Spivakian shift through shedding light on what Spivak sees as two phases in Derrida's deconstruction. Thus, the significance of Derrida's deconstruction and its influence on Spivak's approach will be explained. Then, there will be a brief outlining of the first phase and the second phase of deconstruction through some of Derrida's texts that appear in the footnotes of Spivak's analyses of *Foe* and "Pterodactyl." This resort to Derrida's texts will contribute to coming to terms with the major concepts that constitute Spivak's ethical approach, such as ethical singularity, responsibility and the experience of the impossible. The last part of this chapter will briefly summarise Spivak's use of Derrida's terms in her approach to the 'native subaltern female.'

Spivak suggests that instead of trying to find solutions to the absent voice of the 'native subaltern female,' one should rather be engaged in ethical encounters with her. Not only is retrieving the subaltern voice impossible, but also such retrieval would be correcting the imperialist truth-claim about the 'uncivilised' Other by recourse to another claim –

the claim of knowing the subaltern female's real identity. Because Spivak learnt from de Man's two-step tropological deconstruction that a correction of a truth-claim would entail the recourse to another truth-claim, Spivak rejects the validity of any attempt to retrieve the voice of the 'native subaltern female' and this also leads to her rejection of concepts like nationalism and ethno-centrism which merely reverse the dichotomy coloniser/colonised. Ethno-centrism and nationalism also seem to homogenise the subaltern under a collectivity, and such a homogenisation is politically useful because it brings the subaltern into a unity that can be represented politically. However, political representation may repeat the epistemic violence and manipulate the voice of the subaltern without even realising the differences in the problems, experience and suffering among them. Spivak rejects political solutions and almost all her writings illustrate that the imperialist homogenising of the Other as uncivilised cannot be countered by a process of reverse homogenising. Rather, the imperialist construction of the 'native subaltern female' should be answered by taking up the ethical responsibility towards her, the responsibility that can be achieved by encountering the singular subaltern face to face. Spivak takes most of her ethical concepts, such as responsibility, which is a key term in her ethical approach, from Derrida.

What makes Derrida's deconstruction very useful for Spivak is that it does not offer political solutions and cannot be the basis for a political programme as she emphasises in one of her interviews: "That's the thing that deconstruction gives us; an awareness that what we are obliged to do, and must do scrupulously, in the long run is not OK. But this is not, and could not be, a political theory."[1] In other words, deconstruction for Spivak warns that there are unavoidable strategies like the strategic essentialism that she explains in her engagement with feminism. Spivak quotes from many of Derrida's works and outlines his deconstructive practice as divided into two phases. For the purposes of this book and depending on Spivak's footnotes in her study of "*Foe*" and "Pterodactyl," the focus will be on Derrida's *Of Grammatology* (1967),"Politics of Friendship" (1988), "Force of Law: the 'Mystical Foundation of Authority'" (1989) and *The Gift of Death* (1992).

Translating *Of Grammatology* was Spivak's first engagement with Derrida's thought and it has had its influence on Spivak's work since 1967 in terms of the dichotomies coloniser/colonised and white woman/subaltern woman. Concerning "Politics of Friendship," Spivak read this text one month after presenting "Theory in the Margin." Then, when she

---

[1] Spivak, *The Postcolonial Critic*, 45.

reproduced this article in *A Critique of Postcolonial Reason,* Spivak added to it some ideas from "Politics of Friendship." As for "Force of Law" and *The Gift of Death,* Spivak read both works before her analysis of "Pterodactyl." For Spivak, "Force of Law" contains "the central statement of Derrida's ethical turn" though she says that this turn started since Derrida's "The Ends of Man" (1982) which has been summarised in the first chapter of this book.[2] Spivak continues arguing that if we considered *Given Time* (1991), *The Gift of Death* (1992) and *Aporias* (1993) with "Force of Law," "we will see some major ideas in play," and she means ideas in relation to the ethical turn in Derrida's thought.[3] However, in this chapter the focus will be on "Force of Law" and *The Gift of Death* because they are key texts for an understanding of Derrida's notion of responsibility on which Spivak relies in her reading of *Foe* and "Pterodactyl." The following paragraphs will discuss these Derridean texts according to Spivak's classification of them as belonging to two phases of Derridean deconstruction.

Derrida: the first phase of deconstruction

Spivak views the first phase of Derrida's deconstruction – with texts like *Of Grammatology* – as based on guarding the unanswerable question of being. *Of Grammatology* (1976) is Spivak's translation of *de la grammatologie* (1967). Spivak describes her first encounter with deconstruction as being "touched by deconstruction" and this touch started with *Of Grammatology.* Spivak, however, admits that she had not known deconstruction before and that when she told de Man that she would translate Derrida's work, the former encouraged her saying that he had heard of Derrida. She clarifies that she does not know why she selected Derrida's work:

> How can I describe that first encounter, the moment when I felt that something called 'deconstruction' had touched me? I have described the facts many times, but the fact is I don't remember the details at all.
>   Where was I when I studied the Minuit catalogue? I know it had to be late 1967, since I was planning my first public lecture. What made me order De la grammatologie? As I have recounted many times, I did not know Derrida's name. Did I really read that entire difficult book? And

---

understand it well enough to have written words that fill me with shame now.[4]

Spivak's account of her first encounter with deconstruction shows that it was mere chance. It also shows that *Of Grammatology* was important for Spivak's career as a student who had just finished her PhD and was thinking of her first public lecture. The result was the introduction of Derrida's text to the American academy and Spivak "was forever touched by something that I call deconstruction, with no guarantees that I am ever right on the mark."[5] She also says: "I think *De la grammatologie* deserved a better translator and certainly a more knowledgeable introducer. But what would my life have been if I hadn't gone through that terrific drill?"[6] She is right in estimating how important this translation has been for her career as literary critic. One of the central terms which Spivak finds in Derrida's text and uses in her later writings on the issue of the 'native subaltern female' is "trace."

One can summarise Derrida's approach to the question of 'being' through his criticism of the western use of the structure of the sign. For him, the western metaphysical heritage presents the sign as implying a distinction between two parts: the signifier and the signified, but this structure depended on presence, implying that the signifier refers to a present signified. However, for his part, Derrida believes that the structure of the sign depends on absence rather than presence, that is, the signifier refers to an always absent signified. Reading Derrida leads to the conclusion that the spoken or written word is used because we cannot carry the signified wherever we go to refer to it, which also means that the sign loses its origin and therefore it is not a structure that refers to the truth. Taking the sign 'flower' for example, one says 'flower' when it is not actually there, so this part of the sign refers to an absent signified, the absent flower. Thus, the signified which is one half of this sign is not there. The other half, which is the signifier 'flower,' is not that actual signified. Because of the absence of the signified, the signifier loses its origin and when one tries to explain any sign, like in a dictionary for example, one is led through a series of signifiers that lost their origin and the real signified is never reached and meaning is endlessly deferred.

The always deferred meaning about which Derrida speaks is what he calls the trace, contending that:

---

[4] Gayatri Chakravorty Spivak, "Touched by Deconstruction," in *Grey Room* 20 (2005): 95.
[5] Spivak, "Touched," 95.
[6] Spivak, "Touched," 96.

The trace is not only the disappearance of origin – within the discourse that we sustain and according to the path that we follow it means that the origin did not even disappear, that it was never constituted except reciprocally by a nonorigin, the trace becomes the origin of the origin. [7]

For Derrida, thinking of the signifier and signified as a unity, rather than as difference and deferral, is always caused by the nostalgia for a lost origin. Thus, Spivak makes it clear that the first phase of deconstruction is the realisation that all origins are established by pushing away everything that this origin is not, pushing away the antonyms. Similarly, the self is also deferred because it can only be known as every Other that the self is not; selfhood can only be known through the relationship with the Other. Spivak says:

This irreducible work of the trace not only produces an unrestricted economy of the same and other, rather than a relatively restricted dialectic of negation and sublation, in all philosophical oppositions. It also places our selfhood (ipseity) in a relationship with what can only be 'named' radical alterity (and thus necessarily effaced).[8]

Having read Derrida, Spivak herself defines the trace as "mark of the absence of a presence, an always already absent present, of the lack at the origin that is the condition of thought and experience."[9] This notion of the trace is at work in Spivak's understanding of the sign: 'native subaltern female.' In other words, Spivak's writings in relation to the 'native subaltern female' are concerned with showing that this sign has lost its origin and that the signified, the subaltern female's reality or consciousness, is the trace that is deferred and inaccessible.

Derrida: the second phase of deconstruction

Spivak considers that Derrida's turn from the first to the second phase of deconstruction in 1982, at the conference entitled "The Ends of Man," was a shift from guarding the unanswerable question to the call to the Other.[10] At this conference, she says, "Derrida described a movement in his work as well. It was a turn from 'guarding the question' – insisting on the

---

[7] Jacques Derrida, *Of Grammatology,* trans. Gayatri Chakravorty Spivak (London: the John Hopkins University Press, 1976), 61.

[8] Spivak, *Critique,* 424.

[9] Spivak, "Translator's Preface," *Of Grammatology,* xvii.

[10] Spivak, *Critique,* 426.

priority of an unanswerable question, the question of *différance* – to a 'call to the wholly other.'"[11]

Spivak describes this phase of deconstruction as "affirmative deconstruction" by which she means that deconstruction has to say 'yes' to everything, as she said in one of her interviews: "I think what he [Derrida] began to realise is not that you have to say no to whatever positive stuff you're doing, that is to say 'keeping the question alive.' But that deconstruction obliges you to say yes to that which interrupts your project."[12] According to Derrida, deconstruction is affirmative because first of all it says 'yes' to the future, to the experience, and the Other that are yet to be reached. Simultaneously, deconstruction says 'yes' to the past and does not reject anything completely. For example, in order to produce some new ideas, Derrida did not completely reject Heidegger or Nietzsche, believing that for a new enlightenment to come, one should open these previous discourses to a new future which may include the Other. Derrida stresses this saying:

> Because, however affirmative deconstruction is, it is affirmative in a way that is not simply positive, not simply conservative, not simply a way of repeating the given institution. I think that the life of an institution implies that we are able to criticize, to transform, to open the institution to its own future. The paradox in the instituting moment of an institution is that, at the same time that it starts something new, it also continues something, is true to the memory of the past, to a heritage, to something we receive from the past, from our predecessors, from the culture.[13]

In the case of Derrida, Spivak explains that his relationship to all the philosophers he critiques, such as Kant, Kierkegaard, Heidegger and Levinas, is critical intimacy rather than distance. For example, she mentions that Derrida embraces Levinas' critique of Heidegger. This is the same strategy followed by Spivak, who does not reject any discourse. Instead, she accepts and negotiates philosophies such as Kant's three critiques, as has been discussed earlier in this book. She describes her practice as constructive complicity.[14] What is essential in the second phase of deconstruction is transcending both the binary self/Other and the question of being itself in an attempt to reach the Other. Derrida, in this

---

[11] Spivak, *Critique*, 425.

[12] Spivak, *The Post-Colonial Critic*, 46-7.

[13] John D. Caputo, ed. *Deconstruction in a Nutshell: a Conversation with Jacques Derrida* (New York: Fordham University Press, 1997), 5-6.

[14] Spivak, *Critique*, 3-4.

phase, tries to find ethical strategies that enable one to encounter the Other in a way that leads to responsibility.

Derrida's term "trace" underlies Spivak's definition of the 'native subaltern female,' but as for how this female can be read, Derrida's paper "Politics of Friendship" is one of the texts that provide Spivak with an approach. Derrida presented "Politics of Friendship" in an American Philosophical Association (APA) symposium 1988, where the theme was law and society. Striving to show that the relationship with the Other is prior to any law or society, Derrida's main concern is with the ethico-politico-philosophical discourse of friendship as the relationship with the Other. In this paper, Derrida discusses the concepts of response and responsibility and their role in friendship. First, as this paper was delivered as a lecture, Derrida explains that his presence with the attendants is a response since he responded to an invitation to participate. He starts his lecture with the statement, "O my friends, there is no friend," which he cited from a work by the French renaissance writer Michel de Montaigne, who was quoting Aristotle's repetition of an anonymous statement. Even though Derrida does not start with his own words, he knows that his listeners will consider him responsible for the mere fact that he is speaking. By stressing that he will be considered responsible despite the fact he is only quoting someone rather than saying his own words, Derrida wants to lead his listeners to the conclusion that responsibility is assigned to one by the Other as soon as one starts to sign. Then, he explains his thought on responsibility in the following passage:

> We are invested with an undeniable responsibility at the moment we begin to signify something (but where does that begin?). This responsibility assigns us our freedom without leaving it with us, if one could put it that way. And we see it coming from the Other. It is assigned to us by the Other, from the Other, before any hope of reappropriation permits us to assume this responsibility in the space of what could be called *autonomy*.[15]

The first important point that influences Spivak's approach to the 'native subaltern female' is Derrida's emphasis on the relationship with the Other as an experience of waiting, when he analyses the paradox caused by the statement: "O my friends, there is no friend." On the one hand, Derrida contends that the first part "O my friends" forms an appeal because it signs towards the future in the following manner: there are no friends but I appeal to you to be my friends because I love, or, will love you. Derrida

---

[15] Jacques Derrida, "Politics of Friendship," translated by Gabriel Motzkin and Michael Syrotinski, *American Imago* 50:3 (1993), 634.

continues that the first part is a calling for friendship, which is something that is yet to happen in the future, saying that friendship "is never a given in the present; it belongs to the experience of waiting, of promise, or of commitment."[16] On the other hand, Derrida thinks that the statement signs towards the past, implying that we would not have been together and you listening to me "if a *sort* of friendship had not already been sealed before any other contract: a friendship prior to friendships [...] the one that draws its breath in the sharing of a language (past or to come) and in the being-together that any allocution supposes, including a declaration of war."[17] In brief, this statement shows a call from the speaker for others to be his friends but since he already calls them 'my friends' this means that the relationship he is calling for is a past experience because they are listening to his call. At the same time it is a future experience because it is not complete since he is still waiting for a response.

For Derrida, the relationship with the Other and the responsibility assigned to one by the Other are based on the three dimensions of response, which are: answering for oneself, answering before another or others, and answering to the Other. However, he asserts that the last dimension –responding to the Other – is the most original because one cannot be responsible for oneself or before others without first needing to respond to the Other and it is the Other who calls for this response. Thus, the first stage of responsibility is supposing "the other in relation to oneself."[18] Moreover, the Other who calls for a response and to whom one must respond is singular, which means that Derrida stresses heterogeneity rather than homogeneity. Responding to the Other that is singular happens before some agency which is authorised to represent the Other legitimately like the law. This means that the relationship with the Other is always witnessed by a third party that interrupts the Other's singularity. The law, in turn, requires the person to recognise the alterity of the Other that is also resistant to the generality of the law. So, friendship implies the singular and the universal at the same time. The binary singularity/universality that is at work in friendship produces other oppositions: secret/manifest, private/public, invisible/exposed to witness, and apolitical/political which dominate the interpretation and experience of friendship.

To sum up Derrida's ideas on friendship – which Spivak applies to the relationship with the 'native subaltern female' – one can say that, first, the relationship between the self and the Other is a one-to-one relationship that is witnessed and interrupted by collective relationships like governments

---

[16] Derrida, "Politics," 636.
[17] Derrida, "Politics," 636.
[18] Derrida, "Politics," 638.

and organisations, as well as by the law which governs all relationships. Second, responsibility is a reciprocal process which involves both the self and the Other. Whereas the Other calls for a response from the self, assigning responsibility to the latter, the self must recognise this call and must try to respond. Third, the relationship between the self and the Other is the experience of waiting, a matter of future achievement or as Derrida puts it: "the absolute of an unrepresentable past as well as future."[19] Derrida's emphasis on the singularity of the relationship between the self and the Other and his conviction that the relationship with the Other is prior and more original than the law, organizations and governments make his approach to the discourse of friendship and consequently the relationship with the Other ethical rather than political.

Another Derridean text that Spivak read before writing "Pterodactyl" and that is concerned with responsibility is *The Gift of Death,* which was published in French in 1992. In this text, Derrida discusses the contradictions that arise when one wants to behave responsibly. He argues that there is an aporia caused by the clash between two types of responsibility, the responsibility towards a singular Other and the one towards others generally. In fact, this text is very important for a better understanding of Spivak's ethical approach. Derrida selected the story of Prophet Abraham as a deconstructive exposé of the aporia caused by the responsibility to the singular Other and the responsibility to others generally. Derrida picks his example from *Fear and Trembling* (1843) by the Danish philosopher and theologian Søren Aabye Kierkegaard (1813-1855). The story starts by God ordering Abraham to sacrifice his only son, Isaac. Abraham kept the order secret and decided to resign to God's will without telling anyone, even his wife Sarah and Isaac himself, and he took Isaac to the mountain for the sacrifice. On the way, Isaac asks Abraham about where the lamb to be sacrificed is, but the latter's answer was that God would provide it. At the very moment when Abraham raised his arm to kill his son, God stopped him and provided a lamb for the sacrifice instead of Isaac.

Derrida recalls Kierkegaard's conclusion that Abraham's response to Isaac's question concerning the lamb was neither a silence nor a lie, however; it did not reveal his secret – Abraham's intention to sacrifice his son. For Kierkegaard, by deciding to keep the secret, Abraham sacrifices the ethical order for the sake of obeying God. Kierkegaard defines the ethical order as one's responsibility to other human beings, family, community, friends or nation. Derrida reads Kierkegaard and concludes

---

[19] Derrida, "Politics," 637.

that this story reveals the aporia that is inherent in the concept of responsibility. For him, one can no more speak of responsibility in its usual universal meaning as acting dutifully. Instead, Derrida discusses what he refers to as absolute responsibility to the singular absolute – radical or wholly – Other. He explains his ideas through an analysis of the relationship between Abraham or any human being and God, rendering this relationship as dominated by the secret and sacrifice. Derrida contends that when asked about the sacrifice, Abraham responded and did not respond simultaneously; Abraham said a lot but still he did not say everything and even if he said everything, there was still one thing that did not pass between him and the others that are his family members. The silence [that] "takes over his [Abraham's] whole discourse" demonstrates Abraham as assuming the absolute responsibility to God, the singular absolute Other, to be a secret and a decision to be taken alone.[20] Abraham keeps to the ultimate secret responsibility to God, but he breaks with the responsibility to his family, a responsibility which philosophical reasoning associates with the public or the general. Thus, Abraham is both responsible and irresponsible.

Derrida views Abraham's relationship to God – and his absolute responsibility to God's radical Otherness – as exemplary of everyone's relationship to every singular Other, every singular human Other. He insists that the relationship with God inscribes itself within the order of the gaze that cannot be exchanged or returned. In Abraham's case, there is an intermediary, an angel that speaks between God and him. Accordingly, Derrida comments:

> There is no face-to-face exchange of looks between God and myself. God looks at me and I don't see him and it is on the basis of this gaze that singles me out [...] that my responsibility comes into being [...]. It is dissymmetrical: this gaze sees me without my seeing it looking at me. It knows my very secret even when I myself don't see it [...] the secret that is for me is what I can't see; the secret that is for the other is what is revealed only to the other, that she alone can see. By disavowing this secret, philosophy would have come to reside in a misunderstanding of what there is to know, namely, that there secrecy and that is incommensurable with knowledge and with objectivity.[21]

Moreover, when one is to respond to the call of the singular absolute Other, one also maintains one's singularity by taking the decision on one's

---

[20] Jacques Derrida, *The Gift of Death,* translated David Wills (Chicago: University of Chicago Press, 1995), 59.
[21] Derrida, *The Gift*, 91-2.

own as Abraham did. However, this decision will entail an "absolute sacrifice" since maintaining the singularity of the self and the Other leads one to betray the responsibility to the infinite number of others in their generality.[22] Abraham does this when he decides to kill his son, a sacrifice that would not have been justified and accepted by the public and that might have been an unforgivable crime. Therefore, Derrida emphasises: "I cannot respond to the call, the request, the obligation, or even the love of another without sacrificing the other other, the other others."[23] Responsibility in Derrida's analysis of Abraham's study is the stage that is between listening to God's call or order and the action of killing his son. It is at this stage that Abraham decided to respond to God by obedience disregarding how sacrificing his son would be seen by the general others.

To sum up Derrida's theory of the ethical responsibility towards the Other as it is presented in *The Gift of Death*, one can say that this relationship depends on silence rather than speech. It is based on the gaze and secrecy. The Other looks at one secretly asking for response. This secret gaze assigns one's responsibility to make the decision on one's own, again secretly as was the case in Abraham's story. The relationship with the Other maintains the singularity of the self and that of the Other. The Other is singular and the Other's gaze is directed at the singular self. The Other gazes and knows the self's secret, but the self cannot access any secret. Thus, one cannot know the self and cannot know the Other and the result is that there is a secret that belongs to no one. The only way out is taking the decision clandestinely even if the responsibility to the singular Other will result in the irresponsibility to the other others. This is responsibility. In Derrida's work, ethics associated with the public should be sacrificed for the sake of the ethics of singularity.

It is noteworthy that discussing the second phase of deconstruction in Derrida's work, Spivak highlights the concept-metaphor of the experience of the impossible. The term "experience" is essential in many of Derrida's writings, as in "Politics of Friendship" where he speaks of friendship as the experience of waiting. For an explanation of this concept-metaphor which Spivak uses in her literary readings, one can resort to its definition in a paper delivered by Derrida in 1989 under the title: "Force of Law: the 'Mystical Foundation of Authority.'" In this paper, Derrida clarifies that full experience implies traversal; that is, finding an appropriate passage for travelling to a destination. However, as far as aporia is concerned, experience cannot be full because aporia is "something that does not allow

---

[22] Derrida, *The Gift*, 68.
[23] Derrida, *The Gift*, 68.

passage. An aporia is a non-road."[24] Consequently, an aporia cannot be fully experienced and therefore experiencing the aporia means experiencing the impossible.

Hence, because the singular Other cannot be known or defined and because one's friendship with the Other is an experience of waiting, something that is yet to happen, then our relationship with the Other is an experience of the impossible. Also, the responsibility, which is the ethical approach to the singular Other, is aporetic because when one is responsible to the singular Other, one is irresponsible to the other others. This means that responsibility is also the experience of the impossible.

Spivak's Theory of Responsibility

Spivak, for her part, follows Derrida's example and calls for taking a similar approach to the 'native subaltern female,' an approach which is based on ethical singularity and responsibility. For Spivak, collectivity is only a strategy for political activism but the 'native subaltern female' must be treated in her singularity. Accordingly, responsibility becomes the key concept for Spivak's ethical approach to the 'native subaltern female.' Spivak offers her definition of responsibility in 1993 saying: "I can formalize responsibility in the following way: It is that all action is undertaken in response to a call (or something that seems to us to resemble a call) that cannot be grasped as such."[25] Responsibility in this sense appears through ethical singularity by which Spivak means a one-to-one encounter in which responses spring from both sides. Like in Derrida's *The Gift of Death,* Spivak concentrates on the stage that is between attending to the call of the 'native subaltern female' and the action or response. Responsibility for Spivak, then, is also the decision that must be taken on one's own after listening to the 'native subaltern female.'

Further, Spivak explains what happens in such encounters, contending that "when the philosopher – or anyone – tries and tries to explain and reveal, and the respondent tries and tries to receive the explanation and the revelation, that the something that must of necessity not go through is the secret and changeable 'essence' of that exchange."[26] Similarly, when one encounters the singular 'native subaltern female,' both are supposed to reveal everything but this does not happen in reality; something will

---

[24] Derrida, "Force of Law: the 'Mystical Foundation of Authority,'" translated by Mary Quaintance, in *Deconstruction and the Possibility of Justice*, ed. Drucilla Cornell, Michel Rosenfeld (London: Routledge, 1992), 16.

[25] Spivak, "Responsibility," *Boundary* 2 21(1994): 22.

[26] Spivak, "Responsibility," 21.

remain a secret not because it is meant to be hidden but because it cannot be transmitted from one side to the other. Therefore, in her preface to *Imaginary Maps,* Spivak describes these responsible ethical encounters as secret encounters. As in Derrida, Spivak here means that some secret that belongs to no one remains inaccessible. She describes the ethics that is based on the responsibility towards the 'native subaltern female' as the experience of the impossible. She explains that she does not say that this kind of ethics is itself impossible, but it is yet to be achieved. Consequently, there is no decision that leads to doing the right thing, and, as in Derrida, there is no full experience of responsibility in Spivak's opinion.

Moreover, because the subaltern participates in this ethical responsibility by enticing a response from the other side, Spivak insists that the object of ethical action is not an object of benevolence. Benevolence means the imposition of certain types of help exactly as western colonialism imposed its benevolence as civilising the world. This colonialist practice contributed to the construction of the colonial subject as an incomplete image of the self, a practice that Spivak describes as 'selfing' the Other. For Spivak, then, the ethical approach is not the western benevolence that aims at helping the 'native subaltern female' to have a voice which enables her be a domesticated version of the self as Ray argues: "what is being formalized is not responsibility as a discourse that moves from knowing the other to helping/enabling the other."[27] Responsibility is not the duty of the self only, but the duty of the subaltern as well. In addition, Spivak's ethical approach does not mean to be attentive to the subaltern female in the sense of making her an object of knowledge, which is usually the approach of anthropological studies, because for Spivak "[e]thics are not a problem of knowledge but a call of relationship."[28] Thus, one must read the 'native subaltern female' without claiming full knowledge of her experience.

The following two chapters will deal with Spivak's literary examples that show her shift from the critique of imperialism to the ethics of singularity in the same manner as Derrida shifted from the first to the second phase of deconstruction. The two chapters will be detailed analyses of Spivak's readings of *Foe* and "Pterodactyl" respectively. With slight differences both texts present good examples of the silent subaltern that can be paralleled with the 'native subaltern female'.

---

[27] Ray, *Gayatri Chakravorty Spivak*, 98.

[28] Spivak, "Echo," 32.

CHAPTER SIX

FOE:
THE STAGING OF A FACE-TO-FACE
ENCOUNTER WITH THE WHOLLY OTHER

Spivak includes her article "Theory in the Margin: Coetzee's *Foe* Reading
Defoe's Crusoe/Roxana" along with "Three Women's Texts" in her chapter
on literature in *A Critique of Postcolonial Reason*. She presents *Foe* (1986)
by the South African author J. M. Coetzee as a text that offers an example of
the "wholly otherness of margins" by rewriting the character of Daniel
Defoe's Friday. As we have seen so far, for Spivak there are two kinds of
Other figures: the Other that can be domesticated, or the Ariel, and the Other
that cannot be domesticated, or the Caliban figure. The wholly Other in
Spivak's thought is also the subaltern and the 'native subaltern female'
because all these figures are inaccessible voices. Therefore, everything that
Spivak mentions about the wholly Other also applies to the 'native subaltern
female' with whom Spivak is concerned in her *Critique*. In *Foe,* the wholly
Other is Friday who can never be reached by Susan Barton, the female
castaway, while trying, with the help of the author Mr. Foe, to write her
story which includes Friday's. Whereas Spivak warns against excluding the
'native subaltern female' from the fight for individualism in "Three
Women's Texts", in "Theory in the Margin" she warns against privileging
and trying to give voice to the wholly Other.

This chapter will first attempt to find possible reasons for Spivak's
choice of this text. Then, there will be four main sections that explain why
Spivak views the relationship between Susan and Friday as showing the
discontinuity between the feminist and the racial struggles. The first deals
with Susan rejecting the narrative of motherhood as part of her struggle for
female individualism. The second section deals with her failure in the
project of soul-making represented by her desire to give voice to the silent
Friday. The third section discusses Mr. Foe's role in light of Spivak's
resort to Derrida's ethics. Finally, the chapter analyses how Spivak detects
a new future for the relationship with the wholly Other in the last scene of
Foe.

Ray argues that by choosing this text Spivak wants to "complete the narrative of soul making and subject formation in the worlding of the third world that initiates Spivak's reading of nineteenth century canonical texts," since *Foe* reopens two early eighteenth-century novels.[1] *Foe* is a re-writing of Daniel Defoe's two novels, *Robinson Crusoe* (1719) and *Roxana: the Fortunate Mistress* (1724). The first is the famous narrative of Crusoe the white Christian man cast away on a desert island. Provided with some essential tools, Crusoe is able to produce crops and necessary things. Then, he encounters a native and names him Friday. He teaches Friday his language and religion. With no place for the individualist female, *Robinson Crusoe* only contained stereotypical female characters like the mother, the benevolent widow and the wife who are only referred to, never appearing as characters. The second novel, *Roxana,* is the story of a woman who falls from wealth because her husband abandons her. Then, she abandons her children and becomes a prostitute. Through different relationships with many rich men, she retains the wealthy position and achieves what she calls her freedom. The two novels show what Spivak views as the early eighteenth-century division between the marginal man, as the solitary Christian leading the imperialist soul-making project and the marginal woman, as the entrepreneurial female who depends on her sexuality to secure a social position.

Coetzee's *Foe* is presented in the form of letters from Susan Barton to a professional author, Mr. Foe. The novel dramatises the process of writing a narrative of the story of Susan, who, while searching for her lost daughter, is cast away on an island where she meets Cruso and Friday. She is very curious to know the story of Cruso and Friday's life on this island but, to her disappointment, Cruso does not keep a journal or any register of time. As for Friday, his tongue has been cut out with the possibility of his being castrated as well. After a year of her life on the island, the three are rescued but Cruso dies on the way back to England and Friday remains with Susan. The latter strives to write a narrative about that year but Friday's silence remains a gap that hinders her writing. She resorts to Mr. Foe to write her story, but they have different opinions about speech and writing. Susan and Friday live in Mr. Foe's house where she is haunted by a girl claiming to be her daughter whom Susan rejects. Mr. Foe tries to convince Susan that the story of her search for her daughter should be written but she insists that she is a free woman and can choose what parts of her life to be written. At last, her book is not written. The last section of the novel is narrated by an unidentified 'I' that revisits the wreck, and

---

[1] Ray, *Gayatri Chakravorty Spivak*, 43.

finds Susan and the ship captain dead. Only Friday is alive with a scar on his neck. Friday opens his mouth releasing a stream that fills the island. The visitor says that the wreck is the place where bodies are their own signs.

Spivak's choice of this text is due to her belief that Coetzee is interested in imperialism and the female. Spivak proves this interest by demonstrating how Coetzee changes Defoe's texts. For example, she shows the difference between Coetzee's Cruso and Defoe's Crusoe. Starting with Defoe's Crusoe, Spivak argues that while other critics read Crusoe as an example of capitalist endeavour, basing themselves on Marx's paragraph on *Robinson Crusoe*, she thinks that the same paragraph proves that Marx presented the novel as a pre-capitalist example of the production of use-values. Marx's paragraph on Crusoe is found in the first volume of *Capital* in a section that discusses the fetishism of commodities immediately before Marx's section on the transformation of money into capital. Therefore, for Spivak this novel is an example of the pre-capitalist stage. She maintains that Crusoe for Marx is a producer of use-values, a mode of production which is expressed by time and not money. In other words, this is not a capitalist mode of production because capitalism is based on exchange-values expressed later by money. Spivak notes that Marx is not concerned with the novel itself. He is merely interested in Robinson as representing the appearance of man in nature because, for Marx, use and exchange values are forms of appearance. Marx himself maintains that to satisfy his wants on the island, Robinson makes tools, tames the goats and does other different tasks. His tasks are different forms of the human labour of one person, Robinson. Another important aspect is time which Robinson apportions according to the difficulties and the possibility of overcoming them. He then starts to write a journal containing a list of the objects he made and the operations of producing them. He evaluates the object according to the labour time spent on producing certain quantities of these objects. The watch, ledge, pen and ink he could rescue from the wreck assisted him in keeping a journal of these pieces of information. Marx concludes that the relations between Robinson and his objects contain the elements, human labour and time, needed for determining value.[2]

Spivak finds that the importance of time in Defoe's text is replaced with a focus on spacing and displacement in Coetzee's novel. Spivak reads this shift from the importance of time to that of space as a shift from the

---

[2] Karl Marx, *Capital,* vol. 1 (Moscow: Foreign Languages Publishing House, 1961), 169-170.

interest in pre-capitalism to imperialism. This is the first change that
makes Spivak interested in *Foe*. Marx was not interested in Crusoe's being
a colonist but Coetzee certainly is. Coetzee, she argues, does "not find
Crusoe useful as the normative man in nature making visible a constitutive
chronometry."[3] In *Foe,* Cruso does not even keep tools. What this Cruso
does is related to empire, namely to the theme of the transition from land
to landed capital which is one aspect of imperialism. For instance, he
leaves a space which is lightly inscribed to an indefinite future as Spivak
discerns in the following passage she quotes from the novel: "'The
planting is not for us,' said he. 'We have nothing to plant – that is our
misfortune [...] The planting is reserved for those who come after us and
have the foresight to bring seed. I only clear the ground for them.'"[4] In
addition, Cruso is not interested in keeping a record of time. Susan Barton
does not succeed in finding "carvings, not even notches to indicate that he
counted the years of his banishment or the cycles of the moon" (16). It is
Susan, not Cruso, who is interested in time and she is the capitalist agent.
This is the second change that is interesting. Thus, Spivak shows that by
shifting the focus from time, labour and value to space and dislocation and
then by replacing the normative man with the woman, Coetzee's text is
about imperialism and the female. Of course, Coetzee's interest is
important for Spivak because a feature of the three texts studied in "Three
Women's Texts" is that the western woman was excluded from the soul-
making project and the same applies to Defoe's texts. Therefore, one of
Spivak's aims in discussing *Foe* is to illustrate the differences between the
consequences of undertaking the soul-making project by Crusoe and by
Susan taking into account their unequal gender positions. Whereas Defoe's
Crusoe participates in soul-making and succeeds in turning Friday into a
domesticated subject, Coetzee's Cruso is not interested in this project. On
the contrary, as will be explained in the following sections, it is Susan who
is allowed to attempt participation in soul-making with consequences
different from those in Defoe's text.

   Although there are some common points that link *Foe* to the texts
discussed in "Three Women's Texts," there is one point of departure
which makes Spivak view this novel as offering a different register of the
relationship between self and Other from the one offered in the previous
texts. Spivak analyses Coetzee's novel foregrounding this departure which
is, as Ray says, the staging of the experience of the impossible, which can

---

[3] Spivak, "Theory in the Margin," 161.
[4] J. M. Coetzee, *Foe* (London: Penguin Books, 1986), 33. All subsequent
references will be to this edition and will be shown as page numbers within
parentheses.

be discussed through the representation of the relationship between Susan and Friday.[5] The common points that link *Foe* to the other texts are the following: first, *Foe* contains the woman, Susan, who, like Antoinette, tries to 'self' the Other for the consolidation of her narrative. She also resembles Jane in the fact that she leads the struggle of the female individualist who resists Mr. Foe's attempts to tell her story according to his wish. Second, the wholly Other in this novel is Friday whose native story or knowledge is withheld like that of Bertha, the monster and Christophine. However, the difference here is that Friday is not even given voice to speak the language of the one encountering him. Both Christophine and the monster speak good English and they only withdraw in the end. As for Friday, his tongue is cut out and Susan fails in all attempts to make him speak or write from the beginning to the end of the novel. For Spivak, Susan is involved in a feminist and anti-imperialist struggle, but she fails in leading both struggles simultaneously.

Spivak presents Susan's attempt to participate in both women's and the anti-imperialist struggles as an example of how the western feminist thought that the western woman could be the norm of the free woman who would be able to participate and succeed in all struggles. For instance, in Hélène Cixous' "The Laugh of the Medusa" (1975) was about the need for feminine writing which would "transform directly and indirectly *all* systems of exchange based on masculine thrift."[6] In the time of writing this essay, Cixous could anticipate the emergence of a new history in which woman would take part in all struggles: "[a]s subject for history, woman occurs simultaneously in different places."[7] In Cixous' view, the presence of the female in different struggles at the same time would enable women to prevent the transmutation of any struggle into a form of repression. Based on the same belief that the western woman can struggle for all women, Spivak indicated, feminists within the academy became interested in marginality. However, she says that the enthusiasm of this interest "has sometimes overlooked a problem: that a concern with women, *and* men, who have not been written in the *same* cultural inscription, cannot be mobilized *in the same way* as the investigation of gendering in our own."[8] In other words, the problem that academic

---

[5] Ray, *Gayatri Chakravorty Spivak*, 43.

[6] Hélène Cixous, "The Laugh of the Medusa" in *New French Feminisms: An Anthology,* ed. Elaine Marks and Isabelle de Courtivron (Amherst: Univ. of Massachusetts Press, 1980), p. 252, quoted in Spivak, "Theory in the Margin," 159.

[7] Cixous, "The Laugh," 252, quoted in Spivak, "Theory in the Margin," 159.

[8] Spivak, "Theory in the Margin," 159.

feminism faces is the lack of the awareness of the heterogeneity of the experiences of the marginal: the wholly Other or the subaltern. What Spivak emphasises is that to include the 'native subaltern female,' we must learn new ways which Spivak would later describe as the singular ethical encounters with the subaltern, the ethical approach which Spivak has derived from Derrida's works discussed in the previous chapter. Stressing that "Coetzee's focus is on gender and empire," Spivak studies two strands in the novel: Susan's rejection of the discourse of motherhood and her insistence on participating in the anti-imperialist struggle.[9]

Susan's feminist struggle: the rejection of the text of motherhood

For Spivak, the absence of the female in *Robinson Crusoe,* which is about the project of soul-making, is filled with Susan Barton. However, Susan is not a new character because she comes from Defoe's *Roxana,* a novel where Roxana (whose first name is Susan), uses her sexuality and men's wealth to move to the centre of society. Thus, the division between male and female roles that Spivak exposed in *Jane Eyre* is also at work in Defoe's two novels where the female cannot participate in soul-making and is confined to sexual reproduction. As in her analysis of *Frankenstein,* Spivak's reading of *Foe* shows that Coetzee deconstructs the roles of the male and the female. This time, the project of soul-making, represented by Susan's attempt to construct Friday's voice and identity, is assigned to the western woman who claims her freedom. The inter-textuality between *Roxana* and *Foe* causes an aporia in Susan's relationship with Friday. Spivak illustrates this through her discussion of the mother-daughter sub-plot in *Foe.*

Spivak clarifies that what Roxana and Barton have in common is the story of mothering and that the last episode of Defoe's *Roxana* intervenes in the third section of *Foe,* the section where Susan Barton rejects a girl who claims to be her daughter. In the last episode of *Roxana,* the heroine's daughter, one of the many children abandoned by Roxana, tries to reveal that Roxana is her mother. Yet, Roxana denies and rejects the girl. Then, Roxana agrees to a plot designed by her cunning maid Amy to murder the daughter. Before continuing the argument about the differences between Roxana and Barton, Spivak explains the problems which she detects in Defoe's representation of the female in *Roxana,* problems which Spivak thinks are related to the clash between motherhood and female individualism.

---

[9] Spivak, "Theory in the Margin," 159.

What Spivak had in mind when she discussed the problems of Defoe's representation of the female is Susan Robin Suleiman's "Writing and Motherhood" (1983).   Suleiman criticises the patriarchal narrative of the mother specifically within psychoanalysis. She is mainly concerned with the psychoanalytic neglect of the mother who is always subservient to her children's needs. According to the "traditional psychoanalytic view of motherhood," the main elements affecting the mother's psychology are the feminine will to sacrifice and the child's need for his mother's selflessness.[10] Consequently, the conflict between the mother's desire for individualism or self-realisation and her child's needs has been ignored. It is this conflict that goes on within the mother who is a writer. Suleiman adds that psychoanalysis always puts the artist in the position of the child and considers that the successful artist develops from his earliest relationship with the mother. The mother, then, "is the essential but silent Other;"[11] she is written but she never writes since her creativity finds its place in the production of children. Suleiman also speaks about the guilt that a mother feels when she prioritises her self-realisation at the cost of the needs of her child. One way to calm her crying child, the mother/writer gives him the book, does not write the book, or writes it less well than she could. In addition, for a woman, writing books is considered as a substitute for children if she was not a mother, but for a man it was considered an addition because it becomes a maternal metaphor to be added to his male qualities. This meant that a woman can be either a mother or a writer. Resorting to the radical French feminists like Julia Kristeva, Suleiman declares her opposition to this either /or theory and calls for a reconciliation between motherhood and writing.

By evoking Suleiman, Spivak is telling her readers that Defoe presented this conflict in *Roxana* by making Roxana reject her daughter in order to be a free woman. Thus, the register here is the either mother/or free woman – the either/or theory which Suleiman explains and rejects. Now, the reason why Spivak sees this representation as problematic can be discussed. First, Spivak quotes the following passage from Defoe's text where Roxana recalls the Dutch merchant's marriage proposal. Roxana confesses that she refused to marry this man because she did not want him to share or take her money, but her pretext was that she believed in women's freedom. Roxana says:

---

[10] Susan Rubin Suleiman, "Writing and Motherhood" in *The (M)other Tongue: Essays in Feminist Psychoanalytic Interpretation,* ed. Shirley Nelson Gamer et al (Ithaca: Cornell Univ. Press, 1985), 353.

[11] Suleiman, "Writing and Motherhood," 357.

[T]ho' I cou'd give up my Virtue, [...] yet I wou'd not give up my Money, which, tho' it was true, yet was really too gross for me to acknowledge [...] I was oblig'd to give a new Turn to it, and talk upon a kind of an elevated Strain, [...] as follows: I told him, I had, perhaps, differing Notions of Matrimony, from what the receiv'd Custom had given us of it; that I thought a Woman was a free Agent, as well as a Man, and was born free, and cou'd she manage herself suitably, might enjoy the Liberty to as much Purpose as Men do.[12]

So, the first problem in Defoe's representation of the female for Spivak is that even when Roxana is given the choice between mothering and individualism, the individualism that is offered to her is not a participation in soul-making that was offered to Robinson Crusoe. Spivak illustrates that the individualism that Roxana is claiming is only a disguise that hides her greed for wealth. The second problem is the fact that Roxana's sexuality is the only way that she can use to move to the centre of the social system. A result of using this sexuality as labour power outside marriage, as Spivak argues, is producing children who become commodities that "cannot be legitimately exchanged and may produce an affective value that cannot be fully coded."[13] In other words, when Roxana is offered the choice of female individualism, which is only a claim that covers the desire for wealth, she cannot escape the register of sexual reproduction and mothering even if the children remain illegitimate.

Unlike Defoe, Spivak argues, Coetzee frees Susan from the discourse of *Roxana* and allows her to participate in the anti-imperialist struggle which turns out to be a project of soul-making because Susan tries to construct Friday's identity and voice, as will be explained later in this chapter. Spivak contends that Coetzee's objective is "to represent the bourgeois individualist woman in early capitalism as the *agent* of *other*-directed ethics rather than as a combatant in the preferential ethics of self-interest."[14] For Spivak, Coetzee avoids the problems in Defoe's representation of women in two ways. First, he dismisses the theme of the dissimulation of principles by freeing Susan from the theme of marriage and sexuality as use-value when she is on the island. She does not give pleasure for money and does not advocate female individualism as a pretext to own money, as Roxana does, because Coetzee grants Susan "*full* if unrecognized, unacknowledged, and undeveloped capitalist agency."[15]

---

[12] Daniel Defoe, *Roxana, the Fortunate Mistress* (London: Oxford University Press, 1964), 147.

[13] Spivak, "Theory in the Margin," 164.

[14] Spivak, "Theory in the Margin," 164.

[15] Spivak, "Theory in the Margin," 164.

This agency is expressed in Susan's insistence on the free choice of her story, the use of time and the scrupulous dating of her section. Second, Coetzee avoids the theme of mothering versus female individualism in the way he stages the mother-daughter sub-plot. Susan believes that this plot is a consequence of Mr. Foe's thoughts about woman's dilemma, and therefore it is father-born. The analysis of this relationship between mother and daughter is vital in Spivak's reading because it helps Spivak discuss the extent to which the politics of over-determination is or is not feasible.

Spivak reads this sub-plot as the aporia of the text in terms of other-directed politics. Susan is involved in two kinds of struggle, the first anti-patriarchal and the second anti-imperialist. The anti-patriarchal resistance is represented by her rejection of the mother-daughter relationship. In the third section, while staying at Foe's house, Susan is haunted by a girl, claiming to be her daughter. Susan does not believe the girl, thinking that the appearance of this daughter was designed by Mr. Foe. Susan takes the girl to the forest and tells her that she does not have a mother and that she is only father-born. The girl disappears but then Susan says: "I wake up in the grey of a London dawn with the word still faintly in my eyes [...] Have I expelled her, lost her at last in the forest" (91)? Spivak maintains that these words suggest the forest incident to be a dream within Susan's dream citation from Defoe's texts. Spivak also refers to another letter by Susan in which she tells Mr. Foe about finding a stillborn baby-girl in a ditch: "[t]ry though I might, I could not put from my thoughts the little sleeper who would never awake, the pinched eyes that would never see the sky, the curled fingers that would never open. Who was the child but I, in another life" (105)? Spivak construes 'another life' to be another story and another register. By saying that Susan's is a dream citation of Defoe's texts and that there may be many registers and stories within this dream, Spivak is taking us to psychoanalysis – also using the term 'over-determination' – to prove that Susan's narrative as she wishes it to be written is not possible.

Over-determination in psychoanalysis is used when an object is influenced by more than one cause such as a dream that contains more than one image. As clarified in Laplanche and Pontalis's *The Language of Psycho-analysis,* "[t]aking the hysterical symptom as his model, Freud shows that this 'develops only where the fulfilments of two opposing wishes, arising each from a different psychical system, are able to converge in a single expression.'"[16] Thus, in a dream two wishes can converge into one expression. This means that when Spivak speaks about Susan's dream, she implies that Susan can lead her two struggles in the

---

[16] Laplanche and Pontalis, *The Language of Psycho-analysis,* 293.

dream. However, this becomes not possible when the dream is to be written in a book. Mr. Foe insists that the story should be that of motherhood and Susan insists that it should be the story of the island. Spivak says:

> It is true that we are each of us overdetermined, part historian, part mother, and many other determinations besides. But overdetermination can itself be disclosed when the condensed rebus in the dream has been straightened out in analytical prose. Because of this dislocation, there can be no politics founded on a continuous overdetermined multiplicity of agencies.[17]

In *Foe,* Susan is over-determined by both history and motherhood and she cannot write the two narratives in one book since the book is a dislocation of her dream about the island where she was cast away while searching for her daughter, and where she met Friday. For Spivak, the two texts cannot be written in the same register of language. The dislocation that takes place when Susan's dream is transformed into writing makes it impossible for her to manage both agencies and it also makes it difficult for the male author, Foe, to write a complete narrative about the western woman involved in two discontinuous struggles. The direct implication of this idea is that Susan cannot make Friday's story part of her narrative and, similarly, western feminism cannot make the story of the 'native subaltern female' part of theirs, as Spivak declares saying: "I am suggesting that here the book may be gesturing toward the impossibility of restoring the history of empire and recovering the lost text of mothering *in the same register of language.*"[18] Thus, western feminists cannot construct the voice of the 'native subaltern female' because their signification methods are not the same as those of the 'native subaltern female.' Western feminists must look for new ways to approach the 'native subaltern female.' They must listen to her call and then respond. In other words, the 'native subaltern female' must be involved. Moving to Spivak's reading of Friday, it becomes clear that Susan fails in involving him in the encounter by insisting on teaching him how to express by drawing and writing.

Susan, Friday and the failure of soul-making

Spivak's reading of *Frankenstein* highlights Frankenstein's failure when he undertakes the role of sexual reproduction using his laboratory as an artificial womb. In *Foe,* she reveals how the western female undertakes the

---

[17] Spivak, "Theory in the Margin," 165.
[18] Spivak, "Theory in the Margin," 165.

project of soul-making and fails in contrast with the success of Defoe's Crusoe in teaching Friday English language and Christianity. Spivak clarifies Susan's attempts to domesticate the wholly Other. However, here Friday is tongueless and this prevents Susan from accessing his voice, which also hinders the narrative of her own story. When Cruso asks Friday to say 'La-la-la,' the latter repeats 'Ha-ha-ha' and then Susan discovers that he has no tongue. Spivak indicates that Coetzee deliberately keeps Friday silent and she emphasises Coetzee's focus on *h* since it stands for Friday's muteness. This makes *h* significant to the extent that it is the only sound Friday is capable of learning. Furthermore, Spivak draws our attention to the fact that only the letter *H* is typographically raised and separated from the line in the way of the typeface of the eighteenth century throughout the text. In other words, Spivak shows us that silence is highlighted in *Foe* through the sound *h*.

In the text, we read how Susan tries all the forms of communication which she knows as a western woman like drawing, music, dancing and writing to make Friday tell his story, but in vain. In fact, Spivak stresses these attempts by referring to the incident when first Susan draws a picture of Cruso cutting Friday's tongue out. But then Susan realises that her representation may not be congruent with that of Friday; he might see the sketch as showing a benevolent Cruso putting a piece of fish in Friday's mouth. All her sketches fail in the same manner and when she surrenders, she says: "who was to say there do not exist entire tribes in Africa among whom the men are mute and speech is reserved to women?" (69) This statement, Spivak believes, challenges the good white woman's anguish by "an ignorance that is removable only by anthropology."[19] What Spivak is alluding to here is that western benevolent discourses like anthropology, as discussed in Chapter One of this book, were based on a conviction that the 'native informant' has a culture which can be inscribed only by the west. In other words, Spivak indicates that when encountered by failure to access the wholly Other, the west resorts to anthropology to fill the gap rather than trying to attend to the call of the wholly Other who may be using his/her own ways of signification. Just as Spivak considered Kristeva's encounter with the silent Chinese women as consolidation of the self, Kant's introduction of the New Hollanders as consolidation of the theory of the rational man, and Antoinette's domestication of Christophine as a way to find a place to speak from, so Spivak here suggests that Susan wants Friday as her informant only to consolidate herself and complete her own story. This implies that Susan wants to prove her female individualism

---

[19] Spivak, *Critique,* 196.

by choosing the story she wants to tell and this cannot be fully achieved without Friday's voice. Spivak states: "the account of her [Susan's] anguish as Friday grows dull in London; her longing for Friday's desire and her exasperation at herself; the orchestration of her desire to construct Friday as subject so that he can be her informant, cannot be summarized."[20] Thus, Spivak implies that Susan's is a project of soul-making, a domestication of the wholly Other and the method is giving voice to Friday to make him speak using the signification methods known by Susan herself.

Later, Susan notices that Friday dances in a way that, she supposes, enables him to remove himself from England. Thereupon, she tries to dance with him in order to achieve communication with him. She fails again and finds Friday sleeping sluggishly after she finishes her dance. Spivak refers to this attempt as well quoting Susan's following declaration:

> The story of Friday's tongue is a story unable to be told, or unable to be told by me. That is to say, many stories can be told of Friday's tongue, but the true story is buried within Friday, who is mute. The true story will not be heard till by art we have found a means of giving voice to Friday. (118)

Despite all her failures to make Friday speak, Susan does not give up her project of giving voice to him. To demonstrate the invalidity of this effort, Spivak even raises doubts about whether Susan herself is the voice of *Foe*. Spivak's reading draws our attention to three important points which may indicate that Susan is not the voice of the novel. Spivak argues that Susan only wrote a title: *The Female Castaway,* a memoir and some letters sent to Mr. Foe. The memoir does appear in *Foe* as the first section. However, the title is not used and Spivak asks: "[w]hat happens to *The Female Castaway?*"[21] Spivak is alluding to the fact that the book *Foe* is not what Susan wanted to write. As for the letters, not all of them reach their destination. In light of Spivak's use of letters in her reading of *Wide Sargasso Sea,* we can conclude that by sending the letters to Mr. Foe, Susan is looking for a power which can authorise her story. In "Rochester's" case, Spivak concluded that "Rochester" cannot be a victim because he writes the letter which explains his being a victim of the patriarchal system, but actually he does not send it to his father and he does not use the patronymic.

Therefore, Spivak concludes that this absence of the authority of the name of the father means that "Rochester" is not subject to the oedipal

---

[20] Spivak, "Theory in the Margin," 168.
[21] Spivak, "Theory in the Margin," 162.

exchange. In Susan's case, Spivak is implying that since Susan declares the name of the authority she is seeking and that is the male author, Mr. Foe, this can mean that she is not actually the voice of the book *Foe*, especially since the original title selected by Susan disappears. In addition, in "The Letter as Cutting Edge," Spivak reveals a Lacanian approach to letters and this means that she believes that if a letter does not reach its destination, then the desire is not yet fulfilled and it remains in circulation. Accordingly, the fact that not all the letters reach their destination, for Spivak, may mean the deferral of some parts of Susan's story. Finally and most importantly, Spivak contends that *Foe* starts with a self-citation between quotation marks: "[a]t last I could row no further" (5). Spivak highlights that this is a "quotation with no fixed origin."[22] Here Spivak is drawing on Derrida's *Spurs* where he comments on "I have forgotten my umbrella," a sentence which appears in quotation marks in Nietzsche's unpublished manuscripts.[23] Discussing the possibilities of what this sentence may be or mean, whether a citation or anything else, Derrida says:

> In fact, it is even possible that it is not Nietzsche's sentence, and this notwithstanding any confident certainty that it is indeed written in his hand. What, after all, is handwriting? Is one obliged, merely because something is written in one's hand, to assume, or thus to sign it? Does one assume even one's own signature?[24]

When Spivak highlights that the self-citation with which the novel begins has no fixed origin, she suggests also that it may not be Susan's. This implies that Susan may not be the voice in *Foe*.

If there is doubt whether or not Susan is the voice of the text, then how can she give voice to Friday? Spivak is adamant at showing Susan's failure in giving voice to Friday by commenting on how the words which she tries to teach to Friday lose their referents or, in Spivak's words, "are losing their mode of existence as semes."[25] For example, Susan recounts that when trying to write 'h-o-u-s', "Friday wrote the four letters, or four shapes passably like them: whether they were truly the four letters and stood truly for the word *house* and the picture I had drawn, and the thing itself, only he knew" (145-6). Spivak also chooses another limitation that Susan's project of giving voice to Friday faces; it is her inability even to

---

[22] Spivak, "Theory in the Margin," 162.
[23] Jacques Derrida, *Spurs*, translated by Barbara Harlow (Chicago: the University of Chicago Press, 1979), 123.
[24] Derrida, *Spurs*, 127.
[25] Spivak, "Theory in the Margin," 170.

give him an identity and this is clear in her attempt to teach him the name Africa. Spivak maintains that Africa is a catachresis, referring to Christopher L. Miller's *Blank Darkness* where Miller studies the constructions of Africa in French literature. Miller stresses the fact that naming Africa and its parts is allegorical, not based on realism: "[n]ames for Africa and parts of Africa – those that come from Europe – tend to follow this pattern and to have a peculiarly tenuous relationship both with the thing they describe and with their etymologies."[26] He claims that it is only relatively recently that Africa started to refer to the whole continent. Seeking origins or meanings for 'Africa,' Miller argues, would give many hypotheses of which he mentions ten that attribute the word to Arabic, Latin, Hebrew and other languages. However, this only leads him to the following conclusion: "[Africa] appears to mean whatever one wants, in the language one wants."[27] Spivak also views Africa as a name without a determined referent and says that it is perhaps a Latin word derived from the name of the Berber tribe, Aourigha. Besides, Africa was used by the Greeks to refer to Libya.

Accordingly, Spivak says that the indeterminacy surrounding the names of the places where the marginal is born leads to the conclusion that although nationalism is a proper political agenda for struggling against oppression, it does not provide a guarantee of identity. This leads back to Parry's criticism of Spivak as turning a deaf ear to native agency or nationalism. It must be remembered that Spivak distinguishes between political solutions and the ethical encounter. Speaking of identity, voice and native agency belongs to the domain of political representation. In other words, nationalism can be a strategy for political activism. For her part, Spivak is concerned with the singular ethical encounter with and responsibility towards the subaltern. Moreover, one can further realise how to distinguish Spivak's effort from any political effort by resorting to Neil Lazarus who says:

> Spivak's theory of Subalternity does not seem to me to be a theory of 'native agency' at all, but a theory of the way in which disenfranchised elements of 'native' population are represented in the discourse of colonialism. The subaltern is for Spivak not a colonised person but a

---

[26] Christopher L. Miller, *Blank Darkness: Africanist Discourse in French* (Chicago: the University of Chicago Press, 1985), 6.

[27] Miller, *Blank Darkness,* 11.

discursive figure in a battery of more or less integrated dominant cultural texts. [28]

It can be added here that Spivak's reading of literature, which is part of the cultural arena, shows that she is mainly concerned with how literature played a role in the construction of the 'native informant' as a savage. This construction supported the colonial expansion under the pretext of the civilising mission. As Lazarus clarifies, Spivak's effort is not for liberating the colonised person but to raise awareness of the risks of endowing this discursive figure, the wholly Other, with speech within the text. Even her choice of *Foe* must not be taken at face value. The text is not about Friday fighting for freedom. Rather, it is about Susan trying to free him as a form of benevolence that consolidates the self: Spivak herself quotes Susan admitting: "[h]ow can Friday know what freedom means when he barely knows his name?" (100). Spivak implies that the concern should be with what Friday wants, with Friday's call which Susan is unable to listen to. Spivak is not speaking of struggling against colonialism or imperialism and this is clear in her reading of Friday, a reading which refuses to fix Friday's reactions as resistance, as will be explained in the next section through contrasting the outcome of the project of soul-making in *Robinson Crusoe* to its counterpart in *Foe*.

The last scene in Defoe's text

Spivak highlights the claim of the success of Defoe's Crusoe in soul-making through reference to the last scene of *Robinson Crusoe*. She does this with the aim of showing how the staging of the relationship between Susan and Friday in *Foe* contrasts with the relationship between Crusoe and Friday in *Robinson Crusoe*. Whereas in Defoe's text Friday is turned into a domesticated servant, Friday in *Foe* is the subaltern whose voice cannot be accessed, and who cannot be turned into a copy of the self and consequently cannot be domesticated. *Defoe's* Crusoe, Spivak argues, does not need to learn the marginal language; rather he teaches Friday English. Friday escapes his Otherness and becomes not only domesticated but also an example of the successful colonial subject because he "learns his master's speech, does his master's work, happily swears loyalty, believes the culture of the master is better, and kills his Other's self to enter the

---

[28] Neil Lazarus, "National Consciousness and the Specificity of (post)colonial Intellectualism," in *Colonial Discourse/Postcolonial Theory,* edited by Francis Barker *et al* (Manchester: Manchester University Press, 1994), 205.

shady plains of northwestern Europe."[29] Despite this success in exceeding
the line separating savagery from civilisation, Spivak contends, Defoe
allows Friday to reinforce his savagery in the last scene. In this scene,
Friday offers to entertain the foot-store company that escaped from wolves
with a huge and dangerous bear. He speaks in English to the bear which
understands the language and tone. Then, Friday and the bear dance
together in the trees and finally Friday kills the bear by shooting it in the
ear. Spivak stresses that by replacing the spear with the gun, Defoe's
Friday crosses the line separating animal from human. The master here is
the spectator of this crossing. Spivak implies here that there is no
encounter where both master and servant participate; Crusoe only teaches
and watches the result. He does not listen to Friday or learn from him what
the wholly Other needs.

Spivak contrasts this scene to what happens in Friday's two writing
lessons with which Susan's narrative ends. On the first occasion, Friday
shows a sign of withholding:

> While Foe and I spoke, [Friday filled] his slate with open eyes, each set
> upon human feet: row upon row of eyes upon feet: walking eyes [...]
> 'Give! Give me the slate, Friday!' I commanded. Whereupon, instead of
> obeying me, Friday put three fingers into his mouth and wet them with
> spittle and rubbed the slate clean (147).

Spivak quotes this passage and comments saying: "[a]re those walking
eyes rebuses, hieroglyphs, ideograms, or is their secret that they hold no
secret at all? Each scrupulous effort at decoding or deciphering will bring
its own rewards; but there is a structural possibility that they are
nothing."[30] When asked by an interviewer about considering Friday's
withholding as a type of resistance, a graphemic resistance, Spivak
answers that we can read it as resistance if we want to make it politically
useful. This means that Friday's withholding can be read as resistance if
one wants to support native agency and nationalism as counter-narratives
of imperialism, and perhaps Spivak is alluding to Parry who accused her
of ignoring native resistance. However, for her part, Spivak follows the
Derridean warning that there is no one reading that can be the right one
and that a sign may hold no secret at all. When Derrida comments on
Nietzsche's sentence "I have forgotten my umbrella," he says:

> That inaccessibility though is not necessarily one of some hidden secret. It
> might just as easily be an inconsistency, or of no significance at all. What

---

[29] Spivak, "Theory in the Margin", 169.
[30] Spivak, "Theory in the Margin," 171-2.

if Nietzsche himself meant to say nothing, or at least not much of anything, or anything whatever? Then again, what if Nietzsche was only pretending to say something?[31]

With maintaining the possibility of Friday's slate having no secret at all, Spivak prefers describing his reaction as 'the withholding of writing' rather than resistance. She argues that this withholding can also be distancing oneself from the resistance from above. By the resistance from above Spivak means the resistance in the meaning which can be interpreted as native agency. Although Spivak herself does not try to fix the subaltern voice towards the formation of native agency, she considers that her effort inevitably forms a part of this resistance from above and therefore she admits:

> What is happening here is the withholding of something which might in fact not have the meaning of resistance that we want to give it, in order to make it politically useful. That's very different from resistance as such. In my position as a senior U. S. academic [...] whether I want it or not, however much I work against it, I *am* part of a resistance from above from which Friday is withholding his writing. [32]

Friday's withdrawal might be an attempt at guarding his voice against being usurped or represented by those who resist from above trying to interpret his voice in their own way and to decide what is good for him without listening to him in the same manner Susan does. Hence, if we insist on reading Friday's withholding as resistance, then we are imposing two things on him: first that every sign must have a fixed meaning and second that we can know and represent this meaning. Remembering that her effort is part of the resistance from above leads Spivak to prevent herself from fixing the meaning of Friday's withholding as resistance. The implication that one can get from Spivak's argument is that if one reads Friday's behaviour as resistance, then one is acting like spectators of Friday watching him while forming native agency, just as Defoe's Crusoe is the spectator of Friday when the former watches the latter stepping out of the margin of savagery. Thus, Spivak refrains from the politically useful reading, preferring the ethical reading. She wants us to see Friday's walking eyes as an inaccessible secret as Derrida, in *The Gift of Death,* considers that in the relationship with the absolute Other there is always a secret that is for no one to reach. In other words, *Foe* is a novel that stages

---

[31] Derrida, *Spurs*, 125-18.
[32] Gayatri Chakravorty Spivak, "Naming Gayatri Spivak," *Stanford Humanities Review* 1:1 (1989): 95.

the failure of reading the subaltern as a copy of the self not only because Susan is unable to access Friday's secret but also because those who resist from above, like Spivak herself, cannot. For Spivak, then, the relationship with Friday is the experience of the impossible because it has not been fully lived. It is a matter of waiting, due to Friday's inaccessible secret, and this is what Spivak indicates by saying: "[t]he answers may be in that margin that we cannot penetrate, that we must indeed ignore to go forward."[33] This going forward in Spivak's statement implies the waiting for the future of the relationship with the wholly Other. By ignoring the margin, Spivak does not mean turning a deaf ear to native agency; rather she means that one should avoid fixing that margin and keep one's relationship to the singular marginal as an experience that is yet to be fulfilled. By maintaining the indeterminacy of the margin and going forward, Spivak shows us how her effort relates to affirmative deconstruction because she implies that theory might be more productive because it says 'yes' to the past and 'yes' to the future and will maintain the open end.

The second writing lesson ends Susan's narrative when she beholds Friday dressed in Foe's clothes and writing a series of the letter *o*. Foe takes this as a promising beginning. He says: "'[i]t is a beginning,' [...] 'Tomorrow you must teach him *a*'" (152). Spivak contends that one can disagree with Foe and that *o* could be omega, which means the end and this negates the promise of future writing lessons. The promised lesson does not take place in the novel because it is here where Susan's narrative ends. From another perspective, Spivak has earlier reminded her readers of the use of *'O'* in *Robinson Crusoe* where Friday explains to Crusoe that *'O'* stands for his native people's prayer. She argues that the *'O'* of Friday's people is one of examples of the negation of reason; it is unreason. In other words, Spivak explains that as Defoe's Friday is not easily convinced of Christian doctrines through God's word, so is Coetzee's Friday not convinced of writing as a way of telling his story. For Spivak, Susan, as a teacher of writing, is like Defoe's Crusoe who is not a good religious instructor unable to help Friday, "the merely reasonable savage," access the doctrine of Christianity or revelation.[34] Similarly, Susan encounters the dilemma of making writing accessible to Friday.

Spivak states that Coetzee stages a message between the margins of the first and second days of the writing lessons: "[h]ere is the guardian of the margin. Neither narrative nor text gives pride of place to this bit; miming

---

[33] Spivak, *Critique,* 190.

[34] Spivak, "Theory in the Margin," 171.

the active marginalizing of the margin perhaps."[35] Although Susan expresses her belief that she has control over her story and that she can withhold whatever she wants, it is Friday who actually withholds his story. Spivak also says that Friday is "the curious guardian at the margin" towards the end of her section on *Foe.*[36] Using the preposition *'at'* here is significant, as Ray argues, saying:

> Christophine is imagined by Rhys as the guardian of the margin and is therefore allowed voice within the main text. She speaks from the margins to the center in the language of the center but then must withdraw since such penetration of the center by the margins necessarily entails consequences of which Christophine is well aware. Such margin-center interactions are rendered impossible in *Foe* because Friday is not a guardian of the margins but a guardian at the margins.[37]

In fact, Spivak uses both forms: 'guardian of the margin' and 'guardian at the margin.' As Ray contended, Spivak implies that Friday guards the margin against being constructed by the dominant discourses represented by Susan and Mr. Foe. However, Friday does this while he remains at the margin and this is the success which the novel achieves by not trying to displace the subaltern and give him an identity and a voice, a success that justifies Spivak's choice of this text in contrast to the previous three. Spivak believes that there is always a space of withholding for colonialism and any metropolitan anti-colonialism. This withholding may not be a secret, but it still cannot be unlocked. She adds that the 'native' is a victim as well as agent when he/she guards the margin. One can conclude from this that Friday is a victim because he is not listened to and is an agent because he will not allow the manipulation of any voice or identity constructed as his own.

Mr. Foe

As far as Mr. Foe is concerned, Spivak says that previous to Derrida's paper, "Politics of Friendship", presented in a seminar on law in 1988, she wanted to conclude that Mr. Foe is everyone's foe because he is the violator without whom nothing can be cited. Having listened to Derrida's seminar paper, Spivak changed her opinion concerning considering Mr. Foe as enemy. Instead, she maintains: "I want to say now that this *Foe* in

---

[35] Spivak, "Theory in the Margin," 171.
[36] Spivak, "Theory in the Margin," 172.
[37] Ray, *Gayatri Chakravorty Spivak*, 44.

history, is the site where the line between friend and foe is undone. When one wants to be a friend to the other, it withdraws its graphematic space. Foe allows this story to be told."[38] In other words, the novel illustrates an example of the relationship between Susan and Friday, the wholly Other, which precedes any relationship. Any third party comes after this relationship. Thus, Mr. Foe is neither friend nor enemy; he is only a witness of this relationship that remains as an experience of waiting.

Spivak says that she could read Mr. Foe in this way because she also read *Moral Luck* by the English moral philosopher Bernard Williams. Williams declares that moral value is conditioned by luck. To him, past philosophers of morality like Kant considered humans' experiences of agency had already been tidied up in accordance with the simple image of rationality. Williams argues:

> Anything which is the product of happy and unhappy contingency is no proper object of moral assessment, and no proper determinant of it, either. Just as, in the realm of character, it is motive that counts, not style, or powers, or endowment, so in action it is not changes actually effected in the world, but intension.[39]

By evoking Williams' discussion of moral luck, Spivak implies that one needs not judge Foe depending on the consequences of his endeavour. This also applies to theory which for Spivak "has no con-sequence. It is autosequential rather than automatic."[40] It is through her opinion of Mr. Foe that Spivak expresses her ideas about theory, For Spivak, then, theory is again a witness of any relationship with the wholly Other and therefore, theory must not provide answers or give voices.

The last section of *Foe*

Spivak draws her readers' attention to Susan's desire to father her story and then discusses how the struggle between fathering and mothering is tackled in the novel through Susan's and Foe's intercourse. In addition, she illustrates the openings that result from this intercourse in terms of encountering the subaltern. To better understand Spivak's argument, one needs some textual details surrounding this intercourse. Early in the same evening, there has been a gathering in Foe's flat, including Susan and the

---

[38] Spivak, "Theory in the Margin," 175.

[39] Bernard Williams, *Moral Luck* (Cambridge: Cambridge University Press, 1981), 20-21.

[40] Spivak, "Theory in the Margin," 175.

girl who claims to be her daughter. Susan still insists on her doubts about this daughter whom she thinks is unlike her in many ways. However, she kisses and embraces the girl, who leaves soothed and cheerful. Afterwards, Susan says: "[the girl's] appearances, or apparitions, or whatever they were, disturbed me less now that I knew her better" (136). When they are left alone, Foe, "with a seducer's touch," asks Susan to stay with him during that night.[41] When they are in bed, Susan claims: "'a privilege that comes with the first night' [...] Then I drew off my shift and straddled him (which he did not seem easy with, in a woman). 'This is the manner of the Muse when she visits her poets,' I whispered" (139).

Several critics regard this scene as a reversal of male and female roles. For example, Sue Kossew says that Susan's desire to be "not just Muse and Mother, but also 'father' to her story, refusing to take on the traditionally subservient role of female Muse. This takes the form of a sexual encounter with Foe, with Susan 'straddling the poet.'"[42] Spivak, for her part, does not take this incident as Susan's success in rejecting mothering and in fathering her story. For her, the roles of father/mother or male/female are not reversed here. They are only presented as undecidable due to the male author's difficulty in imagining the woman and "negotiating a gendered position."[43] Spivak poses two questions that reveal this undecidability. First, Spivak thinks of what meaning the term 'father' could take in the novel by asking: "Is that authoritative word *father* being turned into a false but useful analogy (catachresis) here?"[44] The name 'father' as authority does not exist in the novel. Perhaps, Spivak thinks of the term as catachrestic because Mr. Foe is unable to write Susan's story as he wishes it to be. Susan also cannot be a father figure since she cannot write the story according to her wish either. Thus, Spivak negates the previous readings that advocate a reversal of roles. The second option is implied in Spivak's next question: "Or is Coetzee's Susan being made to operate a traditional masculist topos of reversal and making Foe 'gestate?' We cannot know."[45] This question brings the text into comparison with Shelley's *Frankenstein* where Frankenstein is, as it were, given an artificial womb. Thus, like Frankenstein, Foe has acquired feminine properties.

---

[41] Spivak, "Theory in the Margin," 173.
[42] Sue Kossew, *Pen and Power: A Postcolonial Reading of J. M. Coetzee and André Brink* (Amsterdam: Rodopi, 1996), 168-9.
[43] Spivak, "Theory in the Margin," 162.
[44] Spivak, "Theory in the Margin," 162.
[45] Spivak, "Theory in the Margin," 162.

Spivak makes this indeterminacy about male/female roles useful by arguing that this intercourse is a combination of fathering and musing which promises a different kind of future writing. She specifically reads this in the interval that follows Susan and Foe's intercourse which paves the way for new inspirations. After this scene, Susan feels drowsy but Foe speaks about the sea monster. He remembers Susan mentioning Friday's floating among petals and says: "[t]o us [Friday] leaves the task of descending into the eye" (*Foe*, 140-1). Spivak contends that the sea monster is an image derived from *The Tempest.* As in her reading of *Frankenstein,* Spivak here is referring to Caliban the character that she, depending on Retamar, thinks as representing the wholly Other. As she sees Caliban as a blankness surrounded by an interpretable text, she implies that Friday is also a blankness that cannot be filled. Spivak argues that the image of the sea monster is what allows the unidentified 'I' that is the narrator of the last section of *Foe* to visit Friday's home where bodies are their own signs. The implication that we can get from this argument on Spivak's part is that Susan's scene of fathering and musing produces this indeterminate 'I' that ignores the writing lessons given to Friday according to Foe's directions and alerts us that there is a place, a margin, where there is another kind of signification which must be attended to even if the ability to decipher is rendered as an experience of the impossible.

Towards the end of her discussion of *Foe,* Spivak tries to answer the question: Does the book *Foe* recover the margin? The answer in Spivak's opinion is 'no.' The only consequence of this text is undoing Defoe's *Robinson Crusoe.* It deconstructs the subject formation or soul-making project. Friday becomes the arbitrary name for the margin before which we should halt. Spivak finds this deconstruction in the last section of the novel. The last section, Spivak argues, represents an easy reading because the unidentified 'I' who visits the wreck, where the captain and Susan are found dead, finds Susan's unpublished book. Her text, contrary to *Foe,* starts without quotation marks and it is addressed to Mr. Foe. The subject position of the reader is filled with this 'I' – not Foe since the book does not reach him. In addition, Susan is the one who wrote the book and she is not quoting from Defoe. The last section even denies the presence of both *Robinson Crusoe* and *Foe.* Spivak says:

> Nothing is cited, everything is at once real and fantastic, all the permissible indulgences of narrative fiction in the narrow sense are available to the reader, sole shifter on this trip. The ride is smooth, the trip leads not to Crusoe's island but to the second wreck, where Susan Barton lies fat and

dead. *Robinson Crusoe* has not been written, and *Foe* is annulled, for now Barton will not reach Crusoe's island.[46]

Spivak also illustrates that the last section of *Foe* confirms the presence of Friday with his body as his sign. She wonders whether the text's confidence in Friday's presence is guaranteed. In other words, what if Friday does not exist even in the shipwreck? However, Spivak suggests that this confidence in the existence of the margin is what is generating texts and that texts form an expression of the wish to penetrate the margin. Spivak implies that Coetzee's text is a journey towards fulfilling this wish and it is an experience that cannot be fully lived in the first sections of *Foe* because, as Spivak suggests:

> But we cannot hold together, in a continuous narrative space, the voyage of reading at the end of the book, Susan Barton's narrative, and the withheld slate of the native who will not be an informant. Perhaps that is the novel's message: the impossible politics of overdetermination (mothering, authoring, giving voice to the native 'in' the text.[47]

In analysing *Jane Eyre*, *Wide Sargasso Sea* and *Frankenstein,* Spivak has shown that there has always been a claim that the western subject can domesticate the 'native subaltern female' constructed in texts as the savage. However, Spivak detected slippages that deconstruct this claim in the texts discussed in the previous chapters. In reading *Foe,* she shows that this text does not claim the validity of 'selfing' the subaltern figure. On the contrary, this text stages the failure of the relationship between the self and the subaltern on the basis of domestication; thereby illustrating that there must be a different register of such a relationship which Spivak will discuss in her reading of "Pterodactyl." Susan fails in attending to Friday's call, but in "Pterodactyl" there is an example of success in listening to the subaltern and acting according to ethical responsibility. An important conclusion that can be drawn from Spivak's reading of *Foe* is that as readers of literature, we must abandon the resistance from above which means reading the subaltern withdrawal as resistance only because we want it to be resistance. Spivak's call is for avoiding giving determined political meanings to the subaltern withholding. It is more productive to understand this withholding as the subaltern's injunction to us to listen to his/her call. There is nothing that can give guaranteed answers for Spivak. However, the important thing is the attempt to listen to the subaltern and then take the decision, as will be discussed in the coming chapter.

---

[46] Spivak, "Theory in the Margin," 174.
[47] Spivak, *Critique,* 193.

CHAPTER SEVEN

"PTERODACTYL, PIRTHA AND PURAN SAHAY": THE ETHICAL ENCOUNTER WITH THE SUBALTERN

In *A Critique of Postcolonial Reason,* Spivak adds her reading of "Pterodactyl, Pirtha, and Puran Sahay" to "Three Women's Texts." This novella was written by the Bengali journalist, author and activist Mahasweta Devi. It was first published in Bengali in the Bengali literary journal *Pratikshan* in 1987. In 1993, "Pterodactyl" appeared in English in *Imaginary Maps,* translated by Spivak herself. This book starts with a conversation between Spivak and Devi followed by the translator's preface. Part of Spivak's commentary on "Pterodactyl" appears in her appendix at the end of *Imaginary Maps,* another part in *A Critique of Postcolonial Reason,* and another can be found in *Death of a Discipline* (2003). Almost every study written in English about Devi refers to Spivak's reading which has become so influential to the extent that we read comments like: "[reading] Mahasweta in English, is to some degree, reading Spivak,"[1] or "for better or worse, we are indebted to Spivak for setting the terms of critical engagement for Mahasweta Devi's works."[2] As for Devi herself, the significance of Spivak's translation and theorisation of her work is that her stories are internationally published and read. This has allowed the suffering of Indian tribals to reach the world after long years of Devi's effort to develop the subject.[3]

---

[1] Jennifer Wenzel, "Grim Fairy Tales: Taking a Risk, Reading *Imaginary Maps,*" in *Mahasweta Devi: An Anthology of Recent Criticism,* ed. Nivedita Sen and Nikhil Yadav (New Delhi: Penecraft International, 2008), 167.
[2] Nivedita Sen and Nikhil Yadav, "Introduction," in *Mahasweta Devi: An Anthology of Recent Criticism,* 21.
[3] Mahasweta Devi, "Speaking with Mahasweta Devi: Mahasweta Devi Interviewed by Gabrielle Collu," ed. Gabrielle Collu in *Mahasweta Devi: An Anthology of Recent Criticism,* 222-223.

After briefly summarising what "Pterodactyl" presents, the chapter will discuss the relationship between Spivak as translator and Devi since this relationship makes Spivak's reading of this text different from her reading of the previous ones. Then, the chapter will discuss how Spivak views this text as a good example of the ethical encounter with the subaltern through discussing the characters' as well as the author's refusal to be 'native informants.' The chapter will focus on Shankar and the resistance to Development, Puran and his success to make the responsible decision and Bikhia and the pterodactyl as examples of the wholly Other who call for a response from the mainstream Indian.

"Pterodactyl" starts with the Hindu journalist Puran Sahay leaving for Pirtha, a tribal village in the district of Madhya Pradesh, India. People in Pirtha to whom Spivak refers as tribals or aboriginals are dying of a man-made famine. The historical context of the narrative is the green revolution that started in 1961 in India as the Government's reaction to the famine which started in British India in 1943 due to the fact that the British troops neglected food production for reasons related to the Second World War. After independence, the Indian government had to focus on agricultural development, a movement which became known as the green revolution. However, Devi in "Pterodactyl" presents the example of Pirtha to show that during "the government's propaganda about the green revolution, there is a relentless famine in Madhya Pradesh, a supposedly 'no famine' area. Pirtha receives nothing from modern India, and the funds that are embarked for it are siphoned off to build roads that serve the interest of money lending sharks."[4]

In 1991, Devi herself spoke about the suffering of the tribals, saying:

> They [the tribals] do not understand mainstream machination, so although there are safeguarding laws against land-grabbing, tribal land is being sold illegally every day, and usurped by mainstream society all over India, especially in West Bengal. In North Bengal, extensive lands are being converted into tea gardens, fruit orchards. They can't keep their land; there is no education for them [...] They are denied everything.[5]

Thus, we can observe that Devi's description implies that the tribals are suffering mainly because they do not have access to the dominant discourse of mainstream India. In the novella, Puran goes to Pirtha with the aim of preparing a report about this area for his friend Harisharan. There, Puran is introduced to tribals like Shankar who believes that the

---

[4] Sen and Yadav, "Introduction," 15.
[5] Mahasweta Devi, "The Author in Conversation," in *Imaginary Maps,* trans. Gayatri Chakravorty Spivak (Calcutta: Thema, 2001), iii.

state cannot do anything for them. He also meets Bikhia, Shankar's nephew, who drew a cave painting of a pterodactyl, a reptile that lived in the Jurassic Period. Bikhia remains silent. After Puran's arrival, rain falls and the tribals feel indebted to him, believing that he brought them a miracle. It is after this that Puran encounters the pterodactyl that is thought by Bikhia to be the ancestors' soul. Unintentionally, Puran is accepted into the mythic history of the tribals and is trusted by them, and specifically by Bikhia, who allows him to participate in the secret burial of the pterodactyl. Puran feels that the tribals do not want him to tell about their ancestors' soul and he promises not to write a report about it. Realising the harm resulting from the fact that mainstream Indians have not established any communication point with the tribals, Puran leaves Pirtha with the decision that he will not be a distant spectator anymore.

Spivak and Devi

What makes Spivak's reading of this text different from her analysis of the previous ones is that she knows the author well. Minoli Salgado says that Spivak and Devi have "clear class, linguistic and pedagogical affinities."[6] Apart from this, there is a more significant similarity between Spivak's line of thought and that of Devi. Through this similarity, Spivak's shift from the previous texts to this one can be explained. Spivak always stresses the importance of abandoning the discussion of dichotomies like man/woman and coloniser/colonised lest such debates entrench the binaries. She endeavours to move to another stage which is responsibility towards the subaltern by attempting to listen to them, rather than just keeping on criticising colonialism and imperialism. Devi's writings show that she also has the same project and, as Henry Schwarz puts it, "[a]mong the most instructive aspects of Mahasweta Devi's recent work [...] is the relative absence in it of any discussion of colonization or the movement for Indian independence."[7] Her works are more concerned with the nation from within, presenting issues such as national integration after independence. Schwarz adds: "Mahasweta's subaltern perspective unwrites the historical record of colonial subordination and national

---

[6] Minoli Salgado, "Tribal Stories, Scribal Worlds: Mahasweta Devi and the Unreliable Translator," in *Mahasweta Devi: An Anthology of Recent Criticism,* 162.

[7] Henry Schwarz, "Postcolonial Performance: Texts and Contexts of Mahasweta Devi," in *Mahasweta Devi: Critical Perspectives,* ed. Nandini Sen (New Delhi: Pencraft International, 2011), 175.

independence to reveal deep strata of the population that do not recognize these periodizing frames or their liberationist potential."[8]

Spivak personally knows the author and they discussed some points concerning the translation of the text. Besides, Spivak interviewed Devi, allowing the latter to convey the ideas and messages endorsed in her novella. Most commentators on Spivak and Devi agree that this writer-translator relationship is distinguished. However, for Nivedita Sen and Nikhil Yadav, the "disjunction, of course, is between the unimpeachable political commitment of the author and the infamous stridently obscure criticism offered by the translator-critic."[9] While one may agree on the difficulty of Spivak's criticism, one cannot deny that many of the points raised by Spivak about "Pterodactyl" are derived from Devi's interview. Devi's writing and Spivak's theory complement each other as Devi implies in her declaration:

> I don't understand theory much [...] and I haven't read any theory. I always say that all I have read is man. I have seen him, I have known him, and out of that I have written my stories and now so many theories are coming out of it. It's all right. I don't understand so many things. But Gayatri knows. With her I have full understanding. [10]

Reviewing Spivak's translation of Devi's *Draupadi*, the Indian intellectual, Sujit Mukherjee, observes that Spivak's analysis of Devi's stories are placed in a section of the book *In Other Worlds* with the title "Entering the Third World." This entices him to describe Spivak as an "incomparable *dwarapalika* [female doorkeeper]" by whom the "First World" can enter the "Third World" and the door is Devi.[11] In her preface to *Imaginary Maps,* Spivak admitted that there is some truth in this comment saying: "[t]here is some truth in this and I want to perform the doorkeeper's obligation."[12]

Spivak's analysis of "Pterodactyl"

"Pterodactyl" for Spivak is "a story of the journey into the heart (land) of the other."[13] Previously, Spivak demonstrated how eighteenth-century and

---

[8] Schwarz, "Postcolonial Performance," 176.
[9] Sen and Yadav, "Introduction," 22.
[10] Devi, "Speaking with Mahasweta Devi," 222.
[11] Sujit Mukherjee, "Mahasweta Devi's writings – An Evaluation," *Book Review,* XV: 3 (1991): 31.
[12] Gayatri Chakravorty Spivak, "Translator's Preface," *Imaginary Maps,* xxi.
[13] Spivak, *Death of a Discipline*, 66.

nineteenth-century British texts constructed the 'native subaltern female' as savage by recourse to the axiomatics or truth-claims of imperialism. Then, she moved to *Foe* where she presented an example of the author who refused to present a complete narrative of the woman, Susan, and simultaneously refused to give voice to the subaltern, Friday. She also stresses that one should not read Friday's withholding with the aim of giving him the voice we desire as resistance. However, Spivak is adamant in demonstrating that the encounter between Susan and Friday lacks the ethical dimension because Susan in the first three sections of the novel tries to impose her discourse on Friday to endow him with a voice, so that he can complete her own story. Susan is angled towards the subaltern but she does not know how to listen to and be responsible towards him. Within the scope of Spivak's criticism, it can be said that like *Foe*, "Pterodactyl" stages an encounter between the self and the subaltern but it goes a step further from the encounter presented in *Foe* by presenting an example of a responsible encounter in which the subaltern is a participant in producing responses, rather than just a passive recipient of the benevolence represented by the desire to give him/her speech and identity depending on dominant discourses.

The novella is about the singular subaltern who refuses to be a 'native informant.' Spivak says: "[t]he native informant is not a catachresis here, but quite literally the person who feeds anthropology [...] In the story itself there are at least two powerful figures who cannot be appropriated into that perspective."[14] In the texts discussed in "Three Women's Texts," Spivak has selected some figures that she read catachrestically as the 'native subaltern female.' In "Pterodactyl" she declares that she is not reading catachrestically. The two characters who do not accept being manipulated as 'native informants' are Shankar and Bikhia. They abstain from giving information about Pirtha to Puran, the mainstream Indian journalist and by this they guard the margin and the subaltern knowledge. As for Shankar, we must take into account that in light of Spivak's concept of the subaltern, Shankar is not a subaltern figure because he is given voice and expresses what Spivak sees as his resistance to Development.[15] In the text, Shankar is introduced as the most educated man in Pirtha. This could have turned him into an example of the 'native informant,' but it is the following passage that leads Spivak to assert that he cannot be appropriated into such a position. Shankar says:

---

[14] Spivak, *Critique,* 142.
[15] 'Development' is used with capital D because it is thus how Spivak uses it since her article "Supplementing Marxism," in *Whither Marxism*, edited by Bernd Magnus and Stephen Cullenberg (New York: Routledge, 1995).

'I can't see you. But I say to you in great humility, you can't do anything
for us. We became unclean as soon as you entered our lives. No more
roads, no more relief – what will you give to a people in exchange for the
vanished land, home, field, burial ground?' Shankar comes up close and
says, 'Can you move far away? Very far? Very, very far?'[16] (120).

By asking Puran, as a journalist, to move far away, Shankar refuses to
let his voice be appropriated. What Spivak implies is that Shankar does not
want to be the giver of information that can be used by journalism to
publicise Pirtha only through photos and reports written by mainstream
Indians who do not know how to communicate with and listen to the
tribals. Shankar is blaming Development for erasing the tribal history
which can be caught only from songs. The foreigners came and made
tribals subjects and then slaves. He recounts that their land was taken and
that every time they ran away to remain attached to the forest and build
their homes, roads followed them. They did not want roads, schools or
hospitals, the signs of Development which Shankar rejects. Being an
activist in tribal areas, Devi herself witnessed how Development took
away six-year-old boys from Palamu – one of the twenty-four districts of
Jharkhand state, India – and branded their backs as workers in a carpet-
making factory.[17] Interviewed by Spivak, Devi suggests the resistance to
Development as the proper solution for the lack of communication
between mainstream Indians and the tribals. She concludes her interview
with the statement: "[o]ur double task is to resist 'development'
actively."[18]

Spivak's attitude to Development is similar to her attitude to the
civilising mission. Her ideas reveal that she thinks that Development is the
alibi for the world's economic expansion and the subordination of what
was known as the "Third World" to the "First World." Spivak argues that
world organisations, supported by "Third-World" people or governments
having interests in this kind of subordination, lead enterprises in the poorer
countries under the name of aiding them and that Development as such
destroys the lifestyle of the subaltern. In "Supplementing Marxism,"
Spivak says:

For it is impossible to escape the orthodox constraints of a neo-liberal
world economic system which in the name of Development (capital D) and

---

[16] Mahasweta Devi, "Pterodactyl," *Imaginary Maps,* translated by Gayatri
Chakravorty Spivak (Calcutta: Thema, 2004), 120. All subsequent reference will
be to this version and will be introduced as page numbers within parentheses.
[17] Devi, "The Author in Conversation," xv.
[18] Devi, "The Author in Conversation," xvi.

now sustainable removes all barriers between itself and the fragile national economies, so that any possibility of social redistribution is severely damaged. Further, the people who have politico-economic power or consumerist ambitions in much of the old third world share a common interest in and therefore often welcome subordination (invariably represented as aid or collaboration) by dominant global capital.[19]

She also discusses this idea in "Responsibility" where she explains this through the example of the Flood Action Plan (1988). This was a plan for flood control in Bangladesh for which the seven countries in the group involved in this plan donated money. Spivak contends that money was collected and policies were decided without listening to the Bangladeshis about whom she says:

> [T]he Bangladeshi fisher-folk and grass-roots peasants have been used to living with water, even yearly flooding, forever. Every thirty years or so, there are devastating floods. They have learned to bear this, not quite to cope with the extraordinary inundations, but to bend with them and rise again. As for the yearly floods, they have learned to manage them, welcome them, and build a life-style with respect for them.[20]

The consultancies, enterprises and policies, Spivak continues, ignored the fact that Bangladeshi people's rights might be overlooked especially after the organisation is dismantled. In addition, everything in this plan was done according to the standards and requirements of the countries that are the donors since the "de facto law is in the hands of the donors."[21]

Understanding the attitude to western benevolence in Spivak's thought is closely connected with Derrida's ideas of the gift in *Given Time* (1992). In this book, Derrida explains how the gift causes an aporia because it cannot escape the demands of giving and taking. Derrida argues that in order to be genuine, the gift must not be motivated by self-interest and must not entail acknowledgement or recompense even by the polite response 'thank you.' The gift, according to Derrida, can be deployed in many ways. For example, the giver may claim advantage by giving and he may wait for a just response to his giving.[22] When discussing western benevolence like the one offered in Bangladesh in 1988, Spivak shows her awareness of this aporia. She refers to Leonard Sklar, an expert in engineering geology, who said that the "true beneficiaries of the plan will

---

[19] Spivak, "Supplementing Marxism," 114.
[20] Spivak, "Responsibility," 47-48.
[21] Spivak, "Responsibility," 51.
[22] Jacques Derrida, *Given Time,* translated by Peggy Kamuf (Chicago: University of Chicago Press, 1992).

be foreign consultants and contractors who will collect hundreds of millions of dollars in fees, the cost of which will be added to Bangladesh's already crushing foreign debt."[23] Thus, drawing on Sklar's opinion, Spivak declares that the benevolence offered by the FAP is no more than "a bonded donation [which] mortgages the future of the country."[24] What Spivak implies is that this plan with all the efforts and donations is the gift that is deployed to give the donors the advantage as concerns decisions and laws disregarding the Bangladeshi people's desires or rights.

Spivak's concern is not only with FAP itself, but also with the conference that was held in 1993 to give the chance for a dialogue between the proponents of and opponents to FAP. For Spivak, just as in the case of the FAP, decision-making was in the hands of the donors ignoring people's rights, so was the conference another western-centred structure that silenced the subaltern. Spivak's example is Mr. Abdus Sattar Khan who presented a testimony in the conference. It is true that Sattar is not a real subaltern figure and that he was a leader of a peasant movement opposing flood-management methods suggested by the World Bank, but he was presented in the conference as the authentic 'native informant.' Accordingly, Sattar spoke in his own language and style, "an old-fashioned perorative way," trying to offer his native knowledge of the traditional Bangladeshi methods of managing floods.[25] He was given access to an international conference and the place to speak from but actually this was no more than silencing. One of the most important reasons for this, Spivak continues, is the lack of a professional translator from Bengali and the substitute was an imperfect English translation that was read out by another Bangladeshi attendant. What Spivak is adamant to demonstrate here is that if the subalterns do not conform to the western methods of signification and presentation, they will not be listened to. She says that the conference hall was, for the first time during the conference, full of hubbub and this indicates that, though speaking, the 'native informant' is still passive and not participating in the responsibility within the frame of the conference. Spivak comments:

> The way the shape of his words escaped the monumental structuring of the theatre of Old Europe, which determined the 'dialogue,' was pathetically trivial. [...] In order to hear him, "Europe" would need him to represent

---

[23] Leonard Sklar, "Drowning in Aid: The World Bank's Bangladesh Action Plan," in *Multinational Monitor* 13 (1993): 8, quoted in Spivak, "Responsibility," 51, n. 54.

[24] Spivak, "Responsibility," 51.

[25] Spivak, "Responsibility," 60.

responsibility, by reflex, in "Europe"'s way. In other words, he would have to change his mind-set. That is how the old colonial subject was shaped.[26]

Spivak implies that any form of responsibility that requires the subaltern to change his mind-set or signification method for the aim of conforming to the givers, western donors, is not ethical. The responsibility shown at such conferences is the one that does not involve the subaltern, as long as the subaltern is not domesticated, and therefore such a conference is an example of western benevolence which offers solutions without checking whether such solutions are what the subaltern really need. In brief, Spivak considers both FAP and the conference as a form of benevolence where the gift is manipulated to the advantage of the giver at the expense of the subaltern who is silenced by this gift. What Spivak detects in "Pterodactyl" is similar to this argument. Development which Shankar resists is the benevolence presented by the government at the expense of the tribals. Responsibility for Spivak is what happens to Puran when he encounters the subaltern in Pirtha.

Puran Sahay

Spivak parallels Puran with Devi who founded "the radical working-class periodical *Bortika* in which she took the editorial charge of representing marginal writing that included rural peasants, factory workers and tribals."[27] According to Henry Schwarz, Devi as a journalist, "steadfastly criticises the failure of both state and central government policies and practices to a substantial Calcutta-based middle class audience through the daily newspapers."[28] Spivak describes her as an interventionist journalist. Puran is a middle-class Hindu who is placed in a Hindu-majority land where he is a stranger. At the beginning we are introduced into his private life which, in Spivak's opinion, is inscribed within the gender-emancipation of domestic society among the urban lower-middle-class. His wife died and left him a son and the son lives with Puran's mother. The mother fails in convincing Puran to get married. Later, driven by a feeling of loneliness, he decides to marry Saraswati, a teacher, but he fails in developing their relationship and she cannot wait for him anymore. In brief, Spivak maintains that he is presented only as an agent of intellect. Failing to achieve human relationships within this frame, and invited by

---

[26] Spivak, "Responsibility," 61.
[27] Sen and Yadav, "Introduction," 12.
[28] Schwarz, "Postcolonial Performance," 177.

his friend Harisharan, Puran leaves for Pirtha to prepare a report about the tribals' refusal of governmental plans and aids.

Puran succeeds in entering the mythical life of the aboriginals, which means his introduction into subaltern responsibility. Without further textual details, Spivak says that this responsible introduction is staged within the story of funeral rites – which she regards as the heart of the narrative. The context is provided by the tribals who are in mourning for the dead due to viewing a pterodactyl: "[t]hey needed an explanation on the subject of that creature or shadow. They will not get food, water, roads. There will be no hunting. Singing and dancing will become extinct" (113). They think that the soul of the ancestors is angry. Aboriginals' trust in Puran starts when rain falls upon his arrival. They think that he brought them a miracle. It is Harisharan who explains to him saying: "Man! People who have nothing need miracles. For now it's through you [...] now a story will become song [...] and the song will enter the history that they hold in their oral ballads" (144-5). For Spivak, the subalterns in this text are no more passive copies of the self. On the contrary, they are participants because it is they who accept Puran and allow him to share their secret, the appearance of the pterodactyl. Spivak says that "it is they [the tribals] who play subject."[29] In other words, they are not passive receivers of benevolence. Spivak's argument implies that the subalterns accept Puran because they think he brought them what they really want since the rain is what ends their mourning. The rain that comes with him is part of their mythical system and that is why communication has become possible between this mainstream journalist and the subalterns. Hence, the key idea here is communicating with the subaltern in their own ways instead of imposing the dominant discourse under the guise of Development or aid. Later, Puran encounters Bikhia, Shankar's nephew who remains silent all the time. Spivak comments on this encounter in *Death of a Discipline*. Bikhia is so happy with the rain and he tries to entice Puran to a response:

> Bikhia has received his ancestral soul [...] What has Puran received? [...]
> Bikhia keeps pulling him outside and points ahead. Water is running down
> a crack in the rock. Is Bikhia asking him to listen to the music of the
> waters? Puran bunderstands nothing [...] Caves, cave paintings. Bikhia's
> picture. Puran now realizes that the rainfall on the night of his arrival might
> give rise to another legend (144).

When she quotes this passage in *Death of a Discipline,* Spivak changes the word 'a legend' with which the quotation ends into 'a saying.' Spivak does

---

[29] Spivak, *Death of a Discipline,* 67.

not make it clear why she made this change; whether she found 'a saying' a better equivalent for the word used in the Bengali text than 'legend.' However, what is important is how Spivak uses 'a saying.' The answer to Puran's question about what Bikhia is trying to tell him is that the rain will give rise to a saying. Spivak explains that "'a saying' is, literally, 'what is [a person] saying[?]' – a tiny question frozen into a noun, as if ordinary language allows even the object of his [Puran's] understanding to be only a question behaving like an object."[30] The inference that can be drawn from this statement is the following: if Puran's question is answered by the question, 'what is [a person saying]?', then he failed to recognise the correct response to Bikhia's call when Bikhia is pulling Puran and pointing ahead. Spivak concludes that Puran becomes responsible because he fails to find the correct response when "a response has already been entered into myth."[31] In Spivak's opinion, it is this structure that opens the way for responsibility towards the subaltern.

Puran also encounters the pterodactyl that he has first seen in Bikhia's cave painting. The pterodactyl reveals itself to Puran in a material form. It is an empirical impossibility for him as a modern Indian because the pterodactyl belongs to the Jurassic Period, but for the aboriginal Indian it could stand for the ancestors' soul. For Spivak, the two registers, the mainstream and the aboriginal, are aporetic to each other but she says that Devi does not privilege one over the other or judge between them. More importantly, Spivak draws her readers' attention to the fact that Puran encounters the pterodactyl and tries to understand its gaze although she previously says that for Puran the existence of the pterodactyl is empirically impossible. The implication here is that Puran respects the mythical system of the subaltern The passage that Spivak quotes is the following:

> You are moveless with your wings folded, I do not wish to touch you, you are outside my wisdom, reason, and feelings, who can place his hand on the axial moment of the end of the third phase of Mesozoic and the beginnings of Kenozoic geological ages? [...] What do its eyes to tell Puran? [...] There is no communication between eyes. Only a dusky waiting, without end. What does it want to tell: We are extinct by the inevitable natural geological evolution. You too are endangered. You too will become instinct in nuclear explosions, or in war, or in the aggressive advance of the strong as it obliterates the weak, [...] think if you are going forward or back [...] What will you finally grow in the soil, having

---

[30] Spivak, *Death of a Discipline*, 69.
[31] Spivak, *Death of a Discipline*, 69.

> murdered nature in the application of man-imposed substitutes? [...]The
> dusky lidless eyes remain unresponsive. (157-8)

The pterodactyl, in Spivak's reading, is neither a creature of science
fiction nor a symbol. Rather, she prefers to read it as a spectre, saying:
"[Puran] sees the pterodactyl. Or, perhaps, the pterodactyl reveals itself to
him in the peculiar corporeality of the spectre."[32] It is important that
Spivak highlights the fact that it is the pterodactyl that reveals itself to
Puran; this shows that Spivak believes that in this novella the subaltern is
presented as participant in the encounter with the mainstream Indian and
that it is the subaltern who calls for a response from Puran. As for spectre,
Spivak refers here to Derrida's use of the term in *Spectres of Marx*.
Derrida says:

> It [the spectre] is something that one does not know, precisely, and one
> does not know if precisely it is, if it exists, if it responds to a name and
> corresponds to an essence. One does not know: not out of ignorance, but
> because this non-object, this non-present present, this being-there of an
> absent or departed one no longer belongs to knowledge. At least no longer
> to that which one knows by the name of knowledge. One does not know if
> it is living or if it is dead.[33]

Accordingly, Spivak contends that the pterodactyl "remains other; it
cannot dwell, nor can it be buried."[34] Yet, within the fictional scope of the
novella, the pterodactyl dies. Spivak comments on Puran's acceptance of
what he has seen and participation in the burial of the pterodactyl despite
the anthropological information he has read about this Jurassic creature. In
fact, this must not be seen as a paradox. On the contrary, this means that
both registers, the mainstream empirical and the aboriginal mythical, are
presented and respected in the text. This uncertainty surrounding the
pterodactyl's appearance does not lead Puran to deny that the aboriginals
received a message from this appearance. He even tries to receive this
message but he would not receive it in the same manner it is received by
the aboriginals. A communication between Puran and the aboriginals has
been established despite the fact that their registers are aporetic to each
other and this is the ethical encounter which leads to responsibility without
imposing the dominant discourse of the mainstream Indian.

---

[32] Spivak, *Critique*, 144.

[33] Jacques Derrida, *Specters of Marx,* trans. Peggy Kamuf (London: Routledge,
1994), 6.

[34] Spivak, *Death of a Discipline*, 80.

Spivak also concludes that Puran resists the position of the 'native informant' because he refrains from anything which might turn the subalterns into museum objects. Spivak says: "[t]he aboriginal is not museumized in this text."[35] She also says: "Puran has situated his study of anthropology, transcodings of the native informant's speech, as useful but unequal to these encounters [with Bikhia and the pterodactyl]."[36] We can add some textual details to understand why Spivak draws these conclusions. From the very beginning, people in Pirtha ask Puran not to publicise everything he sees because they are afraid of putting "modern man, the media, and foreigners on the trail" (114). They have the desire not to be observed as museum objects; they do not want mainstream people to be their spectators. Puran promises not to take photos or tape anything and he keeps his promise. For example, Bikhia and Puran bury the pterodactyl in an underground river cave with walls replete with pictures of which nobody is aware; nobody knows whether they are old or modern. Spivak refers to these hidden paintings, highlighting the textual lack of interest in making them appear as ancient objects which can be exhibited at museums. This lack of interest in the history of the pictures makes the encounter with the subaltern an ethical encounter; Puran does not look at the subaltern as a source of anthropological information but he tries to attend to the subaltern call and to search for the suitable response.

The appearance of the pterodactyl is not an anthropological phenomenon and also the mourning it causes is not anthropological, as Spivak argues, saying: "[t]his mourning is not anthropological but ethico-political. (Puran has situated his study of anthropology, transcodings of the native informant's speech, as useful but unequal to these encounters [with Bikhia and the pterodactyl]."[37] To understand Spivak's point, one might need to refer to the moment in the text when Puran realises that "[n]o amount of reading on the topic, anthropological surveys, field reports from division officers and *sarpanch* can fill in the absence of explanatory logic that the appearance of this bird has opened for Puran."[38] After seeing the pterodactyl, Puran reads about it but when he compares the bird he saw with the one in the book, he lays down the books lent by Harisharan and then we read the following passage:

> He knows more because he has read the information in the book, and the
> subject of the discussion is physically present in front of him. Yet, he can

---

[35] Spivak, *Critique*, 145.

[36] Spivak, *Critique*, 145.

[37] Spivak, *Critique*, 145.

[38] Sen and Yadav, "Introduction," 34.

know nothing from life [...] modern man is afraid to know life by entering
life. It is much safer to know life by reading books, reading theory. (159)

Puran realises that he cannot merely resort to an anthropological study for
an interpretation of the pterodactyl's gaze and consequently of the tribal's
speech. This interpretation will not be equivalent to their speech. When
Puran leaves Pirtha, he will not mention the pterodactyl because he is
aware that he cannot reproduce the way in which it is perceived in the
aboriginal consciousness. This is the report which Puran does not present
within a journalistic frame. It is this respect for the secrecy and singularity
of the relationship with the singular subaltern which makes Spivak believe
that the relationship between Puran and the subaltern is based on ethical
singularity. This relationship parallels the relationship between Abraham
and God which Derrida explains in *The Gift of Death* to prove that the
relationship with the wholly Other entails singularity and secrecy. Derrida
argues that Abraham was loyal to God at the expense of the others in
general when he decided to sacrifice his son without telling his family or
even his son. Abraham would have done what others would have
described as a crime by being loyal to God and by keeping the secret.
Similarly, Puran has been asked to prepare a report about the tribals'
resistance to the government's aid and plans. This report is meant to be
presented to the public through journalism; it is a report for the others in
general. However, Puran chooses the singular Other when he decides to
keep the secret of the pterodactyl and abstains from publicising what he
has seen in the cave.

In "Responsibility" Spivak argues that responsibility is an intermediary
stage between a call for a response that might be unintelligible – like the
unintelligible smile of Bikhia when rain falls – and starting to act
according to this call. It is actually the decision that follows the subaltern
call and precedes the action according to this call. Puran passes through
this intermediary stage both in his encounter with the pterodactyl and with
Bikhia. Puran does not make sense of Bikhia's look, the cave paintings,
and the pterodactyl's gaze, but he feels that all of them are waiting for his
response and this moves him to love Pirtha and decide to keep their secret
and not to watch from a distance any longer. Puran and all those who want
to approach the subaltern must learn 'love'. Love here is used to simplify
one-to-one responsible encounters, or, in Spivak's terms, love is the
"ethical responsibility-in-singularity."[39] Puran's learning the lesson is
included in the passage which Spivak quotes and calls 'the elegy.' It is
observed by some commentators that the endings of Devi's works "often

---

[39] Gayatri Chakravorty Spivak, "Appendix," in *Imaginary Maps*, 203.

lament the all-pervasive tyranny and injustice that their protagonists are victims of."[40] But for Spivak this elegy is not only a lamentation but a lesson as well. The elegy of "Pterodactyl," which is presented before Puran takes the truck to leave Pirtha, is the following:

> Puran's amazed heart discovers what love for Pirtha there is in his heart, perhaps he cannot remain a distant spectator anywhere in life. Pterodactyl's eyes. Bikhia's eyes. Oh ancient civilization, the foundation and ground of the civilization of India, oh first sustaining civilization, we are in truth defeated. A continent! We destroyed it undiscovered, as we are destroying the primordial forest, water, living beings, the human. A truck comes by. Puran raises his hand, steps up. (197)

This not only shows Puran's responsibility but also Devi's. The elegy also appears before Devi's postscript, and therefore Spivak infers that the subject of the elegy is suspended between the character and the author. Spivak believes that Devi, who discusses the postcolonial state "with minute knowledge, anger, and loving despair,"[41] like Puran has learnt to love and consequently to be responsible.

Spivak argues that after Puran has learnt how to love Pirtha and entered subaltern responsibility, he withdraws. Yet, it is this lesson that makes his withdrawal at the end of the text different from the withdrawal scene of the monster in Frankenstein because the monster is expelled completely from the novel "into an indefinite future."[42] As for Puran, he withdraws into action "within the postcolonial new nation."[43] Spivak does not explain how Puran can act later, but one can draw a conclusion from her statement at the beginning of her discussion of "Pterodactyl" when she contrasts Devi's text with the texts analysed in "Three Women's Texts." Spivak says that instead of the "sympathetic and supportive staging of the situation of the refusal of the withholding of specular exchange in favour of the monstrous colonial subject," Devi's text is associated with "the postcolonial performance of the construction of the constitutional subject of the new nation, in subalternity, rather than, as most often by renaming the colonial subject, as citizen."[44] The issue here is the constituting of the subjects of the new nation but, at the same time, maintaining their subalternity; without changing their mindset or culture. This is a very central point here because to some readers it may appear that Spivak is

---

[40] Sen and Yadav, "Introduction," 14.
[41] Spivak, *Critique,* 143.
[42] Spivak, "Appendix," 207.
[43] Spivak, *Critique,* 143.
[44] Spivak, *Critique,* 141.

contradicting herself when whereas she claims that Devi presents an example of the singular ethical encounter with the subaltern, she also argues that Devi is pushing the subaltern into a hegemony, a structural unity, so that they can be included in the nation.[45] The reference here is to Devi's postscript:

> [In this piece no name- such as Madhya Pradesh or Nagesia – has been used literally. Madhya Pradesh is here India, Nagesia village the entire tribal society. I have deliberately conflated the ways – rules and customs of different Austric tribes and groups, and the idea of the ancestral soul is also my own. I have merely tried to express my estimation, born of experience, of Indian aboriginal society, through the myth of the pterodactyl.] (198)

The novella is about Indian tribals who are not usually approached by mainstream Indians. Spivak declares that "Pterodactyl" speaks about over eighty million original inhabitants in India categorised into three hundred divisions with individual languages belonging to four large language groups. But Devi uses names like Madhya Pradesh in a way that unites the tribals. By so doing, Spivak emphasises, Devi enforces a structural unity upon this vast group in favour of "placing the subaltern into hegemony."[46]

Spivak does not seem convinced of this unifying gesture because the idea of the heterogeneity of the subaltern is the heart of her theory. Therefore, she asks Devi: "[w]ill it be right then to say that you are not trying to keep their separate ethnicities alive," and Devi answers: "[g]eneral tribal as Indian, not only that. They are Indians who belong to the rest of India."[47] Drawing on this quotation, Salgado, who believes that Spivak manipulates Devi's works, declares:

> While Spivak, the translator, is busy advocating the need to address cultural difference and disjunction in Mahasweta's texts, the author herself is keen to focus on the generalized tribal experience in her work and posit the need for the tribal people's insertion into the Indian mainstream – a need, of course, which undermines Spivak's claim that Mahasweta's work punctures nationalist discourse.[48]

It is true that Devi has made efforts to achieve the integration of the tribals in the Indian mainstream not only structurally in a text but also practically. As an activist, Devi has been involved, for example, in the formation of actions of the Tribal Unity Forum in 1986 to stop killing among tribes.

---

[45] Spivak, *Critique,* 142.
[46] Spivak, *Critique,* 141.
[47] Devi, "The Author in Conversation," x.
[48] Salgado, "Tribal Stories," 153.

Spivak does not deny that a kind of collectivity is presented in "Pterodactyl," but her point is that this collectivity cannot be described as nationalism. It is a collectivity that maintains the difference of the subaltern.

When tackling subaltern issues, Spivak rejects two different approaches to collectivity: Fredric Jameson's and Aijaz Ahmad's. She says: "[p]olitically correct metropolitan multiculturalists want the world's others to be identitarians; nationalist (Jameson) or class (Ahmad)."[49] Spivak even insists that Devi's text does not belong to what Fredric Jameson calls 'Third-World' literature. The reference here is to Jameson's "Third-World Literature in the Era of Multinational Capitalism" in which he argues that the structural differences between the culture and tradition of the 'Third World' and those of the 'First World' make the texts of the former unreadable to readers belonging to the latter. The main distinction for Jameson is the national allegory used by 'Third-World' writers:

> All third-world texts are necessarily, I want to argue, allegorical, and in a very specific way: they are to be read as what I will call *national allegories*, even when, or perhaps I should say, particularly when their forms develop out of predominantly western machineries of representation, such as the novel.[50]

Jameson explains that there is no division between the private and the political in 'Third- World' texts and this makes them resistant to the conventional western habits of reading. For example, through a discussion of "Diary of a Madman" by the Chinese author Lu Xun, Jameson tries to prove that psychology in such texts should be read in primarily political and social terms. Spivak criticises Jameson because he generalises from Chinese and African literatures but she does not agree with Ahmad either.

Whereas Jameson sees the 'Third World' as a national collectivity, Aijaz Ahmad advocates class collectivity instead. Ahmad criticises Jameson for considering "nation" a unifying element, declaring that because Jameson depends on the theory of three worlds which can see the 'Third World' only in terms of an experience of colonialism and imperialism, he is left with no other choice but nationalism to describe its literature. Disagreeing with the idea of a coherent "Third-World" literature, Ahmad offers class as a substitute for nation. He can only see the unity of the globe in terms of the struggle between capital and labour:

---

[49] Spivak, *Death of a Discipline,* 56.
[50] Fredric Jameson, "Third-World Literature in the Era of Multinational Capitalism," *Social Text* 15 (1986): 69.

"societies in formations of backward capitalism are as much constituted by the division of classes as are societies in the advanced capitalist countries."[51] For example, he offers examples from nineteenth-century Urdu literature which are more connected with the rise "of a new kind of petty bourgeois who was violating all established social norms for his own pecuniary ends."[52] However, for Ahmad the struggle between capital and labour does not function in the same way in all "Third-World" countries.

Spivak wants to avoid such binaries, insisting that collectivity can appear in more unexpected manoeuvres as is the case in "Pterodactyl." For her, it is difficult to associate Devi with an "ism." Collectivity in Devi's work cannot be studied in terms of political concepts like nationhood, citizenship, constitutionalism and others exported from the European Enlightenment, and for which "no *historically* adequate referent may be advanced from postcolonial space."[53] The collectivity here is that which cannot be contained by nation and which is "outside organized labor."[54] Spivak explains why collectivity in "Pterodactyl" cannot be understood in the frame of nationalism by saying that when independence was achieved, the tribals were not recognised and thus when the reversal of colonialism/nationalism took place, it did not cover the tribals. This exclusion is emphasised by Devi who tells Spivak that although "they fought bravely against the British, they have not been treated as part of India's freedom struggle."[55] The subalterns are consequently doubly marginalised by the colonisers during the age of imperialism and by the Indian elite after independence.

For Spivak, "Pterodactyl" is a text in which "the inevitable themes of tradition and modernity, collectivity and individualism may be in play in many different ways."[56] Of course, this is clear in Spivak's analysis of Puran entering the mythical collectivity of the tribals with his inability to go native. In addition, Spivak discusses aboriginal collectivity in "Pterodactyl" in terms of the relationship with nature which is very complicated as Spivak suggests:

---

[51] Aijaz Ahmad, "Jameson's Rhetoric of Otherness and the 'National Allegory,'" *Social Text* 17 (1987): 9.
[52] Ahmad, "Jameson's Rhetoric,'" 20.
[53] Spivak, "More on Power/Knowledge," in *The Spivak Reader*, 164.
[54] Spivak, "More on Power/Knowledge," 164.
[55] Devi, "The Author in Conversation," iii.
[56] Spivak, *Death of a Discipline,* 66.

Subaltern aboriginal groups read "nature" with uncanny precision. Their weather predictions, altogether confined in geographical scope, are always astonishing to someone less used to living in the eco-biome. The fictive nature of their inclusion of Puran as rainmaker is therefore more complex than a lack of 'scientific' savvy.[57]

Nature is an important element in Devi's work and this is related to the issue of forest dwellers. The old relationship between tribals and the forest is not only dependent on its being their source of livelihood. The forest is also associated with their traditional system of farming which is imbued with religious sentiment and mythical expression. Because of their sensitivity to nature, the tribals possess knowledge that gives them access to deep parts of the forest. This knowledge can be fully appreciated or comprehended only by the tribals themselves. Colonialism introduced technology to use nature for industrial purposes, thereby rupturing the tribal social organisation. Devi explains how the tribals' lands have been usurped by mainstream Indians using false tribal names. She says that they cannot keep their lands and they are denied everything although they "understood ecology and the environment in a way we cannot yet imagine."[58] The fact that there is a sense of collectivity in the text does not contradict Spivak's belief that "Pterodactyl" is a text that addresses cultural heterogeneity because the collectivity presented in the text maintains the locality and lifestyle of the tribals who want to run away from roads. Devi tries adamantly to show that mainstream people should listen to the tribal's desire to live in the forest and keep his lands. Spivak herself has learnt this lesson and she used to go to tribal areas to listen to the subaltern. In an interview, Devi says that Spivak used to go with her to tribal areas and that once tribal women composed songs expressing their sadness because Spivak was going to leave after staying for six days and sharing their life. Devi quotes Spivak saying: "'I go to the villages to learn, not to teach. I go to learn. I listen to them, in reverence.' It's fantastic. It is quite an experience to go with Gayatri to the remote tribal areas."[59]

Furthermore, the collectivity offered in "Pterodactyl" is the collectivity which includes the subaltern in the Indian mainstream but which at the same time maintains the subaltern situation through respecting the tribals' relationship to their myth and to nature. This is what Spivak means when she says that Devi is associated with constituting the new subject in

---

[57] Spivak, *Death of a Discipline,* 68.
[58] Devi, "The Author in Conversation," ii.
[59] Devi, "Speaking with Mahasweta Devi," 223.

subalternity, not as a citizen. Citizen is a term which resulted from the reversal of the colonial/the national and it is a term which is not appropriate to refer to the subalterns since from the very beginning it did not include them. Again, it should always be remembered that Spivak does not exclude collectivity completely because she believes in it as a strategy for political action. However, her own concern as a critic is with the subaltern as a discursive figure in cultural texts. Devi's text does not allow us to constitute the subaltern as a sign with a fixed meaning, consciousness and speech and this is what is most important for Spivak. For her, political activism and decision making must be accompanied with singular encounters with the subaltern. These encounters are the experience of the impossible which according to Derrida is the experience that cannot be fully lived. Perhaps, Spivak concentrates on Puran's decision not to watch from a distance because it is a promise of a future that is still to come and a relationship that is yet to be fulfilled. This deferment or waiting for the fulfilment of the relationship with the subaltern is in itself a characteristic of the experience of the impossible.

Puran abstains from any representation of what he has seen in the report. This unwritten report reaches us only in the rhetorical space of the novella and as Morton declares, the narrative of the pterodactyl is an "unrepresentable sign" of subaltern knowledge.[60] Even by placing her postscript outside the text, Devi demonstrates that responsibility for the subaltern cannot be achieved only through learning about them in literature or socio-historical documents. Spivak implies that Devi is warning us that her text is her own experience and that we must not take it as a source of learning about the subaltern. Devi, Spivak continues, assures us that she will not be a 'native informant' who "feeds anthropology."[61] Spivak, in turn, refuses "to museumize Mahasweta Devi as the authentic witness of tribal living and being," as Ray observes.[62] In "Three Women's Texts" Spivak argues that the philosophy of the Enlightenment and British fiction were the sources of the image of the Other as savage because it was read as a true representation and this supported the civilising mission. Here, Spivak warns against committing the same mistake and argues that postcolonial texts should be read with the recognition that truth in fiction is aporetic: she says: "[w]e cannot 'learn' about the subaltern only by reading literary texts, or, mutatis mutandis, sociohistorical documents."[63] In other words, the novella only presents an example of the experience of

---

[60] Morton, *Gayatri Spivak,* 33.
[61] Spivak, *Critique,* 142.
[62] Ray, *Gayatri Chakravorty Spivak,* 39.
[63] Spivak, *Critique,* 142.

encountering the subaltern which Devi is inviting her readers to do. Everyone can do what Puran has done to achieve communication with the singular subaltern and perhaps by encountering the subaltern on a one-to-one basis helps each one of us make a responsible decision which may or may not be the same as Puran's. Spivak's message is that we must experience ethical responsibility rather than take Devi's example as the stereotypical one just as Puran found that everything is different when he escaped the journalistic sphere which takes facts from a distance and believes them.

Where is the 'native subaltern female' in "Pterodactyl?"

Before discussing Spivak's opinion of the position of the 'native subaltern female' in Devi's text, one should refer to Devi's refusal to be associated with feminism. She declares that she does not consider herself a feminist and she mainly writes about poor people including men, children and women because she believes that "[t]here men, women are not isolated at all."[64] She also says: "Yes, a woman in the poorer class, she suffers because of her class, she suffers because of her body. That is always there. That has to be brought up but that does not mean that I am especially gender-biased."[65]

Spivak argues that what we have in "Pterodactyl" is "an effortfully established rather than effortlessly generalized male scene."[66] She also says that the woman "is in the interstices of Pterodactyl."[67] Spivak's argument then is that Devi intentionally postpones dealing with the 'native subaltern female.' She actually credits Devi for this postponement since she thinks that Devi cannot be taken as representing "Third World feminism" and that feminism is inaccessible to subaltern women.[68] Spivak adds that, due to her political activism, Devi is pushing the subalterns into hegemony, while maintaining their mind-set and culture, so that feminism can be one of the accessible discourses to the 'native subaltern female.' Feminism as it is now still cannot embrace the 'native subaltern female' because there is no ethical encounter with and no ethical responsibility towards this female. Spivak makes it clear that although she does not represent the 'native subaltern female' in the ethical encounter with Puran, Devi still depicts the situation of this female who is not listened to through

---

[64] Devi, "Speaking with Mahasweta Devi," 225.
[65] Devi, "Speaking with Mahasweta Devi," 224.
[66] Spivak, *Death of a Discipline,* 67.
[67] Spivak, "Appendix," 205.
[68] Spivak, "More on Power/Knowledge," 162.

the attitude to family planning imposed by the government. Spivak contends that the "bitter humour with which she [Devi] treats the Government's family planning posters shows us that the entire initiative is cruelly unmindful of the robbing of the women and men of Pirtha of the dignity of their reproductive responsibility."[69] Spivak does not quote the text but if we refer to the text, we will understand her point better. Devi does deal with the issue of family planning with bitter humour as it appears in the Sarpanch's following explanation:

> Yes ... they [the family-planning posters] cover cracks if you put them up on the wall, they stop the cold if you spread them on the floor, I distribute them a lot. But no more than one child! Here you are unjust [...] You can't do family planning in a poor area. A poor household needs many children." (139).

The Sarpanch then explains to Puran how each child in a poor household takes a part in order to provide for the family. Concerning the 'native subaltern female,' as Spivak argued in her participation in the conference on reproductive rights in Cairo (1994), many children may mean the woman's social security and stability.[70] The point that can be drawn here is that these people are very poor and the government, supported by world organisations, wants to deprive them of the right to have children without even asking them about their desire. In their conversation in *Imaginary Maps*, Spivak and Devi reveal that the capitalist system is economically encroaching on the tribals' land to make roads and factories, which as Devi says, takes the subalterns' children. This system which destroyed the barriers between its economy and the fragile economies of the South is making these people poor and marginalised and then sends solutions and aid without listening to them. The capitalist system increases the tribals' poverty and then tries to address the problem of poverty by depriving them of children. Accordingly, Spivak says: "[c]apitalism, based on remote-control suffering, is obliged to reject the model of the acknowledgement of being inserted into responsibility as unprogressive; in order to be able to justify itself to passive capitalist members in society."[71]

In brief, the 'native subaltern female' must be listened to and no solutions must be imposed on her out of the claim that we know the best for her. She must participate in solving her problems. This cannot be achieved through international conferences where feminists from the

---

[69] Spivak, "Appendix," 205.
[70] Spivak, "Public Hearing," 3.
[71] Spivak, "Appendix," 205-6.

North speak in the name of the 'native subaltern female.' The best way in Spivak's estimation is "the slow effort at ethical responding."[72] The example of the ethical responding has been presented in "Pterodactyl" in the relationship between Puran and Bikhia. If we ask ourselves why this encounter privileges the male subaltern, Spivak has provided the answer by arguing that because the woman is doubly marginalised, by neo-colonialism and the male, all discourses of freedom are not accessible to her until subaltern freedom is achieved. Spivak argues that as Devi "works actively to move the subalterns into hegemony, in her struggle in the field, she pushes them toward that other episteme, where the 'intuitions of feminism become accessible."[73] So, this is not a privileging of the male subaltern but an awareness of the complication of the relationship with the 'native subaltern female' as an experience that is yet to come. Above all, Spivak demonstrates that even the freedom of middle-class women is not continuous with subaltern freedom and therefore, Puran's fiancée and Harisharan's wife remain outside the text, being activists in other places. Spivak says that the "narrative of subaltern freedom and even middle-level indigenous female (self-) emancipation cannot yet be continuous."[74] Thus, Devi's text succeeds in preventing us from forming the subaltern figure, male or female, as a sign that can be represented as a voice in the text. Devi's text is an invitation to experience ethical responsibility.

---

[72] Spivak, "Appendix," 206.
[73] Spivak, "More on Power/Knowledge," *The Spivak Reader,* p. 164.
[74] Spivak, *Critique,* p. 144.

CONCLUSION

Through critiquing Spivak's reading of a key cluster of colonial and postcolonial texts, this book has demonstrated a shift in Spivak's approach to literature, the shift towards the ethics of literary interpretation. The previous chapters have shown that this shift has been enabled by two versions of deconstruction: the de Manian and the Derridean. The chapters have also carefully illustrated Spivak's main tools and strategies, the most important of which is the parabasis which enables the process of 'learning from below' with the hope of welcoming subaltern participation in the production of knowledge. This concluding chapter will first discuss the complexity and difficulty of Spivak's literary criticism, a complexity that has been the greatest challenge while writing this book. It will explain why this complexity, contrary to what some critics argue, does not prevent us from speaking of a unified Spivakian theory of literary interpretation. Then, it will summarise Spivak's theory of the ethics of postcolonial literary interpretation, which can be concluded from her reading of the five texts chosen for this book and which will be described as the affirmative postcolonial literary interpretation. Finally, it will refer to Spivak's *An Aesthetic Education in the Era of Globalisation* (2012) to see whether Spivak still calls for the same ideas she has previously advocated, whether literature is still an important domain for her ethics and whether her thought promises other prospects or phases.

The question of whether a unified theory can be drawn from Spivak's literary readings has always been hindered by the complexity and difficulty of her theoretical engagements. One of the aims of this book has been to explore the possibility of finding a consistent theory underlying Spivak's reading of literary texts. There have been different opinions with regard to the complexity of Spivak's writings. Some commentators criticise Spivak for this characteristic in her work and others justify it. For example, Terry Eagleton argues that Spivak's texts are overstuffed and that she wants to say everything at once.[1] Moreover, he criticises her work for the "endless digressions and self-interruptions" in addition to her

---

[1] Terry Eagleton, *Figures of Dissent: Reviewing Fish, Spivak, Žižek and Others* (London: Verso, 2003), 160-161.

"inability to stick to the point."[2] In contrast, Robert Young contends that "[Spivak] attempts a number of things at once, not out of disparateness or lack of focus but as a result of an awareness of the complexity of the undertaking in which she is engaged."[3]

Spivak's difficult writing is due to her strategic use of different theoretical tools. Since 1981, all her tools, whatever their source, have been used for two objectives: revealing the foreclosure of the subaltern and seeking the inclusion of the subaltern in the production of knowledge. Spivak uses the terms 'strategy' and 'strategic' repeatedly in commenting on her own work. One example is her justification of her engagement in essentialist feminism, describing this as 'strategic essentialism.' Spivak makes it clear that strategic essentialism gave her access to feminism and gave her the place to speak from. Then, she justifies introducing anthropology to read Kant 'mistakenly' by saying that Derrida accepted anthropologising philosophy 'strategically' in order for the philosophies of Europe's Others to be included. In her preface to *Of Grammatology*, Spivak admits that she acts like a 'bricoleur,' a term which she takes from the French anthropologist and ethnologist Claude Lévi-Strauss. She quotes Levi Strauss's definition of the bricoleur "as a man who undertakes odd jobs and is a Jack of all trades or is a kind of professional do-it-yourself man,"[4] and explains: the bricoleur "makes do with things that were meant perhaps for other ends."[5] As has been demonstrated in different parts of this book, Spivak resorts to psychoanalysis when she evokes Lacan in reading Kant and *Wide Sargasso Sea*, she evokes Marxism through Althusser's 'interpellation,' feminism as is the case in evoking Barbara Johnson in the discussion of *Frankenstein*; and there are many other examples. However, she uses all these theoretical strands for the main purpose of deconstructing the texts she is reading. Although it makes dealing with her writings difficult and complicated, Spivak's strategic method is not a negative aspect of her work. On the contrary, it shows that she is more concerned with the productivity of theory than with sticking to one approach which may lead to one answer, meaning or solution.

Some critics may find it invalid to give shape to Spivak's work in the form of a unified theory. Such critics rely on Spivak's preference for interruptions to the extent that she even interrupts herself. John Clifford, for instance, considers that Spivak advocates self-deconstruction and,

---

[2] Eagleton, *Figures of Dissent*, 160.
[3] Young, *White Mythologies*, 158.
[4] Claude Lévi-Strauss, *La pensee sauvage* (Paris, 1962), quoted in Spivak, "Translator's Preface" in Jacques Derrida, *Of Grammatology*, xix.
[5] Spivak, "Translator's Preface," *Of Grammatology*, xix.

commenting on her perspective on rhetoric, he considers attributing consistency to her approach a "risk of *accusing* [her] of consistency."[6] He also thinks that analysing Spivak's ideas using a form of writing which belongs to the conventional humanist discourse such as the essay is "the antithesis of Spivak's enigmatic, circuitous, tentative, and contradictory train of thought."[7] One may agree with Clifford's opinion that the complexity of Spivak's theoretical engagements makes her thought, which he describes as certainly containing "rhythms," not instantly accessible. However, this does not mean that it is not possible to find a consistent theory in her writings; even when Spivak herself re-examines her articles to collect them in a book, she becomes a new reader and tries to discover what brings these articles together. She believes that one can draw a theory out of any piece of writing. For example, in the preface of *An Aesthetic Education*, she says that in collecting the essays this book contains she followed "the rule of 'In literary criticism, when you look for something, you find it,'" and then she says: "I've found it."[8]

As this book has revealed, the unifying element of Spivak's theoretical manoeuvres in her chapter "Literature" is deconstruction in its de Manian and Derridean versions. Her theory can be described as: affirmative postcolonial literary interpretation. It is affirmative because, in most of its aspects, it is closer to Derrida's affirmative deconstruction. Spivak analyses literary texts without pre-determined conclusions as she emphasises in an interview, saying:

> So, I try, although this is almost impossible, I try to read deductively in this way. I do not know. Some things can't be helped, but I resist the assumption with which I enter the text, if you know what I mean. Let the book teach you to change your assumptions, or try to have as few assumptions as possible as you look at it.[9]

This means that for Spivak, reading a literary text is the experience of the impossible; she reads a book without pre-determined conclusions and waits for what is coming. In the same interview, she declares that past texts are useful. Examining past canonical texts with no pre-determined conclusions waiting for a non-determined future belongs to Derrida's experience of the impossible; this means that she approaches literary texts

---

[6] John Clifford, "Toward a Productive Crisis: A Response to Gayatri Spivak," *JAC: Journal of Advanced Composition* 11:1 (1991): 195. [emphasis added]

[7] Clifford, "Toward a Productive Crisis," 192.

[8] Spivak, *An Aesthetic Education*, ix.

[9] Spivak, "What is it for? Gayatri Chakravorty Spivak on the Functions of the Postcolonial Critic," *Nineteenth Century Contexts* 18:1 (1994): 76.

traversing through aporias and using whatever tools which come to her hand. It is as Derrida says; "[t]o experience is to advance by navigating."[10] Although Spivak knows her objectives – which are related to the relationship with the subaltern and the 'native subaltern female' – she does not know what will result from her reading with these objectives in mind. She does not know whether the relationship will come and how it will be.

Affirmative postcolonial literary interpretation is affirmative because it says two 'yeses,' one to the past canonical texts and one to the future of the subaltern inclusion. It is an ethical theory which depends on the relationship between two contradictory elements: the dominant discourse of western philosophy and literature, and the subaltern call which may lead to the subaltern participation in the production of knowledge. The gap between the two is filled by ethics. Ethics for Spivak is a matter of relationship, but ethics is an aporia as Spivak herself stresses when she says that ethics is one of the "structureless structures" because it is "neither available nor unavailable."[11] Applied in the field of literary criticism, when a literary critic encounters a subaltern character within a text, the critic should again distinguish between two approaches: 'resistance from above' (benevolence presented by the dominant) and 'learning from below' (responsibility shared by both dominant and subaltern).[12] The gap between the two approaches is also filled by ethics.

Spivak invites us to abandon the 'resistance from above' and adopt the 'learning from below.' In other words, when readers approach any canonical text which presents a subaltern character, they should be aware that they cannot interpret this character's silence or gestures as resistance because, in this way, readers will be using their own discourse. The consequence of this is that readers may claim authority over the subaltern's voice. In addition, 'resistance from above' is the kind of interpretation which achieves self-interest for two reasons. First, like benevolence, reading the subaltern as agent is like doing a favour for her/his since her agency may mean her freedom and then she can become a copy of the western feminist self. Second, fixing the subaltern as a sign means that readers can do away with it as Spivak makes clear when she contends that to have the subaltern speak "is like Godot arriving on a bus.

---

[10] Jacques Derrida, *Points: Interviews,* ed. Elisabeth Weber, translated by Peggy Kamuf *et al* (Stanford: Stanford University Press, 1995), 376.

[11] Gayatri Chakravorty Spivak, "From Haverstock Hill Flat," 17.

[12] Spivak mentions the 'resistance from above' while discussing Friday's withheld slate in an interview by her under the title "Naming Gayatri Spivak" ed. Maria Kounoura, *Stanford Humanities Review* 1:1 (1989). See Chapter Six of this book.

Readers may want it to disappear as a name so that they can all speak."[13] In other words, 'resistance from above' achieves self-interest because the determination of this sign gives us the ground from which we can start to theorise.

Instead, Spivak advocates 'learning from below.' So, the approach of Spivak's theory is affirmative but the strategy is 'learning from below.' In fact, one can explain how 'learning from below' achieves Spivak's aims in the following manner: resorting to 'learning from below,' the reader can approach canonical western texts by applying tropological deconstruction to discover the figures of parabasis which interrupt them allowing the reader to question the norms presented by them. Then, the reader may discover that the subaltern is excluded from such norms and that this foreclosure justified colonialism, neo-colonialism and even globalisation in our age. Finally, this leads the reader to think ethically of the subaltern, a way of thinking which leads to avoiding the kind of representation which usurps and manipulates the subaltern voice. The alternative is, of course, respecting the subalterns, trying to attend to their signification methods when they call for our response and finally taking the ethical decision. Spivak has shown the literary example of this in "Pterodactyl" when Puran abandons all governmental and journalistic representations of the tribals and decides to respect the tribals' desire to protect their culture against being publicised, museumised or encroached on by factories and roads, which only serve economic and capitalist agendas.

As it were, 'learning from below' in Spivak's thought requires us to be involved with both sides, the dominant and the subaltern; one cannot question western texts without having access to the dominant discourse and cannot think from a subaltern viewpoint without encountering the subaltern. For instance, reading of Kant's third critique Spivak says: "if in Kant's world the New Hollander (the Australian Aboriginal) or the man from Tierra del Fuego could have been endowed with speech (turned into the subject of speech), he might well have maintained that [...]."[14] In other words, Spivak tries to imagine what questions the subaltern might have asked had he/she been listened to, questions like: what does Kant's universal of the rational man offer to the 'native informant'? And what does feminism's celebration of the 'female individualist' offer to the 'native subaltern female'? Of course, Spivak's answer is that the 'native informant' and the 'native subaltern female' are excluded from the freedom offered by western texts. This shows that 'learning from below,'

---

[13] Spivak, "Gayatri Spivak on the Politics of the Subaltern," 91.
[14] Spivak, *Critique,* 26.

enables Spivak to play two contradictory roles: the intellectual and the subaltern. However, saying this does not mean that Spivak is taking the position of the subaltern or claiming knowledge of the subaltern consciousness. She is only asking: where is the subaltern? Why is the subaltern represented in terms of the binaries human/not human, civilised/uncivilised or free/bound when he/she does not have access to the role of narrating history? Thus, she is imagining the subaltern position only to reveal the absence of the subaltern voice rather than fill this absence. For her, imagination is the ability of "thinking", not defining, "absent things."[15] Later, in her book *An Aesthetic Education,* Spivak would use 'learning from below' to propose a training of the imagination with the purpose of preparing a generation for the future of the subaltern. Although *An Aesthetic Education* is thirteen years later than *A Critique of Postcolonial Reason,* and although the former is more interested in pedagogy than literary theory, Spivak's approach is still affirmative and her strategy is still 'learning from below,' depending on parabasis. However, before discussing Spivak's persistence in advocating the same approach in 2012, it is useful for Spivak's reader to discover, what has changed for her throughout the years separating *A Critique of Postcolonial Reason* and *An Aesthetic Education.*

In 1999 Spivak tracked the foreclosure of the subaltern which was still ongoing when she published *A Critique of Postcolonial Reason.* She also warned at that time that the postcolonial subject, who had started to be manipulated as the 'native informant,' should refuse to be an informant.[16] She emphasised that if the postcolonial subject became an informant and spoke in the name of the subaltern, the subaltern would remain foreclosed. In *An Aesthetic Education,* Spivak stresses that globalisation is the power which has been increasingly invading the world, including the academic sphere, during the years she has been teaching. This book is a collection of some of Spivak's articles, concerned with pedagogy, published over around twenty-three years with some of them written around the same period as the pieces discussed in the previous chapters. Spivak stresses that when she wrote many of the essays included in *An Aesthetic Education,* globalisation had not fully flourished. Then, the more globalisation flourished the more the study of the humanities was minimalised. Spivak is aware that whereas humanities were useful in constructing the colonial subject during the age of colonialism, in this age of technology and data, literature is not important for the dominant capitalist system which is more

---

[15] Spivak, *An Aesthetic Education,* 16.

[16] Spivak, *Critique,* ix.

interested in the quantity rather than the analysis of available information. Therefore, she states that globalisation has destroyed reading and knowing, which are her main concerns as a critic and an academic.[17]

In addition to globalisation as the main challenge which Spivak's ethical approach encounters, the dilemma which Spivak has emphasised since writing "How to Teach a 'Culturally Different Book'" in 1991 has been the lack of a prepared generation of readers, teachers and students who can read the texts coming from the South without taking them as the generalised cultural representations of the nationality or identity of the people about whom these texts speak.[18] In "How to Teach a 'Culturally Different Book,'" "The Burden of English," and "Teaching for the Times," Spivak tackles issues related to education and curriculum reform as a way of changing the mind-set of readers and students of literature. As a literary critic, Spivak shifts the attention to postcolonial texts. Similarly, as a teacher of literature, she calls for a curricular reform by adding texts from the South to the literary curriculum. It is in *Death of a Discipline* (2003) where Spivak offers one possible way to address the problem of the unprepared mind-set.

In *Death of a Discipline*, Spivak suggests that the discipline of Comparative Literature is where preparing the mind-set for the participation of the literature of the South in the production of knowledge can start. She encourages the learning of languages like Sanskrit, Arabic, Chinese and others and this suggests that she is calling for the inclusion of the literatures written in these languages in the curriculum. At the same time, this implies the importance of reading the texts from the South in the original language rather than in "global English."[19] Thus, in 2003, Spivak's recommendation was including other languages and literary texts in Comparative Literature, but what happened during the period that separated *Death of a Discipline* from *An Aesthetic Education*? In *An Aesthetic Education*, Spivak shows that her ethical approach is still encountering the same dilemma, an unprepared generation in the grip of globalisation. The humanities are more and more minimalised. In the preface and introduction of the book, she reveals an increasing hopelessness in the role which can be played by literary studies and the humanities in general in minimalising the globalised homogenisation. Therefore, Spivak re-emphasises her suggestion of training the

---

[17] Spivak, *An Aesthetic Education*, 2.
[18] Spivak, "How to Teach a 'Culturally Different Book,'" in *The Spivak Reader*, 261.
[19] Spivak uses 'global English" in her essay "How to Teach a 'Culturally Different Book'" in *The Spivak Reader*, 238.

imagination, describing this training as an aesthetic education suitable for the era of globalisation. Of course, this book has been concerned with Spivak's suggestions for the reader of literature, and although these suggestions are inseparable from issues of teaching literature, this is not the place to discuss these issues in detail. Referring to *An Aesthetic Education* here is meant to give an idea of whether Spivak's aesthetic education is based on the same ethical approach she recommended in her chapter "Literature."

Spivak particularly refers to "The Burden of English," the first essay in *An Aesthetic Education*. This essay was originally presented as part of a collection of seminar papers (1988/89) and then published in *Orientalism and the Postcolonial Predicament: Perspectives on South Asia* in 1993. With this essay, Spivak declares, the responsibility of her turn to ethics started because it was concerned with teaching English literature in India.[20] As mentioned in Chapter One and Chapter Two of this book, Spivak highlighted her belief that teaching English literature in colonial India constructed the Indian colonial subject. With Spivak's *An Aesthetic Education,* teaching English literature in colonial India can now be described as the aesthetic education which presented truth-claims. Such truth-claims became the norms and were exploited to justify colonialism. According to the discussion presented in the previous chapters, Spivak started to change her way of thinking in 1981 and used deconstruction as her tool until she achieved the ethical shift in reading postcolonial texts. The ethical shift helped Spivak include postcolonial texts in the production of knowledge in the interest of the subaltern in an age when globalisation, Spivak sees, replaces territorial colonialism and imperialism. However, it seems that Spivak in 1988 realised that ethical attention to the subaltern call, achieved through her approach to reading literature, was not enough and that she must take her responsible decision and displace her ethical approach to the arena of education. Therefore, in *An Aesthetic Education,* she declares the need for "producing epistemological change, rather than only attending upon the ethical, in subaltern and intellectual alike."[21] Hence, this book, published thirteen years after *A Critique of Postcolonial Reason*, still advocates the same ideas: the importance of the role of literature in constructing the subject, now described as aesthetic education, and changing the mind-set, now described as the epistemological change achievable through aesthetic education. In addition, Spivak is still insistent on the importance of her critique of Kant, Schiller and de Man leading to

---

[20] Spivak, *An Aesthetic Education,* ix.
[21] Spivak, *An Aesthetic Education,* 3.

the necessity of committing the intended 'mistake' and parabasis is still one of Spivak's favourite tools. This is clear when she says: "[i]t is still the story of that parabasis that was for me the most sustained lesson of Paul de Man: displacing the lesson of Paul de Man to another theatre."[22]

Above all, in *An Aesthetic Education,* Spivak adds a psychological explanation to her strategy 'learning from below' if this strategy is to be used by a teacher of literature. She stresses the necessity of training the imagination to play the double bind. Spivak uses the concept of 'double bind' in the sense it is used in the work of the English anthropologist and social scientist, Gregory Bateson. Bateson, Spivak argues, suggests that a therapist dealing with a schizophrenic patient can create benevolent double binds for the patient to gradually lead the latter to freedom from the original double bind which caused schizophrenia. The difference between the orginial double bind of the patient and the therapeutic double binds is that the therapist is not himself involved in the struggle; the patient can be healed and the therapist does not live the struggle himself. Displacing this argument to the field of teaching literature, Spivak implies that the role of the teacher of literature should be the same as that of the therapist in Bateson's work. What Spivak is suggesting through the concept of the double bind is that the aesthetic education she is proposing is based on training the imagination of students and readers to play the double binds, the contradictory instructions of intellectual and subaltern, so that they can imagine questions related to the subaltern without thinking that they can speak as or in the name of the subaltern. In this way, it becomes possible to prepare a generation for subaltern participation in the production of knowledge. This training, in Spivak's opinion, is the duty of the educators. In other words, Spivak's message in *An Aesthetic Education* is mainly directed to the teachers of literature. She says:

> In the contemporary context, we can call this double bind of the universalizability of the singular, the double bind at the heart of democracy, for which an aesthetic education can be an epistemological preparation, as we, the teachers of the aesthetic, use material that is historically marked by the region, cohabiting with, resisting, and accommodating what comes from the Enlightenment. [23]

Spivak clarifies that the new aesthetic education is playing the double bind with the intellectual at one end and the subaltern at the other, and in fact Spivak opens her introduction by discussing learning from below as a

---

[22] Spivak, *An Aesthetic Education,* 34.
[23] Spivak, *An Aesthetic Education,* 4.

double bind because it involves both the philosophy of the Enlightenment and the subaltern questions. As for Derrida's influence, again it is still clear in Spivak's thought because the relationship with the subaltern is still the experience of the impossible. It is still something to come and it is the only hope for Spivak.[24]

Now, speaking of the phases of Spivak's career, as shown in the previous chapters, can be re-emphasised. Although this book has not discussed the first phase, it must be said that Spivak's writings during that phase focused on W. B Yeats, some Renaissance poets and also on French feminism and the translation of Derrida's *de la grammatologie*. The second phase ranged over the period of 1981-1988. The year 1981 marks Spivak's shift to third-wave feminism when she highlighted the exclusion of the so-called 'Third-World' woman. After that date, Spivak was busy dealing with the tropological deconstruction of western woman/'native subaltern female' in a series of literary texts. The third phase started with Spivak's reading of Derrida's "Politics of Friendship" while writing the conclusion of her "Theory in the Margin." Spivak then started to go beyond all binaries and to think of the relationship with the subaltern as the experience of the impossible following Derrida's example. This shift was accompanied by Spivak writing about issues related to pedagogy which she took as her ethical responsibility. In her preface to *An Aesthetic Education,* Spivak dates her realisation that her ethical responsibility is advocating an aesthetic education in the interest of the subaltern back to "The Burden of English" presented in the same year as "Theory in the Margin." Thus, the third phase is the phase of Spivak's ethical responsibility.

In conclusion, like Puran in "Pterodactyl," Spivak encountered the subaltern both in literature and outside it.[25] She has respected the heterogeneity of the subaltern and especially the 'native subaltern female.' This respect was followed by ethical responsibility which was behind her decision to displace her ethical approach to the arena of education. Since Spivak has stressed that ethical responsibility is the stage between the subaltern call and action, this means that she is now in the middle stage which promises her readers and students of a new phase which might contain action on the level of academic literary curriculum and syllabus design.

---

[24] Spivak, *An Aesthetic Education,* 2.

[25] Spivak has run teacher training courses in India and she mentions this in many interviews like "Mapping the Present" "Mapping the Present: Interview with Gayatri Spivak," ed. Meyda Yegenoglu and Mahmut Mutman, in *New Formations,* 45 (2001). She also opened schools in rural parts of India.

Bibliography

Primary Texts

Brontë, Charlotte. *Jane Eyre*. London: Penguin Books, 1994.

Coetzee, J. M. *Foe*. London: Penguin Books, 1986.

Devi, Mahasweta. "Pterodactyl." In *Imaginary Maps*. Translated by Gayatri Chakravorty Spivak, 95-198. Calcutta: Thema, 2001.

Rhys, Jean. *Wide Sargasso Sea*, ed. Angela Smith. London: Penguin Books, 1997.

Shelley, Mary. *Frankenstein, or the Modern Prometheus*. London: Penguin Books, 2006.

Spivak, Gayatri Chakravorty. *A Critique of Postcolonial Reason: Toward a History of the Vanishing Present*. Cambridge, Mass.: Harvard University Press, 1999.

—. "Theory in the Margin: Coetzee's Foe Reading Defoe's Crusoe/Roxan." In *Consequences of Theory*, edited by Jonathan Arac and Barbara Johnson, 154-177. London: Johns Hopkins University Press, 1991.

—. "Three Women's Texts and a Critique of Imperialism." *Critical Inquiry*, 12 (1985): 243-261

Secondary Sources

Aijaz Ahmad, "Jameson's Rhetoric of Otherness and the "National Allegory." *Social Text* 17 (1987): 3-25.

Althusser, Louis. *Lenin and Philosophy and Other Essays*. Translated by Ben Brewster. New York: Monthly Review Press, 2001.

Arneil, Barbara. *Politics and Feminism*. Oxford: Blackwell, 1999.

Ashcroft, Bill, Gareth Griffins and Helen Triffin. *Key Concepts in Post-Colonial Studies*. London: Routledge, 1998.

Azim, Firdous. *The Colonial Rise of the Novel*. London: Routledge, 1993.

Berman, Carolyn Vellenga. *Creole Crossings: Domestic Fiction and the Reform of Colonial Slavery*. London: Cornell University Press, 2006.

Bohls, Elizabeth A. "Standards of Taste, Discourses of 'Race,' and the Aesthetic Education of a Monster: Critique of Empire in *Frankenstein*." *Eighteenth-Century Life*, 18 (1994): 23-36.

Brenkman, John. "Narcissus in the Text." *Georgia Review,* 30 (1976): 293-327.

Budgeon, Shelley. *Third Wave Feminism and the Politics of Gender in Late Modernity.* Basingstoke: Palgrave Macmillan, 2011.

Caputo, John D., ed. *Deconstruction in a Nutshell: A Conversation with Jacques Derrida.* New York: Fordham University Press, 1997.

Chakravorty, Swapan, Suzana Milevska and Tani E. Barlow, eds. *Conversations with Spivak.* London: Seagull, 2006.

Childs, Peter, and Patrick R.J. Williams. *An Introduction to Postcolonial Theory.* Essex: Pearson Education Limited, 1997.

Chrisman, Laura. "The Imperial Unconscious? Representations of Imperial Discourse." *Critical Quarterly* 32:3 (1990): 38-58.

—. *Postcolonial Contraventions Cultural Readings of Race, Imperialism and Transnationalism.* Manchester: Manchester University Press, 2003.

Cixous, Hélène. "The Laugh of the Medusa." In *New French Feminisms: An Anthology,* ed. Elaine Marks and Isabelle de Courtivron, 90-98. Amherst: Univ. of Massachusetts Press, 1980.

Clifford, James, and George E. Marcus, eds. *Writing Culture: The Poetics and Politics of Ethnography.* Berkeley: University of California Press, 1986.

Clifford, John. "Toward a Productive Crisis: A Response to Gayatri Spivak." *JAC: Journal of Advanced Composition* 11:1 (1991): 191-196

De Bouvoir, Simone. *The Second Sex.* Translated by H. M. Parshley. London: Jonathan Capt Ltd, 1953.

De Man, Paul. "Kant and Schiller." In *Aesthetic Ideology,* 129-162. Minneapolis: Univ. of Minnesota Press, 1996.

—. "Phenomenality and Materiality in Kant." In *Aesthetic Ideology,* 70-90. Minneapolis: Univ. of Minnesota Press, 1996.

—. *Allegories of Reading*: *Figural Language in Rousseau, Nietzsche, Rilke and Proust.* London: Yale University Press, 1979.

Defoe, Daniel. *Roxana, the Fortunate Mistress.* London: Oxford University Press, 1964.

Derret, J. M. *Hindu Law Past and Present: Being an Account of the Controversy which Preceded the Enactment of the Hindu Code, and Text of the Code as Enacted, and Some Comments Thereon.* Calcutta: A. Mukherjee and Co. 1957.

Derrida, Jacques. "Force of Law: The 'Mystical Foundation of Authority." In *Deconstruction and the Possibility of Justice,* 3-67. Translated by Mary Quaintance. Edited by Drucilla Cornell, Michel Rosenfeld. London: Routledge, 1992.

—. *Points: Interviews*, edited by Elisabeth Weber. Translated Peggy Kamuf and others. Stanford: Stanford University Press, 1995.

—. "Politics of Friendship." *American Imago* 50:3 (1993): 353-391.

—. "The Ends of Man." In *Margins of Philosophy*. Translated by Alan Bass, 111-136. London: Harvester, 1982.

—. *Given Time*, trans. Peggy Kamuf. Chicago: University of Chicago Press, 1992.

—. *Specters of Marx*. Translated by Peggy Kamuf. London: Routledge, 1994.

—. *Spurs*. Translated. Barbara Harlow. Chicago: the University of Chicago   Press, 1979.

Devi, Mahasweta. "Speaking with Mahasweta Devi: Mahasweta Devi Interviewed by Gabrielle Collu," edited by Gabrielle Collu. In *Mahasweta Devi: An Anthology of Recent Criticism*, ed. Nivedita Sen and Nikhil Yadav, 221-228. New Delhi: Penecraft International, 2008.

Doane, Mary Ann. "Film and the Masquerade: Theorising the Female Spectator." *Screen* 23 (1982): 74-87.

Donawerth, Jane. *Frankenstein's Daughters: Women Writing Science Fiction*. New York: Syracuse University Press, 1997.

Eagleton, Terry. *Figures of Dissent: Reviewing Fish, Spivak, Žižek and Others*. London: Verso, 2003.

Eagleton, Terry. *Myths of Power: A Marxist Study of the Brontës*. London: Macmillan, 1975.

Emery, Mary Lou. *Jean Rhys at "World's End": Novels of Colonial and Sexual Exile*. Austin: University of Texas Press, 1990.

Fabian, Johannes. *Time and the Other: How Anthropology Makes its Object*. New York: Colombia University Press, 1983.

Fox-Genovese, Elizabeth. "Placing Women's History in History." *New Left Review* 133 (1982): 5-29.

Jameson, Frederic. "Third-World Literature in the Era of Multinational Capitalism." *Social Text* 15 (1986): 65-88.

Freud, Sigmund. "Fetishism." In *The Standard Edition of the Complete Psychological Works of Sigmund Freud*, vol. XXI, 152-7. Translated by James Starchey. London: The Hogarth Press, 1964.

Freud, Sigmund. *The Interpretation of Dreams*. Translated by Joyce Crick. Oxford: Oxford University Press, 1999.

Gilbert, Sandra and Susan Gubar. *The Madwoman in the Attic: The Woman Writer and the Nineteenth-Century Literary Imagination*. New Haven: Yale University Press, 1979.

Gramsci, Antonio. *Selections from the Prison Notebooks*, edited and translated by Quintin Hoare and Geoffrey Nowell Smith. London: Lawrence and Wishart, 1971.

Hallward, Peter. *Absolutely Postcolonial: Writing between the Singular and the Specific*. Manchester: Manchester University Press, 2001.

Harrison, Nancy Rebecca. *Jean Rhys and the Novel as Women's Text*. Chapel Hill: University of North Carolina Press, c1988.

Howells, Coral Ann. *Jean Rhys*. Hemel Hempstead: Harvester Wheatsheaf, 1991.

Hulme, Peter. "The Locked Heart: The Creole Family Romance of Wide Sargasso Sea." In *Colonial Discourse/Postcolonial Theory*, edited by Francis Barker, Peter Hulme and Margaret Iverson, 72-88. Manchester: Manchester University Press, 1996.

Jacobus, Mary. "Is there a Woman in this Text?" *New Literary History* 14 (1982): 117-141.

Johnson, Barbara. "Introduction: Truth or Consequences." In *Consequences of Theory*, edited by Jonathan Arac and Barbara Johnson, viii-xiv. London: The John Hopkins University Press, 1991.

—. "My Monster/Myself." *Diacritics* 12:2 (1982): 2-10.

Kant, Immanuel, "Toward a Perpetual Peace." In *Political Writings*. Translated by H. B. Nisbet. Cambridge: Cambridge University Press, 1991.

—. *Critique of Judgement*. Translated by Werner S. Pluhar. Cambridge: Hackett Publishing Company, 1987.

—. *Critique of Practical Reason*. Translated by J. M. D. Meiklejohn. Chicago, 1952.

—. *Critique of Pure Reason*. Translated by Paul Guyer and Allen W. Wood. Cambridge: Cambridge University Press, 1998.

—. *Groundwork for the Metaphysics of Morals*. Translated by Arnulf Zweig, ed. Thomas E. Hill, JR. and Arnulf Zweig. Oxford: Oxford University Press, 2002.

Kossew, Sue. Pen and Power: a Postcolonial Reading of J. M. Coetzee and André Brink. Amsterdam: Rodopi, 1996.

Lacan, Jacques. "The Mirror Stage as formative of the function of the I as revealed in psychoanalytic experience" (1949). In *Écrits: A Selection*, 1-7. Translated by Alan Sheridan. New York: W. W. Norton & Company, 1977.

—. *The Psychoses: The Seminar of Jacques Lacan*, edited by Jacques-Alain Miller. Translated by Russell Grigg. London: Routledge, 1981.

Lambert, David. *White Creole Culture: Politics and Identity During the Age of Abolition*. Cambridge: Cambridge University Press, 2005.

Laplanche, Jean and J. B. Pontalis. *The Language of Psycho-Analysis*. Translated by Donald Nickleson Smith. New York: Norton, 1974.

Lew, Joseph W. "The Deceptive Other: Mary Shelley's Critique of Orientalism in *Frankenstein*." In *Studies in Romanticism* 30:2 (1991): 255-283.

Marks, Elaine and Isabelle de Courtivron. *New French Feminisms: an Anthology*. Sussex: The Harvester Press, 1981.

Marshall, David. *The Surprising Effects of Sympathy*. Chicago: the University of Chicago Press, 1988.

McLeod, John. *Beginning Postcolonialism*. Manchester: Manchester University Press, 2000.

Meyer, Susan. "Colonialism and the Figurative Strategy of Jane Eyre." In *Macro-politics of Nineteenth Century Literature: Nationalism, Exoticism, Imperialism*, ed. Jonathan Arac and Harriet Ritvo, 159-183. Philadelphia: University of Pennsylvania Press, 1991.

Miller, Christopher L. *Blank Darkness: Africanist Discourse in French*. Chicago: the University of Chicago Press, 1985.

Mishra, Vijay. "Review of Gayatri Chakraborty Spivak, *A Critique of Postcolonial Reason*." *Textual Practice* 14:2 (2000): 412–421.

Mohanty, Chandra Talpade. "Under Western Eyes: Feminist Scholarship and Colonial Discourse." *Boundary 2* 12:13 (1984): 333-358.

Moore-Gilbert, Bart. *Postcolonial Theory: Contexts, Practices, Politics*. London: Verso, 1997.

Morton, Stephen. "Subalternity and Aesthetic Education in the Thought of Gayatri Chakravorty Spivak." *Parallax* 17:3 (2011): 70-83.

—. *Gayatri Chakravorty Spivak*. London: Routledge, 2003.

—. *Gayatri Spivak: Ethics, Subalternity and the Critique of Postcolonial Reason*. Cambridge: Plity, 2007.

Mukherjee, Sujit. "Mahasweta Devi's writings – An Evaluation." *Book Review* XV.3 (1991): 30-31.

Ovid. "Narcissus and Echo." In *Metamorphoses*, 109-116. Translated by David Raeburn. London: Penguin Books, 2004.

Parry, Benita. "Problems in Current Theories of Colonial Discourse." *Oxford Literary Review* 9 (1987): 27-58.

Plasa, Carl. *Charlotte Brontë*. Basingstoke: Palgrave Macmillan, 2004.

Ray, Sangeeta. *Gayatri Chakravorty Spivak: In Other Words*. Sussex: Wiley-Blackwell, 2009.

Retamar, Roberto Fernández. "Caliban: Notes Towards a Discussion of Culture in Our America." In *Caliban and Other Essays*, 3-55. Minneapolis: University of Minnesota Press, c1989.

Rhys, Jean. "Jean Rhys Interviewed by Elizabeth Vreeland." *The Paris Review* 76 (1979): 219-237.

Rhys, Jean. *Jean Rhys Letters*, 1931-1966, edited by Francis Wyndham and Diana Melly. London: Deutsch, 1984.

—. "From Haverstock Hill Flat to U.S. Classroom." In *What's Left of Theory? New York on the Politics of Literary Theory*, edited Judith Butler, John Guillory and Kindall Thomas, 1-39. New York: Routledge, 2000.

—. "Gayatri Spivak on the Politics of the Subaltern: Interview by Howard Winant." *Socialist Review* 20 (1990): 81-97.

—. "How to Teach a 'Culturally Different Book.'" In *The Spivak Reader*, 237-266.

—. "Imperialism and Sexual Difference." *Oxford Literary Review* 8 (1986): 225-240.

—. "In a Word: Interview." In *The Second Wave: A Reader in Feminist Theory*, edited by Linda Nicholson, 356-378. New York: Routledge, 1997.

—. "Learning from de Man: Looking Back." *Boundary 2* 32:3 (2005): 21-35.

—. "Mapping the Present: Interview with Gayatri Spivak." *New Formations* 45 (2001): 9-23.

—. "More on Power and Knowledge." In *The Spivak Reader*, 141-174.

—. "Naming Gayatri Spivak." *Stanford Humanities Review* 1:1 (1989): 84-97.

—. "Public Hearing on Crimes Against Women." *WAF* 7 (1995): 3-4.

—. "Resp

Rosaldo, M. Z. "The Use and Abuse of Anthropology: Reflections on Feminism and Cross-Cultural Understanding." *Signs* 5:3 (1980): 389-417.

Rosenfeld, Claire. "The Shadow Within: the Conscious and Unconscious Use of the Double." In *Stories of the Double,* edited by Albert J. Guerard. Philadelphia: J. B. Lippincott, 1967.

Roy, Ayon. "Hegel contra Schlegel; Kierkegaard contra de Man." *PMLA* 124:1 (2009): 107-126.

Russell II, Keith A. "Now every word she said was echoed, echoed loudly in my head": Christophine's Language and Refractive Space in Jean Rhys's *Wide Sargasso Sea*." *Journal of Narrative Theory* 37:1 (2007): 87-103

Salgado, Minoli. "Tribal Stories, Scribal Worlds: Mahasweta Devi and the Unreliable Translator." In *Mahasweta Devi: An Anthology of Recent Criticism,* 148-165.

Sanders, Mark. *Gayatri Chakravorty Spivak: Live Theory*. London: Continuum International Publishing Group, 2006.

Schwarz, Henry. "Postcolonial Performance: Texts and Contexts of Mahasweta Devi." In *Mahasweta Devi: Critical Perspectives*, 175-189. New Delhi: Pencraft International, 2011.

Sen, Nivedita and Nikhil Yadav. "Introduction." In M*ahasweta Devi: An Anthology of Recent Criticism*, 11-40.

Shakespeare, William. *The Tempest*. Cambridge: Cambridge University Press, 2002.

Shakti Jaising. "Who is Christophine? The Good Black Servant and the Contradictions of (Racial) Liberalism." *MFS Modern Fiction Studies* 56:4 (2010): 815-36.

Mary Eagleton. *Feminist Literary Theory: a Reader*. Oxford: Blackwell, 1986.

Sklar, Leonard. "Drowning in Aid: The World Bank's Bangladesh Action Plan." *Multinational Monitor* 13 (1993): 8-13.

Spivak, Gayatri Chakravorty. "Neocolonialism and the Secret Agent of Knowledge," *The Oxford Literary Review* 13 (1991): 220-251.

—. "A Moral Dilemma." In *What Happens to History: the Renewal of Ethics in Contemporary Thought*, edited by Howard Marchitello, 215-239. London: Routledge, 2001.

—. "Can the Subaltern Speak?" In *Marxism and the Interpretation of Culture*, edited by Cary Nelson and Lawrence Crossberg, 271-313. London: Macmillan Education Ltd., 1988.

—. "Criticism, Feminism and the Institution," *Thesis Eleven* 11 (1984/85): 175-186.

—. "Echo." In *The Spivak Reader: Selected Works of Gayatri Chakravorty Spivak*, edited Donna Landry and Gerald MacLean, 175-202. London: Routledge, 1996.

—. "French feminism in an International Frame," *Yale French Studies* 62 (1981): 154-184. onsibility." *Boundary 2* 21 (1994): 19-64.

—. "Strategies of Vigilance: An Interview." *Block* 10 (1985): 5-10.

—. "Supplementing Marxism." In *Wither Marxism: Global Crises in International Perspective*, edited by Bernard Magnus and Stephen Cullenberg, 109-119. London: Routledge, 1995.

—. "The Burden of English." In *Orientalism and the Postcolonial Predicament: Perspectives on South Asia*, edited by Carol A. Breckenridge and Peter van der Veer, 134-157. Philadelphia PA: University of Pennsylvania Press, 1993.

—. "Touched by Deconstruction." *Grey Room* 20 (2005): 95-104.

—. "Translator's Preface." In Jacques Derrida, *Of Grammatology*. Translated by Gayatri Chakravorty Spivak, ix-lxxxvii. London: the Johns Hopkins University Press, 1974.

—. "What is it for? Gayatri Chakravorty Spivak on the Functions of the Postcolonial Critic." *Nineteenth Century Contexts* 18:1 (1994): 71-81.

—. *An Aesthetic Education in the Era of Globalization*. London: Harvard University Press, 2012.

—. *In Other Worlds: Essays in Cultural Politics*. London: Routledge, 1988.

—. *The Postcolonial Critic: Interviews, Strategies, Dialogues*, edited by Sarah Harasym. New York: Routledge, 1990.

Stoler, Ann Laura. *Race and the Education of Desire: Foucault's History of Sexuality and the Colonial Order of Things*. Durham: Duke University Press, 1995.

Stone, Alison. "On the Genealogy of Women: A Defence of Anti-Essentialism." In *Third Wave Feminism: A Critical Exploration*, edited by Stacy Gillis, Gillian Howie and Rebecca Munford, 16-29. Basingstoke: Palgrave Macmillan, 2007.

Suleiman, Susan Rubin. "Writing and Motherhood." In *The (M)other Tongue: Essays in Feminist Psychoanalytic Interpretation*, edited by Shirley Nelson Gamer, Claire Kahane and Madelon Sprengnether, 352-77. Ithaca: Cornell Univ. Press, 1985.

Swift, Simon. "Kant, Herder, and the Question of Philosophical Anthropology." *Textual Practice* 19:2 (2005): 219-238

—. "The Lesson of Gayatri Spivak." *Parallax* 17:3 (2011): 84-97.

Thompson, Edward. *Suttee: A Historical and Philosophical Enquiry into the Hindu Rite of Widow Burning*. London: George Allen and Unwin, 1928.

Ward, Andrew. *Kant: the Three Critiques*. Cambridge: Polity Press, 2006.

Wenzel, Jennifer. "Grim Fairy Tales: Taking a Risk, Reading Imaginary Maps." In *Mahasweta Devi: An Anthology of Recent Criticism*, 166-189.

Williams, Bernard. *Moral Luck*. Cambridge: Cambridge University Press, 1981.

Young, Robert. *White Mythologies: Writing History and the West*. London: Routledge, 1990.